WITHDRAWN

**The Guns N' Roses Encyclopaedia**
by Mick O'Shea

A CHROME DREAMS PUBLICATION
First Edition 2008

Published by Chrome Dreams
PO BOX 230, New Malden, Surrey,
KT3 6YY, UK
info@chromedreams.co.uk
WWW.CHROMEDREAMS.CO.UK

ISBN 978 1 84240 423 2
Copyright © 2008 by Chrome Dreams

Edited by    Cathy Johnstone
Cover Design   Sylwia Grzeszczuk
Layout Design   Marek Niedziewicz

Printed in the UK by CPI William Clowes Ltd, Beccles, NR34 7TL

# GUNS N'

## ENCYCLOPAEDIA

# ROSES

BY MICK O'SHEA

# INTRODUCTION

It was Saturday 31 August, 1991, and there was an extra spring in my motorbike-booted step as I clambered into my mate's car that particular morning. For our destination was Wembley Stadium, and the concert ticket nestled in my back pocket said Guns N' Roses: admit 1. And although I saw the Gunners perform live on their subsequent visits to our shores, this is the show that stands out in my memory. The afternoon was largely spent avoiding being crushed by a collapsing human pyramid or ogling those girls sporting enough to expose their breasts on the giant video screens mounted at the side of the stage, which was much more appealing than *Evil Dead II* minus the sound. Hell, now I think about it, it was even more enjoyable than the support acts, Nine Inch Nails and Skid Row. Needless to say, the 72,000 crowd went ballistic when Guns N' Roses hit the stage – albeit eighty minutes later than advertised – and I don't think my feet touched the ground during the opening number 'Perfect Crime'. I joyously sang – or more likely screeched – along to the songs taken from *Appetite* and *GNR Lies*, and was left slightly envious of those around me who appeared familiar with the *Use Your Illusion* numbers – even though neither album would be released in the UK for another two weeks. The atmosphere beneath the twin towers was absolutely electric throughout the Gunners' entire two hour+ set, but if I had to choose a moment where I was at one with the cosmos, then it would have to be when Slash clambered atop one of the stage monitors and began stroking the opening, chiming chords to 'Paradise City'.

I will readily admit that my having cut my musical teeth on punk rock meant that I didn't get into Guns N' Roses straight away. I had heard their name, but nothing of their music and, believing them to be just another bunch of long-haired L.A. thrash-metal merchants, paid them scant attention. But, like every other incurable romantic on the block, I couldn't help but be captivated by the sentimental lyrics of 'Sweet Child O' Mine', and if any further evidence was required that I should maybe check this band out, then it came upon seeing the video to their hard-rockin' debut 'Welcome To The Jungle'.

Back in the day, everyone had their favourite Gunner and as I was a rhythm guitarist in a band at the time, mine was Izzy Stradlin. Izzy was just born to play guitar, and was also the epitome of cool, but little did I know that the Wembley show would be his last as a full-time member of the band. By this time of course, the Gunners had already parted company with drummer Stephen Adler, and, although the *Illusion* albums are both fantastic, Izzy's departure, closely followed by the less-than-savoury *Spaghetti Incident?* left me with a bad taste regarding all things G N' R . And believing the band had run its course, I barely raised an eyebrow as Slash, Matt, and Duff all subsequently followed Izzy out of Axl's revolving door.

It has of course been impossible to ignore the on-going shenanigans surrounding *Chinese Democracy*, and while the press has had a field day over the album's never-ending, impending release, the *Greatest Hits* album having occupied the coveted #1 slot on both sides of the Atlantic proved that Guns N' Roses are still close to many a rocker's heart. New rumours that the album was coming out (this time 11 February, 2008) surfaced whilst I was putting the finishing touches to the first draft of this Guns N' Roses A - Z, and although I'm looking forward to finally hearing Axl's grand opus, let's just say I'm not holding my breath...

Mick O'Shea
*(Still using my Illusion)*

Professional thanks to Rob and everyone at Chrome Dreams, and to Alan Parker for putting my name in the frame.
Personal thanks to my wife Jakki for taking a back seat while Guns N' Roses pervaded our everyday life, Paul Young (not the singer), Drezzy, Daz and George from Phrenic, the guys at Quantum Finance, Steve "Roadent" Connelly, Steve Diggle, and the rest of the Cambridge Circus Militia, Andy, Dave, Jo, Amandine and everyone else connected with the Spice of Life pub.

## ABBRUSSEZE, DAVE

Dave Abbrusseze is the hard-hitting, ex-Pearl Jam drummer who was brought in by Axl Rose to work on *Chinese Democracy* in 1997.

Abbrusseze first came to prominence as the drummer with Pearl Jam. And he remained with Eddie Veder's band from 1991 through to 1994, during which time he recorded the albums *Vs* and *Vitology* (although he would no longer be in the band by the time of the latter album's release in August, 1994). His trademark hard-hitting style, heavy use of splash cymbals and double-stroke roll technique, has seen him credited by some as having influenced a generation of drummers in the early 1990s. He was brought in by Axl in 1997 primarily to beef up the percussion on *Chinese Democracy* and was understandably overwhelmed upon entering the complex where Axl and the gang were housed, and seeing the vast array of state-of-the art equipment at their disposal. "You could hunt buffalo with his rig," he later recalled. "It had a lot of blinking lights, a lot of things that you stepped on. It sounded like a freight train that was somehow playable."

Abbrusseze was born on 17 May, 1968 in Stamford, Connecticut, but grew up in Mesquite, Texas. As with his G N' R predecessors, Steven Adler and Matt Sorum, Abbrusseze honed his drumming technique on a succession of ceramic and metallic household objects before finally mustering enough cash to purchase his first drum kit. And having decided that the academic life was not for him he dropped out of school and formed a band called Dr. Tongue, a three-piece funk-orientated outfit that played in the Dallas area.

## ADLER'S APPETITE

Adler's Appetite is an L.A.-based rock band which features ex-G N' R drummer Steven Adler.

In January, 2003 Steven Adler joined ex-L.A. Guns guitarist – and one-time Slash's Snakepit collaborator – Keri Kelli's occasional band Suki Jones, which also included Faster Pussycat guitarist Brent Muscat, bassist Robbie Crane and Jizzy Pearl on lead vocals. The band then underwent an immediate name-change to Adler's Appetite, which was obviously aimed at gaining greater exposure having combined the ex-G N' R drummer's surname with the multi-platinum selling album with which he was widely associated. In the initial stages, however, the line-up was extremely fluid owing to Muscat's long-term commitment to Faster Pussycat, and Kelli's ongoing touring commitments with Mötley Crüe frontman Vince Neil's solo project. Muscat finally left the band for good in October, 2004 and Pearl departed the following March to be replaced by Sheldon Tarsha.

Following on from the release of their eponymously-titled EP in July, 2005, the band began collaborating with L.A. Guns frontman, Tracii Guns, with a view to going over to Asia to perform as Guns N' Roses Revisited. The idea was swiftly abandoned, however, once Axl got wind of the project and threatened the band with swift and severe legal action. In December, despite having recorded an album's worth of material, Kelli, Crane and latest recruit, guitarist Craig Bradford, were summarily dismissed and replaced by Michael Thomas (the guitarist who had filled in for Kelli whilst the latter had been out on the road with Vince Neil), guitarist JT Longoria and ex-Enuff Z'Nuff bassist Chip Z'Nuff. But by January, 2006 the in-house friction between Steven and the

other members led to the band announcing a split in the midst of a European tour.

In May, 2006 it was revealed that Adler's Appetite would be supporting Muscat's Faster Pussycat on the latter band's latest tour. Steven confirmed the news via his website and also announced that bassist Chip Z'Nuff would be joining him for several of the intended dates. And although the band did participate in the tour, the line-up was in a constant state of flux, with Steven even failing to appear at several of the venues. The situation was verging on crossing from the sublime to the ridiculous when Kelli, Crane and Pearl revealed that they had formed a legally-binding partnership with Steven which meant they co-owned the band's name.

In the midst of all the legal wrangling, Steven further muddied the waters during an appearance on a Mexican radio station when he asked to borrow the bemused DJ's phone so he could get in contact with his one-time G N' R buddy Izzy Stradlin, as the guitarist had been working on a new Adler's Appetite album. Although there is no way of establishing whether Steven did manage to renew contact with Izzy, the aforementioned album has yet to see the light of day. That said, however, in April, 2007, the previously unreleased track 'Sadder Days' was posted on Steven's MySpace site. The song, which was written by Sheldon Tarsha, had originally been recorded whilst Kelli and Crane

were still with the band, which would seem to suggest that they and Steven have reached an amicable understanding.

In July, 2007, Adler's Appetite resurfaced with Steven on drums, as well as ex-members Sheldon Tarsha, Michael Thomas and Chip Z'Nuff, along with new recruit, guitarist Kristy Majors.

## ADLER, STEVEN

Steven Adler was Guns N' Roses' original drummer, and remained with the band until his dismissal in 1990.

The Gunners original stickman, with a penchant for drums, girls, getting stoned (the first time he remembers getting "wasted" was in his grandmother's bathroom – with the old woman's stash – when he was just eight years-old), rock music, hockey and motorcycles, was born in Cleveland, Ohio in 1965 but waved goodbye to the 'Buckeye State' when his family moved to Los Angeles when he was 7 years-old.

Having wanted to be a rock star ever since he could remember, Steven started out as a guitarist, but abandoned the six-string in favour of the drums upon realising L.A. was already awash with wannabe axemen. As with Axl, Izzy, and Slash, Stephen also succumbed to the Dionysian allure of heroin, but unlike his fellow Gunners he seemed incapable of getting his act together and, following the band's initial success, became something of a regular at the Betty Ford Clinic. One such occasion led to him missing the band's performance at the 1989 American Music Awards with Don Henley being asked to take the drum stool for the occasion. The official excuse given for his absence at the ceremony was that he was suffering from a bout of flu. But nothing stays secret for long along Sunset Strip, and rumours soon began to circulate that the drummer had been placed on probation by the rest of the band. Despite repeated warnings, Steven's lapses were becoming more and more frequent, and with rehearsals underway for what would become the *Use Your Illusion* albums the band was forced to audition for a replacement – amongst those considered were Pretenders stalwart Martin Chambers, and Adam Maples from the Sea Hags. Duff, however, found rehearsing without his rhythm section buddy too much and walked out of the session which saw Steven promptly reinstated, albeit on the proviso that he sign a sobriety contract promising to get his shit together, only for him to then fall off the wagon again.

Every rocker dreams of living the 'sex, drugs and rock 'n' roll' lifestyle, but Steven's capacity for one was negating his capability for the others, and with valuable studio recording time also being wasted, the rest of the band were forced into a decision and he was out for good. Axl had once told the inner circle that Steven would one day talk himself out of the band, but if he thought he'd heard the last from their erstwhile drummer he was in for a surprise. Whilst the band had been out on the road promoting the *Use Your Illusion* albums, Steven had been consulting with his lawyers and filed a $2 million lawsuit against the band accusing them of having defrauded him, and of defaming his character. He claimed the others – with the possible exception of Duff – had used him as their scapegoat. Not only had they each partaken of heroin, but had actively encouraged him to take the drug, only to then toss him aside once his addiction started getting in the way of his 9 - 5.

On 23 August, 1993 Axl and Steven shared the spotlight together one last time when the case was brought before the Los Angeles Superior Court. Axl must have thought the case was a no-brainer, but if so, he was in for a rude awakening. The sobriety contract he and the others had forced the drummer to sign wasn't worth the paper it was written on

as Steven hadn't had his lawyer present at the signing, which, in effect, negated its contents. The contract may have been worthless in the legal sense but to Steven it was worth a fortune. A $2.3 million fortune to be exact, which is the amount Guns N' Roses paid him in an out-of-court settlement on 24 September. Steven also received $100,000 from past and present managers Alan Niven and Doug Goldstein. The fact that Axl is still smarting over the lawsuit some 13 years later leaves little chance of there being a reconciliation between the two – let alone their sharing the same stage. Having finally received his dues, one might have thought Steven

would have gone away and put the rest of his life in order, but before the year was out he overdosed so badly on heroin that he suffered a stroke which left him partially paralysed.

Those closest to Steven must have feared life was imitating art, for the drummer's chronic drug dependency made him a real-life candidate for the fictional 'dead pool' from the 1988 movie of the same name starring Clint Eastwood, in which he and the other Gunners had a fleeting cameo role. Indeed, Axl may have had a side bet on how long Steven would last, but Slash wasn't prepared to stand by and wait to see his friend's name in the obituary column. In his entertaining, yet oft harrowing, eponymously-titled autobiography, the guitarist informs us he has been helping to ween Steven off the smack, crack and Jägermeister, which was slowly, yet surely, killing him.

# AEROSMITH

Aerosmith, whose career has spanned three decades, and have to date sold in excess of 150 million albums worldwide, invited Guns N' Roses to open for them on the US leg of their *Permanent Vacation* tour in July, 1988.

It is no secret that the pre-signed Gunners modelled themselves – in both artistic and addictive terms – on their hard-rockin' and one-time hell-raisin' heroes, Aerosmith. Indeed, so high was their opinion of Messrs. Tyler, Perry, Whitford, Hamilton and Kramer, that anyone not familiar with the Boston rockers' sizeable back catalogue was given exceedingly short shrift, as one not-so-savvy female record company exec. found out to her cost whilst trying to tempt the Gunners to put pen to paper.

The decision to invite Guns N' Roses onto the *Permanent Vacation* tour could have been a logistical disaster as the guys from the 'Smith had recently cleaned up their act while the G N' R boys were still happily sniffing, snorting and smoking anything they could lay their hands on. As the now not-so-Toxic Twins, as Tyler and Perry were once known on the circuit, didn't want to appear churlish, their manager, Tim Collins – who two years earlier had passed on the chance to manage the Gunners – devised a plan which saw the younger band agreeing to restrict their drug intake to the confines of their own dressing room. Although getting wasted was always high on the G N' R agenda, all five members held Aerosmith in the highest esteem and were looking forward to 'hanging' with their heroes. So much so, that they were extra careful to observe the rules whenever they found themselves in the older group's company. The press naturally had a field day with what they saw as Aerosmith's condescending attitude towards Guns N' Roses, but nothing could have been further from the truth. Before the opening show of the tour at the Celebrity Theatre in Phoenix, Arizona, on 9 July, 1987 Tyler summoned Izzy, from whom he had occasionally bought his stash, as well as Slash and Duff to his dressing room to ensure they understood the reasoning behind the guidelines. And just to show that he, Perry and the other guys in the band were all well travelled on William Blake's road of excess, he handed out specially-made T-shirts, which instead of the customary tour dates; bore the names of the many rehab centres they had each visited. Not to be outdone, when the tour drew to a close, Collins and the rest of

Aerosmith's management team presented the five itinerant Gunners with brand-new aluminium Halliburton travel cases.

Apart from the odd slip-up, the Gunners managed to keep their nefarious activities out of sight and the two bands got along famously. And it was a measure of the older band's esteem for the group which many critics were touting as being usurpers of Aerosmith's throne, that they chose to watch the Gunners shows, with Tyler and Perry often joining the band onstage to perform 'Mama Kin'. Although Guns N' Roses were simply happy to be playing with their heroes, and certainly weren't looking to topple them, *Appetite For Destruction* was outselling Aerosmith's latest offering and later that same month finally reached #1 on the Billboard chart. And if further confirmation was needed that Guns N' Roses had surpassed their headlining heroes then it surely came when *Rolling Stone* arrived to do a story on

Aerosmith only to end up putting Guns N' Roses on the cover.

Although Aerosmith are known as the 'Bad Boys from Boston', none of the band members are actually from the Bay State's capital. Indeed, only guitarist Joe Perry was born in Massachusetts. Having signed to Columbia in 1972, the band released their eponymous blues-rock, double platinum-selling debut album – which contained 'Mama Kin' – the following year. The 1974 follow-up album *Get Your Wings* went one (1 million sales) better by achieving triple platinum status, but it was 1975's *Toys In The Attic,* that featured the hit singles 'Sweet Emotion' and 'Walk This Way', that helped catapult Aerosmith into the major league. The 'Smith's' fourth album, the raucous and deliciously raw *Rocks*, which went platinum upon its release in 1976, and has since been cited as having been a major inspiration on the glam-metal class of '86, brought even greater

acclaim and it seemed as though the band could do no wrong. The next album, 1977's *Draw The Line*, which should have been called 'Snort The Line' owing to the band's then voracious drug intake, however, proved the progenitor of the band's fall from grace. Although the album has since gone on to accrue sales in excess of two million, it wasn't initially well received – either by the fans or the critics – which in turn led to in-house squabbling. And when 1979's aptly-named *Night In The Ruts* failed to stop the rot, Joe Perry announced his departure from the band.

Steve Tyler and the rest of the group decided to continue with Jimmy Crespo drafted in as Perry's replacement, and their decision to do so seemed justified when the *Greatest Hits* album,

released in 1980, went multi-platinum. This, however, proved to be a false dawn for, aside from losing rhythm guitarist Brad Whitford in 1981, the band's seventh studio album *Rock In A Hard Place* (1982) was considered a commercial failure having barely scraped gold status. Aerosmith limped on through five uneventful – and largely forgettable years – before undergoing what proved to be the first stage of their 'phoenix from the ashes' rebirth when – having already signed to Geffen – Joe Perry and Brad Whitford returned to the fold in April, 1984. The second stage of the comeback came in 1986 courtesy of Run D.M.C whose latest album *Raising Hell* featured a cover of 'Walk This Way'. When the hip-hop kings decided to release the song as a single they invited Tyler and Perry into the studio. The rap-rock collaboration reached #4 on the Billboard Hot 100, and not only helped cement rap into the mainstream, but also helped introduce Aerosmith to a whole new audience.

Despite being relegated to yesteryear heroes status by the emergence of Guns N' Roses, Aerosmith have continued doing what they always did best, and their 1989 album *Pump* sold in excess of seven million copies and spawned three Top 10 singles: 'Janie's Got A Gun'; 'What It Takes' and 'Love In An Elevator', while the equally-successful 1993 follow-up *Get A Grip* gave the 'Smith their first US #1 album. Aerosmith have continued recording and touring to the present day and their fifteenth – as yet unnamed – studio album is slated for release in spring 2008

## AMERICAN MUSIC AWARDS

The annual American Music Awards, which is regarded as one of America's 'Big Three' music award ceremonies, was created by Emmy Award-winning American television and radio personality Dick Clark in 1973 to compete with the Grammys.

On 30 January, 1989 Guns N' Roses were invited to perform live at that year's awards, which was being held at the Shrine Auditorium in Los Angeles. Although the Gunners had won the 'Favourite Rock/Pop Single' award for 'Sweet Child O' Mine', having staved off competition from Britain's Rick Astley and Steve Winwood, they performed 'Patience', which was scheduled for imminent release as the band's next single. Steven's drug use was so chronic at this stage; however, that former Eagles singer/drummer Don Henley was drafted in

as a last-minute replacement. As the show would be going out live, there was no backstage alcohol on offer to the nominees other than a few bottles of complementary wine. But unfortunately for the Geffen execs in attendance, Dick Clark and the ABC network – not to mention the TV viewing audience – Slash and Duff laid siege to the wine as though prohibition was about to be reintroduced. And although it has never been established how much the pair imbibed, it must have been a considerable amount as by the time they went up on to the podium to receive the award they could barely walk – let alone speak in a coherent manner. When one of the red-faced Geffen execs later demanded an explanation, Slash was heard to reply "It was only a little bit of wine", to which the equally bleary-eyed Duff rejoined "Yes, but it was a very fine wine."

Slash was to prove the guiltier culprit, however, and if Dick Clark's nerves were jangling when the guitarist uttered the word 'shit', not-quite-as under his breath as he'd thought, then the show's host was having palpitations when Slash began his thank you speech: "I want to thank fuckin' oops..." But instead of smiling sheepishly and sloping off back to his seat, Slash pressed ahead with his 'must remember to thank list' and only got as far as expressing his gratitude towards Alan Niven and Doug Goldstein before uttering the dreaded 'F' word for a second time. And although the network's director hastily cut to a commercial break, the ABC switchboard lit up like the Las Vegas strip as hundreds of enraged viewers called in to log their complaints. Needless to say, the story made the front pages of several leading US newspapers the following morning, including the *Los Angeles Times* and the *New York Times*.

## ANDREADIS, TEDDY

Teddy 'Zig Zag' Andreadis is a respected keyboardist and harmonica player who appeared on both Use Your Illusion albums, and also went out on tour with Guns N' Roses.

Andreadis was born to respectable Greek parents in Perth Amboy, New Jersey and music was the centre of his existence almost from the moment he could walk when his father bought him his first musical instrument, an accordion. In the years that followed, he also learnt keyboards, guitar and harmonica, and his musical versatility led to his jamming and performing live with fellow New Jersey musicians Southside Johnny and Bruce Springsteen.

By 1991 he'd acquired worldwide recognition as a keyboardist and harmonica player, as well as a musical arranger, and was invited to tour with Guns N' Roses on the band's *Use Your Illusion* world tour, and also appeared on both of the *Use Your Illusion* albums.

And having acquired a reputation as a skilled cameraman through his work on videos for Michael Jackson's 'Give In To Me' and Carol King's *In Concert* album, he was subsequently invited to work on the G N' R videos for 'November Rain', 'Yesterdays', 'Garden Of Eden' and 'Estranged'. His involvement with G N' R did not end there, however, as he also lent his considerable talents to the first Slash's Snakepit album, as well as several of Gilby Clarke's solo projects. His own debut solo album, *Innocent Loser*, which was released in 1996, features contributions from Slash, Duff and Matt Sorum.

In 1999, by which time he'd shared the stage with a diverse assortment of musical talent ranging from actors Bruce Willis and Billy Bob Thornton, through to guitar legends Chuck Berry and Bo Diddley, the Los Angeles Music Awards voted Teddy 'Outstanding Keyboardist of the Year'. The multi-faceted Teddy has also done TV commercial voice-over work for corporate giants such as McDonalds, Kellogg's, and Toyota as well as contributing to several movie soundtracks including *Tapeheads*, Keenan Ivory Wayan's *I'm Gonna Get You Sucka* and *Breakfast With Einstein*.

Today, Teddy is something of an L.A. luminary, and not just for his having worked with West Hollywood's most-famous musical exponents, but also due to his standing room only ad-hoc jam sessions with his band The

Screaming Cocktail Hour at the city's legendary blues haunt The Baked Potato, which on occasion features Gilby Clarke in its line-up. Teddy still lives in Los Angeles with his wife Lisa Gioch, the one-time stand-up comedienne and co-host of the Marc Germain Show.

## APPETITE FOR DESTRUCTION

*Appetite For Destruction*, Guns N' Roses' debut album, was released worldwide on 31 July, 1987 and hit #1 on both sides of the Atlantic. The twelve songs contained on the album are as follows:

*Welcome To The Jungle* (4:31); *It's So Easy* (3:21); *Nightrain* (4:26); *Out Ta Get Me (4:20); Mr. Brownstone* (3:46); *Paradise City* (6:46); *My Michelle* (3:39); *Think About You* (3:50); *Sweet Child O' Mine* (5:56); *You're Crazy* (3:15); *Anything Goes* (3:25); *Rocket Queen* (6:13).

LP, CD & Cassette
Geffen Records, 1987.

Having failed to procure the services of KISS' Paul Stanley, who'd earlier expressed an interest in working with Guns N' Roses before then crying off, as well as legendary Canadian producer Bob Ezrin, who'd worked on eight albums with Alice Cooper, but proved reluctant to get in the ring with the Gunners, Geffen's Tom Zutaut approached Mötley Crüe's Nikki Sixx. Sixx, however, although perhaps best qualified to handle Geffen's latest acquisition, was at the time far too preoccupied with exorcising his drug demons to even consider the idea, and in desperation Zutaut turned to Baltimore-born Mike Clink, who, at the time, was best known for his engineering work with 'soft rock' producer Ron Nevison.

With Clink ready to take the helm, Geffen booked the band into Rumbo Studios in the southern suburb of Canoga Park, Los Angeles. The 10,000 square foot, three room recording studio, which shares a parking lot with the Winnetka animal clinic, was originally designed, built, and until 2003, owned by the 1970s husband and wife singing team Captain and Tennille (Daryl Dragon and Toni Tennille), perhaps best known for their 1975 US hit 'Love Will Keep Us Together'. Although Rumbo has since welcomed the likes of Megadeth, Bad Religion, Rage Against The Machine and Smash-

ing Pumpkins, back in 1987 one was more likely to run into Barry Manilow shooting pool with Kenny Rogers within the sedate setting of the studio's Billiards Room, which made it a strange choice of studio for a rock band to record their debut album.

One reason was that Rumbo was relatively cheap compared to other L.A. studios such as Hit City, Conway, Cherokee or A & M. Another was that it would be more productive as the five band members would have to live together close to the studio. Within a matter of weeks, however, Geffen was forced to find alternative accommodation following the band's eviction from the place they were staying. Clink later recalled one incident – of which there were many – when the five band members returned to the apartment following yet another late-night drunkfest to find they had locked themselves out. Instead of calling Clink, or perhaps a locksmith, they instead put a rock through one of the windows trying to make it look like an attempted robbery. Fortunately, the put upon producer, who had already enforced a 'no drugs' policy, was willing to ignore such boisterous behaviour as long as it didn't interfere with the album.

Although Clink wasn't sure just for how long the wayward and seemingly uncontrollable Gunners would, or could, keep themselves together, he knew this was his chance to step out from Nevison's shadow and strike out on his

17

own. He also knew Guns N' Roses would require a harder-edged sound than the acts he and Nevison usually worked with, such as Chicago, Heart and Survivor, and got the ball rolling by enquiring as to which records the individual members were listening to. Duff was happy to go with the flow just so long as the music kept the Gunners' punky edge, while Izzy was equally keen to ensure the band stuck to its Stones-esque garage blues roots. Slash had happily rhymed off Aerosmith's back catalogue, while Axl was looking for a production sound akin to that on Metallica's *Ride The Lightning*.

The initial idea was to record each of the twelve tracks live in order to capture the Gunners' on-stage energy, and to keep the overdubs to an absolute minimum. But Axl was anxious to explore every avenue, and sorely tested everyone's patience by demanding endless retakes to nail down each song exactly as he heard it inside his head. Axl's tenacity wasn't Clink's only headache, however, for although Izzy, Steven and Duff laid down their respective parts with consummate ease, Slash – having hocked most of his equipment to score heroin – was far from happy with his three remaining guitars, or their sound. The problem was solved by manager Alan Niven who not only booked Slash into Take 1 studios to redo his guitar parts, he even provided the guitarist with a brand-new axe – a hand-made

1959 flame-top Les Paul replica with Seymour Duncan pickups.

Of the twelve tracks which aren't listed elsewhere in the book, the first up is 'It's So Easy', which was written by Duff and West Arken, and released as Guns N' Roses debut double A-side UK single in June, 1987 to coincide with the band's three-night residency at The Marquee in London that same month. The "ya-ya hippie" song as Axl has since referred to its slower, more laid-back pre-album version, received its first-known public airing at the Whisky A Go-Go on 16 March, 1987. Legend has it that the song was inspired in part by a car smash that Axl and the rest of the band witnessed whilst in New York, yet according to the excellent www.gnrontour.com website, the band didn't actually play in the Big Apple until October of that year.

Next up is 'Nightrain', the Gunners' paean to the cheap gut-rot red wine of the same name which ensured an evening's oblivion for the princely sum of $1.25. Slash and Izzy came up with the initial riff – probably during an evening imbibing on the stuff – before Duff and Axl knocked it into a more recognisable shape. It was released as a single in 1989, but, unlike every other G N' R release, didn't have the luxury of an accompanying promo video, which probably accounts for its lowly #93 placing on the Billboard 100. 'Out Ta Get Me', another autobiographical offering which was often used to open the proceedings at the band's early shows, was Axl's scathing rant against the Indiana authorities back in his hometown of Lafayette, who – in his eyes at least – always seemed out to give him a hard time. The fact that the teenage Axl got himself arrested on four separate occasions for various misdemeanours would have been enough to see him a constant on the cops' radar. While Tippecanoe County Court records show that in the two year period between July, 1980 and September, 1982, Axl spent a total of ten days in the County Jail on charges of public intoxication, criminal trespass, battery and contributing to the delinquency of a minor.

If the moral do-gooders over at the RIAA (Recording Industry Association of America) were worried that 'Nightrain' might be encouraging substance abuse, then the Izzy-penned 'Mr. Brownstone', with its blatant references to both the taking of heroin, and the all-consuming need of a heroin addict (Brownstone being street slang for the highly-addictive drug), would have had Tipper Gore beseeching her hubby Al, the then Senator for Tennessee and future Vice-President, to nuke downtown Los Angeles. 'Think About You', another of Axl's odes to his then love Erin Everly, was an innocuous filler, and by the end of the year it had been scratched from the Gunners' set. In 2001, however, it resurfaced unexpectedly and has since featured regularly on the on-going

*Chinese Democracy* tour set-list, usually when Izzy joins the band on stage for the encore. The rather self-explanatory 'You're Crazy' was – according to the liner notes on *GNR Lies,* where it appears in its original, acoustic glory – originally written shortly after G N' R signed to Geffen Records, only to be transformed both live, and in rehearsals, into the souped-up electric version which appears on *Appetite*. And finally, 'Anything Goes', which – aside from 'Think About You' – is perhaps the weakest offering on the album and dates back to the days of Hollywood Rose when it was better known as 'My Way Your Way'.

Having borrowed the title and front cover artwork from a paint-ing by legendary L.A. fantasy artist Robert Williams, *Appetite For Destruction* went on world-wide release on 31 July, 1987. Although both the band and Mike Clink believed they had excelled themselves in the studio, the suits over at Geffen – including head honcho David Geffen himself – were somewhat less enthused with the finished album, and began braving themselves for a sizeable deficit against the Gunners $750,000 advance. Despite the exertions of the label's promotions team, headed by the indomitable Al Coury, no TV or radio station was willing to promote an album which featured a futuristic rape scene on its front cover, brazenly championed drug use

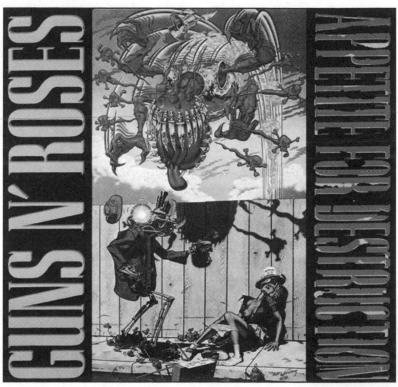

and contained an unacceptable number of expletives (the word 'fuck' features thirteen times). The total lack of media exposure – and a lukewarm response from the critics – meant that only the G N' R cognoscenti were aware of the album and resulted in US sales of around 200,000.

Although Geffen were moderately happy with the sales figures, they believed the record had done all it was going to and instructed Zutaut to concentrate on the band's follow-up album. Zutaut, however, refused to concede defeat. He still believed the album was a smouldering powder keg, and that all it required was for someone or something to light the fuse. Sensing that his words were falling on deaf ears within Coury's hard-pressed promotions department, Zutaut bypassed the normal Geffen chain of command and made his petition directly to David Geffen. Geffen was moved by his chief A&R man's pleas and agreed to help by calling in a favour from MTV's chief executive Tom Freston, to get the 'Welcome To The Jungle' video aired on the world's most famous – and most-watched – music channel. Freston reluctantly agreed, but the deal was for a one-off showing only, at midnight on the East coast, 3am in Los Angeles. Today, it is unbelievable that Guns N' Roses' future 20 year-to-date career rested on those five late-night minutes, but Zutaut knew the majority of America's rock fans were night owls, and one showing was all it

took to create the required buzz and excited fans began bombarding the channel's switchboard demanding repeat plays. Within a matter of weeks the 'Welcome' video was on heavy rotation and sales figures for the parent album doubled and then quadrupled, and still it carried on selling.

By the end of 1987, *Appetite For Destruction* had entered the rarefied air of the *Billboard 200*'s Top 20, but Zutaut still had one more ace up his sleeve in 'Sweet Child O' Mine'. Now that America's mainstream record-buying public was finally attuned to the Gunners sound, it was sure to embrace Axl's heartfelt paean to the transient nature of young love. Zutaut was right, and on 23 July, 1988 (Slash's 23rd birthday), with the ballad storming up the charts, *Appetite For Destruction* hit #1 on the *Billboard 200,* where it remained for three weeks. That was merely a taster, however, for one month later 'Sweet Child O' Mine' claimed the #1 slot on the singles chart to send the parent album back to the coveted top spot where it remained for another five weeks. Within eighteen months the album had sold around nine million copies in the US alone, and has gone on to sell 35 million worldwide, making it one of the best-selling albums of all time.

Needless to say, *Appetite For Destruction* has accrued countless accolades. In 1989, *Rolling Stone*, which chose to ignore the album upon its release, ranked it as the 27th best album of the 1980s, and subsequently listed it as #61 on their 500 Greatest Albums of All Time. In 2003, VH1 placed it at #42 on their Greatest Albums list, while in 2007 the rock monsters at *Kerrang!* made it #1 on their 100 Greatest Rock Albums Ever list.

In 1999, Axl surprised everybody by announcing he'd brought *Appetite* into the 21$^{st}$ century by re-recording the album using the latest state-of-the-art technology. But as the original version was still shifting upwards of 10,000 copies per year, the record company was of the opinion that there's no need to oil what ain't a squeakin'.

# ARKEEN, WEST

West Arkeen, who was a talented musician/songwriter, is often referred to as having been the sixth member of Guns N' Roses.

He was born in Neuilly-sur-Seine, France on 18 June, 1960, but grew up in San Diego, California where he taught himself to play guitar before moving to Los Angeles aged 21 to pursue a career in the music industry. It was there that he befriended a bunch of ragtag musicians called Guns N' Roses and would go on to co-write 'It's So Easy', 'Patience', 'Bad Obsession', 'The Garden' and 'Yesterdays' with the band.

In 1995, West started his own band, The Outpatience, and their debut album *Anxious Disease* featured contributions from Slash, Duff and Axl, who sang backing vocals on the title track as well as co-writing another track with Izzy. Izzy and Duff are perhaps the two Gunners most closely associated with West as he co-wrote two songs on Duff's solo album *Believe In Me*, and played bass on Izzy's debut solo album *Izzy Stradlin and the Ju-Ju Hounds*. The three also collaborated together on a side project aptly named 'The Drunkfux'.

On 30 May, 1997 West was found dead in his Los Angeles home. His management company issued a statement stating that the musician's death was the result of an "accidental opiate overdose" whilst he was recuperating from severe third degree burns which were the result of an accident when his barbecue exploded. Some believe that the badly disfigured West had purposely taken his own life.

His memory will live on, however, as G N' R's *Live Era '87 – '93* album was dedicated to him.

# B'

## BACH, SEBASTIAN

Sebastian Bach is the ex-Skid Row frontman and long-time friend of Axl Rose.

Sebastian Philip Bierk, despite his Germanic-sounding name, was born on 3 April, 1968 in Freeport, Bahamas before relocating to Canada with his family. He was raised in Peterborough, Ontario, where he, along with his two siblings, attended the nearby Lakeside College School. Sebastian's brother Zac would find fame as a goaltender in the Canadian National Hockey League, while his sister Dylan became an actress. Having decided he wanted to be a rock star, Sebastian honed his singing skills in local no-hope bands such as Kid Wikked, Madam X and one-gig wonders VO5, before being offered the role in Skid Row in 1987 after impressing the band's guitarist Dave Sabo whilst crooning at famed rock photographer Mark Weiss' wedding.

It was whilst on a promotional tour in support of Skid Row's eponymously-entitled debut album in 1989 that Bach suffered a "homophobe" backlash similar to the one experienced by Axl over the lyrical content of 'One In A Million', when he took to the stage wearing a T-shirt bearing the slogan 'AIDS Kills Fags Dead', which parodied a well-known TV ad slogan of the day. The success of the Skid Row debut – in conjunction with Bach's pretty boy appeal – led to his being invited to join Axl, Slash and Duff, and Metallica's James Hetfield and Lars Ulrich, in an ad hoc combo which performed together as GAK at *RIP* magazine's birthday party celebrations held at the Hollywood Palladium on 9 November, 1990. This in turn led to Skid Row being invited to accompany Guns N' Roses on the first US leg of the *Use Your Illusion* tour in 1991 as well as various European shows, including one at Wembley on 31 August, 1991 where the charismatic frontman memorably ended the band's set by informing the crowd he was going to "Have a smoke, a Jack n' coke, and sit back and watch Guns N' Fuckin' Roses!"

Despite the release of two more studio albums: *Slave To The Grind* (1991) and *Subhuman* (1995), mainstream success seemed destined to elude Skid Row, and it was Sebastian who paid the price for said failure by being fired from the band in 1996.

That same year, Sebastian formed the Last Hard Men, which

was a rock supergroup of sorts as it included Smashing Pumpkins drummer Jimmy Chamberlin and Breeders guitarist Kelley Deal. The band recorded an album for Atlantic Records who then, rather surprisingly, opted not to release it. (The record eventually came out with little or no fanfare as a limited pressing of 1000 copies in 1998 on Deal's own label, Nice Records.)

In 2000, Sebastian, although still playing regularly with his band Sebastian Bach and Friends, followed in his sister's thespian footsteps by appearing in Broadway productions of *The Rocky Horror Show*, in which he was cast as Riff Raff, as well as the title role in *Jekyll & Hyde*. And in October, 2002 he signed up to play Jesus in a national touring production of Andrew Lloyd Webber's *Jesus Christ Superstar* and garnered favourable reviews before being dismissed for alleged diva-like behaviour.

In May, 2006, Sebastian, having rekindled his friendship with Axl Rose after some 13 years of not speaking, joined the new G N' R incarnation on stage to perform 'My Michelle' at three of the band's four warm-up shows at New York City's Hammerstein Ballroom. This also led to his being invited to accompany the band to Europe where he made several more guest appearances. In June, 2007, he put his own band together for a four-date mini-tour of Japan before joining up with Guns N' Roses to support them on the Australian and

New Zealand legs of their *Chinese Democracy* tour.

As Sebastian had also contributed vocals to the *Chinese Democracy* album he jokingly sent Axl a text suggesting that he should return the favour by appearing on his new solo EMI backed album *Angel Down* (his first solo offering since 1999's *Bring 'Em Bach Alive*) which was scheduled for US release in November, 2007. To his amazement Axl readily agreed and appears on three tracks. The original idea had been for Axl to guest on the album's title track, but he subsequently changed his mind even though he believed it to be a "great rip-your-head-off song". The three tracks he does feature on are: 'Love Is A Bitchslap', perhaps not surprisingly, earmarked as the first single; 'Stuck Inside', which Axl described on the G N' R website as a "kind of call and answer part" and allowed him the freedom to write his own words and melodies, while the third is a cover-version of Aerosmith's 'Back In The Saddle'. Axl also expressed his gratitude to his old friend "Bas" for the opportunity to get involved in the album. "For me," he says on the website posting, "the three songs together are a good package. They are all different, with different approaches and styles from each other and from material I have on the upcoming Guns N' Roses record. For me, the timing couldn't be better and I'm quite surprised to be on one song, let alone three!"

# BAKER, ROY THOMAS

The legendary British-born producer who has worked with a diversity of bands ranging from Dusty Springfield through to The Stranglers, was another producer brought in by Axl to try and make some sense of *Chinese Democracy*.

Although Baker's association with G N' R was brief, he has surely earned a lasting place in rock folklore for his production

work on Queen's first six albums – including the band's ground-breaking 1975 world-wide hit 'Bohemian Rhapsody'.

# BARBER, JUSTIN

Justin Barber was a finance analyst who was said to have been inspired by the lyrical content of 'Used To Love Her' to murder his wife in 2003.

When the 33-year-old stood trial for his life in St. Augustine, Florida, the prosecuting council suggested it was his having listened to the Guns N' Roses track 'Used To Love Her' which drove him to murder 27 year-old April Barber. April, who was found dead on a remote stretch of beach near the family home, had been shot in the head at close range. In his defence Barber claimed that he and his wife had been attacked by a mugger whilst taking an evening stroll, and that the mugger had left him for dead after shooting him four times in the upper body.

In a surreal moment, the courthouse fell silent as forensic computer analyst Christopher Hendry – who worked at the Florida State Crime Laboratory, and had found the G N' R track amongst the deleted files on Barber's hard drive – placed a laptop on the witness box and played the song for the jury whilst the lyrics appeared on a large poster board which had been set up especially for that purpose. Hendry, whilst under

questioning, stated he had found further damning evidence on the hard drive of Barber's company-issued laptop, including a Google search for 'trauma cases gunshot tight chest' and another on 'Florida divorce'. And although the analyst had found some 1,700 songs contained on the hard drive – including 'November Rain' – 'Used To Love Her' was the only one found to have been deleted. Under cross-examination, however, the analyst was forced to concede that there was no way of knowing whether Barber had listened to that particular song on the night of the murder.

Although it was never established how many of the jurors were fans of Guns N' Roses or indeed were familiar with the band's work, they took less than an hour to establish Barber's guilt and an 8-4 majority recommendation for the death penalty. In what was a rare legal move, however, Judge Edward Hedstrum departed from the jury's recommendation and instead sentenced Barber to life imprisonment

## BARBIERO, MICHAEL

Michael Barbiero was a New York-based engineer who worked on *Appetite For Destruction*.

Shortly after the 12 tracks slated for *Appetite For Destruction* were recorded, Slash accompanied Alan Niven to New York to meet up with Michael Barbiero and his then long-term collaborator Steve Thompson, who passed their audition by mixing 'Mr Brownstone'. According to Slash, Niven had also been hoping for a shot at mixing the album, and had recorded a mix of the song. Unfortunately for Niven, his effort was considered too hollow and linear, while the New York duo had rocked the house.

Barbiero started out as a staff producer at Paramount Records, where, aged just 23, he received his first Grammy nomination for his production work on the soundtrack album to the 1973 Al Pacino movie *Serpico*. All told, the engineer has received nine Grammy nominations, winning on three

occasions. The first was in 1985 for Cutting Crew's *Broadcast*, the second in 1994 for Blues Traveller's *Runaround*, and lastly for Ziggy Marley's 1997 album *Fallen Is Babylon*.

During the disco era of the late-70s and early-80s, Barbiero also made a name for himself as a specialist re-mixer, and applied his engineering skills to 12" remixes for legendary soul divas Aretha Franklin and Whitney Houston, as well as The Jacksons, Earth, Wind and Fire, Mick Jagger and Madonna. When he and Thompson decided to shift over from disco to mainstream rock, one of the first projects was for Geffen's recent acquisitions City Kidd who would subsequently change their name to Tesla. In 1995, Barbiero began working with Gov't Mule for whom he has either produced or co-produced eleven separate projects – including the band's awarding-winning albums *The Deepest End* and *Deja Voodoo*. Aside from Guns N' Roses Barbiero has worked with a diverse range of revered artists such as John Lennon, The Velvet Underground, Alice Cooper and Cypress Hill.

# BARNEY'S BEANERY

The famed West Hollywood restaurant and bar located on the old Route 66, now known as the Santa Monica Freeway, where legend has it that Alan Niven held a meeting with the latest – and certainly the brashest – addition to the Geffen roster, and proceeded to match the Gunners drink for drink whilst laying out his game plan.

Barney's was founded in 1920 by John 'Barney' Anthony, and should not be confused with the one located on Santa Monica's fashionable 3rd Street Promenade, which, in the eyes of its current clientele – including Stiff Little Fingers guitarist Ian 'Stick' McCallum – is little more than a "Disneyland for tourists". Almost from its inception, Barney's became a favourite watering hole for Hollywood's acting elite such as Clara Bow, John Barrymore, Errol Flynn and Clark Gable. And the emergence of a burgeoning music scene on the nearby Sunset Strip during the '60s led to rock luminaries such as Jim Morrison and Janice Joplin becoming regu-

lars. Indeed, it is said that Janice spent her last evening on earth here, and her car was found parked out back the following morning. Ironically, given the future controversy over the lyrical content of 'One In A Million', Anthony fell foul of L.A.'s homosexuals for blatantly displaying a sign that read 'FAGOTS – STAY OUT' (sic). It is believed the sign first appeared sometime during 1940 and regardless of steadfast opposition form the local gay community and an article by *Life Magazine,* was still on display at the time of Anthony's death in 1968. It would take an organised picket by the Gay Liberation Front on 7 February, 1970 before the new owners agreed to take down the offending sign, and even then it reappeared again on several occasions during the 1970s before finally coming down for good.

## BEAVAN, SEAN

Beavan, the Cleveland-born producer who is perhaps best known for his work with Nine Inch Nails and Marilyn Manson, has also been involved in the production on *Chinese Democracy*.

Beavan, however, has more than one string to his bow, and other than producing and mixing, he is also a talented bass player (he collaborated with fellow Clevelander Eric Carman on the song 'Hungry Eyes' for the *Dirty Dancing* Soundtrack), and certainly knows

his way around a mixing desk. It was while he was working as a sound engineer at the Right Track Studio in downtown Cleveland in the late '80s that he met Nine Inch Nails frontman Trent Reznor, whose daytime job was as the studio's in-house producer. As Reznor was familiar with Beavan's capabilities, he asked him to mix the demos for what would subsequently be NIN's debut album *Pretty Hate Machine*, as well as the follow-up, *The Downward Spiral*. Beavan also went out on the road with the band to mix the sound for their live shows, and the more successful NIN became, the more his reputation grew. Through Reznor, he was invited to mix several tracks on future Goth God Marilyn Manson's debut album *Portrait Of An American Family* (Would that be the Arnold family from TV's Wonder Years?) This led to his mixing and co-producing Manson's follow-up album *Antichrist Superstar*, as well as the opportunity to mix front of the house on the *Antichrist Superstar* world tour.

In 1997 Beavan moved into Manson's home high up in the Hollywood Hills to start production on the artist's third album, *Mechanical Animals*. Once the record was complete he remained in Los Angeles to produce and mix for artists as diverse as God Lives Underwater, System of a Down, Slayer and Kidneythieves. He also worked on G N' R bassist Tommy Stinson's solo album, which in turn led to his being invited to work on *Chinese Democracy*.

Beavan also mixes and produces for his own band 8mm, which is proving very popular on the L.A. scene and includes his wife Juliette in the line-up. Their debut album, *Songs To Love And Die By* was released in late 2006.

# BENEDETTI, ROBERT

Robert Benedetti was Guns N' Roses' in-house tattooist during their rise to stardom, and as a thank you was forever immortalised within the sleeve notes on *Appetite For Destruction*. Not surprisingly, this led to a steady increase in business at his Sunset Strip parlour.

# BLACK RANDY

Black Randy was a Los Angeles-based musician who generously provided the then unsigned

Guns N' Roses with the money to record their first demos.

Randy, born plain old Jon Morris on 5 January, 1952, fronted the L.A. avante-garde punk band Metro Squad during the late 1970s and early '80s, which at one time featured future Go-Go Belinda Carlisle in its line-up. It is fair to say that Metro Squad would probably have been just another L.A. band had it not been for Randy's amusing – and often controversial – lyrics. Their first single, 'Trouble At The Cup', caused uproar upon its release as the lyrics appear to advocate attacking the police. But as with all Randy's songs, it was merely tongue-in-cheek. The group's one and only album, *Pass The Dust, I think I'm Bowie*, which includes covers of both James Brown's 'Say It Loud, I'm Black and I'm Proud', and Isaac Hayes' theme tune from the cult Blaxploitation film *Shaft*, was released on Dangerhouse Records, the label they themselves had helped to establish.

Metro Squad shows had always been regarded as chaotic affairs owing to Randy's predilection for drink and drugs, but by 1980 his intake was so great that he was a shadow of his former self and could only stagger about the stage barely remembering the words to his own songs. Although the other musicians tried to salvage the shows, the writing was on the wall in stark lettering, and the band finally imploded in 1980. Although Randy remained an active presence on the L.A. scene and championed up-and-coming bands such as Guns N' Roses, he did nothing to curb his wayward lifestyle and on 11 November, 1988 he succumbed to an AIDS related illness brought on by his chronic drug use.

## BOWIE, DAVID

David Bowie, the multi-faceted entertainer whose career has spanned five decades fell foul of Axl Rose in 1989 for having paid too much attention to Axl's then girlfriend Erin Everly.

Bowie, the self-styled 'Thin White Duke' and creator of the androgynous '70's space-age superstar 'Ziggy Stardust', was keen to see for himself whether Guns N' Roses justified their reputation and called in at the Cathouse where the Gunners were performing one of two warm up shows for the forthcoming Rolling Stones dates at the Los Angeles

Coliseum. Whether he was aware of Erin and Axl's relationship is a matter for conjecture, and while such behaviour would normally have resulted in the offender being indelibly inked on Axl's 'shit list', this was not the case with Bowie. Several months after the event, the two singers even went out for a conciliatory meal, where, perhaps not surprisingly, the main topic of conversation was the music business, and its potential pitfalls. Axl was so impressed with Bowie's nous and know-how that he went so far as call him "sick", which, at the time, was apparently the highest accolade the G N' R frontman could bestow.

## BUCKETHEAD

The mysterious, inverted KFC bucket, and plastic facemask-wearing oddball who describes himself as a "guitar mutant virtuoso", joined Guns N' Roses in 2000 and remained with the band until 2004.

The comics and Kung Fu flicks-loving guitarist, who was born plain-old Brian Carroll in Southern California in 1969, first came to musical prominence in 1992 as a member of avant-funk outfit Praxis. And aside from his four-year tenure with G N' R, has also worked with Bootsy Collins, Tom Waits and ex-Faith No More frontman Mike Patton. Although he is something of a multi-instrumentalist, having also mastered bass, banjo and piano, it is the guitar which has proved his forte. He is also a prolific composer having released 36 solo albums to date, which cover a variety of musical genres including thrash-metal, electronica, funk and jazz.

Unlike most lead guitarists, Buckethead is something of an introvert, often uncomfortable on stage, and it was this that led to him adopting his now trademark disguise. The white plastic facemask was in homage to the boiler-suited psychopathic slasher, Michael Myers from the *Halloween* horror movie franchise, while the bucket-on-the-head idea came to him one night after eating fried chicken. It is said that the original bucket came from the lesser known Deli Chicken chain, but the guitarist inevitably switched to KFC on account of it being 'finger-pickin' good'. Like many of G N' R's old school following, I was bemused upon learning the name of Axl's idiosyncratic recruit. But then again, back in the day there were quite a few eyebrows raised at the top-hatted guitarist who went by the name of 'Slash'.

As if taking to the stage sporting a fried chicken receptacle on his head wasn't enough, Buckethead went on to develop a bizarre chicken fetish, which saw him claiming in subsequent interviews that he had been raised by chickens in a coop. He also stated that his long-term ambition was to bring attention to the on-going chicken holocaust in fast-food outlets the world over, which explains why two of his solo offerings, *KFC Skin Piles* (2001) and *Enter The Chicken* (2005), are in homage to free-range poultry.

The guitarist's stage antics are also left of centre as he is known to intersperse his fretwork skills with robotic break dance routines and nunchaka displays – the latter often conducted whilst continuing to play. He also has a tendency to dish out small gifts and sweets to the audience, and even claimed that his sole reason for accepting Axl's invitation to join Guns N' Roses was because the singer had presented him with a rare collector's edition of the Leatherface doll from *The Texas Chainsaw Massacre* movie, which he took as a good omen.

The portents didn't appear quite so promising when G N' R's 2001 summer tour was pulled at the eleventh hour owing to – according to official sources – the guitarist having been ordered to rest due to his suffering 'internal haemorrhaging of the stomach'. Although it could have simply been a coincidence, *Chinese Democracy*'s release date was put back from June – as previously touted by Doug Goldstein – until the autumn, pending some fine-tuning. Rumours soon began to fly, however, that the real reason behind the tour cancellation was Axl's ire over the timing of the release of Buckethead's latest solo recording, *Somewhere Over The Slaughterhouse* (5 June), which he believed the guitarist would overtly promote whilst out on a tour intended to promote the yet again delayed Guns N' Roses album.

Although Buckethead toured with G N' R in 2002, and was also involved in the recording of *Chinese Democracy*, he left the band in May, 2004 shortly before they were due to fly out to Lisbon, Portugal, to take part in the fourth Rock in Rio festival. The guitarist gave no reason for his sudden departure, but Axl give his version of events in the following press release:

"The band has been put in an untenable position by guitarist Buckethead and his untimely departure. During his tenure with the band Buckethead has been inconsistent and erratic in both his behaviour and his commitment, despite being under contract, creating uncertainty and confusion and making it virtually impossible to move forward with recording, rehearsals and live plans with confidence. His transient lifestyle has made it near impossible for even his closest friends to have nearly any form of communications with him whatsoever. There is not a member of this camp that is not hurt, upset and ultimately disappointed by this event. Regardless of anyone's opinions of me and what I may or may not deserve, clearly the fans, individuals in this band, management, crew and our support group do not deserve this type of treatment. On behalf of Guns N' Roses and myself, I apologise to the fans who planned to see us at Rock in Rio."

2005 saw the release of Buckethead's first DVD, *Secret Recipe*, which was initially only avail-able for sale at touring venues, before becoming widely available in March, 2006. His follow-up DVD *Young Buckethead*, which features rare live footage of the guitarist from 1990 and 1991, was released in November, 2006, while another album, *Pepper's Ghost*, was released in March, 2007.

# BUCKMASTER, PAUL

Paul Buckmaster, the British-born arranger and composer perhaps best known for his work with David Bowie and Elton John, was brought in by Axl Rose to work on *Chinese Democracy* in 2004.

After graduating from London's Royal Academy of Music where he'd won a cello scholarship, Buckmaster served as cellist and composer in several English jazz and progressive groups before a life-changing encounter with legendary jazz trumpeter Miles Davis in 1969 which saw him accompany Davis to New York to study under the great man. He subsequently wrote several arrangements and played electric cello on Davis' 1972 album '*On The Corner*'.

The following year he worked on Elton John's eponymously-titled second album, which has resulted in a collaboration stretching over Elton's four decade long career. His CV also includes the Rolling Stones (having been credited with the idea for a gospel choir backing on the band's 1969 single 'You can't Always Get what You Want'), Grateful Dead, Mott The Hoople, Harry Nilsson, Carly Simon and the Backstreet Boys. In 2001, he won a Grammy Award for 'Best Arranger' for his sweeping arrangement on Train's second album *Drops of Jupiter*.

## BUMBLEFOOT

Ron 'Bumblefoot' Thal, a successful musician and producer in his own right, is another to fill the role of Guns N' Roses' lead guitarist.

Thal, who was born 25 September, 1969 in Brooklyn, New York, supposedly received his less-than-savoury moniker, which is the term for an inflammatory bacterial infection afflicting only birds and rodents, whilst helping his wife study for her veterinary exams. His penchant for Vigier Guitars led to the company presenting him with a custom-made model shaped like a human foot at the NAMM (National Association of Music Merchants) convention in January, 1998. The guitar also has a black and gold striped finish, and decorative wings which extended from the body whenever the whammy bar was activated.

Aside from his prowess on the guitar, Thal is also a talented songwriter and producer and has recorded seven solo albums either as Ron Thal: *The Adventures of Bumblefoot* (1995); *Hermit* (1997); *Hands* (1998); *Uncool* (2000); *911* (2001), or as Bumblefoot: *Forgotten Anthology* (2003) and *Normal* (2005). He replaced the departing Buckethead in May, 2006 and made his live debut with the band that same month at the Hammerstein Ballroom in New York City. When he isn't touring with the Gunners, Thal can be found in his studio in Princeton, New Jersey, writing background music for video games and reality TV shows such as *The Osbournes* and *The Real World*.

## CAMP FREDDY

Camp Freddy is a musical collective of well-known and established L.A-based musicians who took their name from Tony Beckley's character in the 1969 Michael Caine movie, *The Italian Job* – which coincidentally features a character called Bill Bailey.

The collective's core members are ex-Jane's Addiction duo Chris Chaney and Dave Navarro, ex-Cult guitarist Billy Morrison, Donovan Leitch Jr. and Velvet Revolver's Scott Weiland and Mat Sorum, while guest musicians range from Billy Duffy,

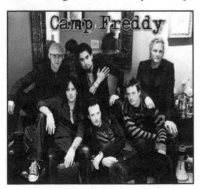

Billie Joe Armstrong, Billy Idol, Dave Kushner, Izzy Stradlin, Slash, Sebastian Bach and Steve Jones to name but a few. Camp Freddy also have their own two-hour radio show which is broadcast every Saturday night on the Los Angeles-based indie 103.1 where the musicians – mostly Navarro and Morrison – play their favourite tracks and discuss wide-ranging topics.

Camp Freddy's debut single – a cover-version of the Cheap Trick hit 'Surrender' – was released in September, 2006 and also features in the Jessica Simpson movie *Employee Of The Month*, while the follow-up, a cover of Slade's 1973 festive perennial, 'Merry Xmas Everybody' was only made available on iTunes that same December. They are currently working with producer Mike Clink on an album which is intended to mirror their live performances with guest musicians being invited in to perform on each track.

## CATHOUSE THE

The Cathouse – or Cat Club, as it's sometimes referred to – is the West Hollywood venue where Guns N' Roses showcased the four songs which appeared on their *Live?!*@Like a Suicide* EP.

In October, 1986, in keeping with the rise of the West Hollywood glam-metal scene, future Headbanger's Ball host Rikki

Rachtman approached the owner of a rundown dance-music orientated bar and, with the help of his roommate, Faster Pussycat frontman Taime Downe, and influential KROQ DJ and record store owner, Joe Brookes (who tipped the wink to Tom Zutaut regarding Guns N' Roses), transformed it into a decadent Tuesday night rock 'n' roll hotspot.

Despite the failure of the newly-named Cathouse's grand opening to pull in the expected crowds, Rachtman persevered, and each week saw a few more people walking through the door – including members of Mötley Crüe and Aerosmith. Needless to say, when word got out that bands were hanging out at the club, the girls came in their droves, which in turn brought in the guys.

In December, 1986, Rachtman was approached by some friends of his who happened to be in a band, asking if they might use the club to showcase some songs intended for their first record. The band's name was Guns N' Roses. Rachtman readily agreed, and two days before Christmas the Cathouse played host to the group, who performed an all-acoustic set, with Downe's Faster Pussycat, L.A. Guns, and another aspiring L.A. quartet called Jetboy providing support. By the time the Gunners next performed at the Cathouse on 21 January, 1988, which included a guest appearance from Mötley Crüe's Vince Neil, it was regarded as the hottest venue in town with bands such as Motor-

head, Megadeth, Black Crows, Pearl Jam and Alice In Chains all clamouring to play. Faster Pussycat, Alice Cooper and Mötley Crüe have even gone so far as to name-check the venue in one of their songs. The Cathouse also featured in the movie *Decline of Western Civilisation ?: the Metal Years*, and the club's profile was heightened even further when the *LA Times* and *LA Weekly* began writing favourable features. And

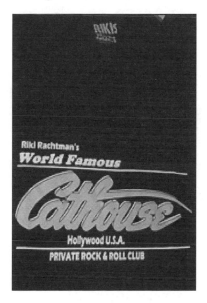

as the audience was predominantly female, the Cathouse also made the pages of *Women's Wear Daily* and *Californian Apparel News*.

Guns N' Roses returned to the Cathouse in October, 1989 for two 'warm-up' shows performed over consecutive evenings in preparation for the band's forthcoming Coliseum dates supporting the Rolling Stones later that month. The first of the shows, on 10 October, included the video shoot for 'It's So Easy', which led to the now-famous incident when Axl took offence to David Bowie having shown a little too much attention to Erin Everly and proceeded to chase the Thin White Duke out of the club. Fortunately for Bowie, the Cathouse's strict 'no cameras' policy saved him from potential tabloid humiliation.

The Cathouse hadn't seen the last of Guns N' Roses, however, for on 22 June, 2000, Axl, making his first public appearance in six years, joined the club's houseband, The Starfuckers, which included ex-G N' R guitarist Gilby Clarke and the venue's new proprietor, former Stray Cats drummer, Slim Jim Phantom, on stage for impromptu renditions of two Rolling Stones numbers; 'Wild Horses' and 'Dead Flowers'. The story goes that Slim Jim and Gilby, having spotted Axl's long-serving bodyguard, Earl, standing at the bar, believed the thickset guy sporting a baseball cap pulled down low over his eyes standing beside Earl vaguely resembled Axl. The pair duly went over to get a closer look with Gilby even going to far as to tap the guy on the shoulder. But just as Gilby was turning away again, convinced they'd made a mistake, Axl's pinched face split into a huge grin and he greeted the guitarist like a long-lost brother.

The lawsuit and counter lawsuits of six years earlier were immediately forgotten, and aside

from agreeing to join Gilby on stage – much to the delight of the 250 or so astonished punters – the two sat chatting into the small hours. But, despite several firm assurances that he would keep in touch, Gilby never saw nor heard from Axl again.

## CHINESE DEMOCRACY

*Chinese Democracy* is the title of Guns N' Roses' long-awaited sixth studio album.

Although there is no way of knowing what – if ever – the $13 million+ album's final track-listing will be, it is safe to assume that the following songs will appear in one guise or another: *Chinese Democracy; Better; The Blues; I.R.S; Madagascar; Sorry* and *There Was A Time,* while the remainder will most likely be culled from the following demos: *Oh My God; Today, Tomorrow, Forever; Silk Worms; Hearts Always Get Killed; Rhiad & The Bedouins; Cock-a-roach Soup; This Life; Closing In On You; Something Always; Catcher In the Rye; No Love Remains; Strange Disease; Suckerpunched; Oklahoma; Friend Or Foe; Never Had It; This I Love; Prostitute; Zip It.*

Given the disappointing reaction to *The Spaghetti Incident?* Geffen were naturally keen to get the Gunners back into the studio at the earliest opportunity. But, although the rest of the band got to work on new ideas, Axl sat in his Malibu 'ivory tower' mansion fixated with idea of delivering the greatest rock album ever made, and rejected each one out of hand. Slash and Duff may have yearned to get back to their hard-rockin' roots, but Axl was of the opinion that the past was a field already well-furrowed and he had no intention of picking up the plough. In his eyes the follow up album would need to supersede the *Use Your Illusion* double-albums in both form and content.

And it wasn't a subject to be held up for debate.

The music press – which had had a field day tearing into the band for releasing an album consisting entirely of covers – were naturally eager to see whether the Gunners had anything in their artistic arsenal to wrestle the rock crown back from Nirvana, but found itself reporting on the departures of first Gilby, then incredibly Slash, Matt and finally Duff.

From here on in Axl would sail the ship alone, albeit with an ever-changing line-up that would each have their respective parts stripped from the mix following their own departures. It wasn't only guitarists and drummers that came and went through the studio's revolving door, for a succession of highly-respected producers such as Roy Thomas Baker, Youth, Sean Beavan, and Moby, were called in to occupy Mike Clink's now-vacant hot seat, only to have their efforts and advice spurned in equal measure. In 2006, however, Axl appeared to have found his man in one time Faith No More producer Andy Wallace. Despite Wallace having worked for the enemy (Nirvana), as well as the opposition (Velvet Revolver), both Axl and his Interscope paymasters were said to be delighted with the results.

The fans' patience was finally rewarded in 1999 with the release of 'Oh My God', but the song's harsh industrial-rock sound failed to strike the right chord, and as a result barely scraped into the US Top 40. It also appeared on the soundtrack to Arnold Schwarzenegger's movie *End Of Days*, but as with Arnie, Axl's salad days were well behind him. One new song – especially one devoid of Guns N' Rose's trademark guitar sound – was never going to turn many heads. And with the world inexorably creeping towards a new millennium, and the G N' R bandwagon having seemingly lost direction, the by now reclusive singer – and his grand opus – were in danger of slipping into sepia-tinged memory.

It was only following Axl's sudden re-emergence in June 2000 that titbits began to filter through the music press indicating that the long-awaited album did actually exist. It also had a name: *Chinese Democracy*. And in order to prove the new songs existed outside of Axl's imagination, the singer – ably accompanied by a line-up consisting entirely of session musicians and a guitarist sporting an upturned fast-food receptacle on his head – went out on the road. But as to an actual release date, there was no word.

In September, 2003, New York DJ, Eddie Trunk announced on air that his studio guest, Oakland Athletics baseball star Mike Piazza, had brought along a CD bearing a new Guns N' Roses song called 'I.R.S'. Piazza, having been presented with the CD by his buddy Axl, wrongly assumed that it was his to do with whatever he chose. He was wrong. And the day following Trunk's airing of the song, the radio station received a polite letter from Axl's lawyers warning them not to repeat their mistake. These days the internet is awash with links purporting to feature the best versions of the songs slated to appear on the as yet unreleased album. The last designated release date was 6 March, 2007, and although the album failed to appear, four tracks – 'There Was A Time', 'The Blues', 'I.R.S' and 'Better' – were played on the internet over the preceding weekend. As a result of this, 'I.R.S' was added – albeit briefly – to the rotation list of several US radio stations, which saw the song reach #49 on the trade magazine *Radio & Records* Active Rock National Airplay chart, before Axl's lawyers again intervened.

## CHINESE DEMOCRACY WORLD TOUR

The *Chinese Democracy* tour, which commenced on 1 January, 2001 at the House of Blues in Las Vegas, Nevada, was supposed to promote Guns N' Roses' as yet unreleased studio album of the same name.

### First Leg:
### 1 January, 2001–31 December, 2001.
### US and Europe:
### 4 dates played, 26 cancelled.

The New Year's day show at the compact 2,000 capacity House of Blues in Las Vegas was Guns N'

Roses first live performance since the final night of the *Use Your Illusion* world tour some seven-and-a-half years earlier, and the first to feature none, save Axl, of the band's original line-up. Although the two-hour 21-song set, which commenced with 'Welcome To The Jungle', and saw the reintroduction of 'Think About You' (which hadn't been performed since 1986), relied heavily on material from the G N' R back catalogue, the 2,000 fans, that had paid between $150 - $250 for their tickets, were treated to six new songs intended for the long-awaited new album: 'Oh My God'; 'The Blues'; 'Oklahoma'; the title track 'Chinese Democracy'; 'Madagascar' and 'Silk Worms'.

Next up was an appearance at the third *Rock In Rio* extravaganza on 15 January, which saw Axl bring his housekeeper Beta out onto the stage to act as his interpreter while he addressed the matter of what he termed "the old band". He informed the 150,000 crowd that his former friends – surely a veiled reference to Slash and Duff – had supposedly done their utmost to prevent him from being there. He then singled out Paul Huge for having "worked through the darkness underground for the last seven years, and that without whom there would be no Guns N' Roses." After lauding Dizzy Reed for his being the only member of the old line-up to have remained loyal and hard-working, Axl gave the cue for 'Live And Let Die'.

As *Chinese Democracy* was due for a 5 June release – and Guns N' Roses were already scheduled to appear at several European festivals in the summer – the band announced a 14-date European tour, including four UK shows in London, Manchester, Glasgow and Birmingham. But, with tickets already on sale, the tour was pulled just two weeks before the opening date in Nuremburg on 1 June. The official reason given for the cancellations was that Buckethead had been ordered to rest having been diagnosed with internal haemorrhaging of the stomach. The 14 European dates were rescheduled for December, only to then be cancelled indefinitely in November by a somewhat embarrassed Doug Goldman, who sheepishly informed an unbelieving world media that he had forgotten to tell Axl about the rearranged dates. Goldstein's official statement read as follows: "To ensure Guns N' Roses fans the album they deserve, Axl Rose has spent every waking minute of every day during the past five years writing, recording, and producing Guns N' Roses' first album of all

new material since 1991. Following the euphoria of Rock in Rio, I jumped the gun and arranged a European tour as our plan was to have the new album out this year. Unfortunately, Buckethead's illness not only stopped the tour but also slowed progress on *Chinese Democracy*. As a result, touring right now is logistically impossible. I am very sorry to disappoint our fans, but I can assure them that it's not what Axl wanted nor is it 'Another page from the Howard Hughes book of rock' as some of the media will no doubt portray it. I made a plan and unfortunately it did not work out. The good news is that everyone is ecstatic with the album and we will be meeting with the label to schedule its release, following which we will announce the rescheduled dates to coincide. Guns N' Roses look forward to seeing everybody next year, and once again, please accept my apologies for the way this has played out".

To add to the confusion, Axl said that he hadn't even been aware of the proposed tour, and had only found out about it having then been cancelled whilst surfing the internet. The band had also pulled out of the European festivals, and the album's release date was put back again until the autumn.

On 29 December, 2001, by which time the album was still sans release date, Guns N' Roses returned to Las Vegas for a show at The Joint, the 1400 capacity venue housed within the Hard Rock Café. This show, however,

was only intended as a 'warm-up' for the one held in the Hard Rock Café itself two days later, on New Year's Eve. In 2000, Slash, in response to the constant questioning as to whether he would agree to a reunion of Guns N' Roses' original line-up, said that in order for that to happen then all five members would need to have straightened out their heads enough so they could get together in the same room. So when the guitarist, who happened to be in Las Vegas for the New Year celebrations, heard about the show, he thought he might as well test the water by calling in on his erstwhile buddy Axl, as well as check out the new band. To his astonishment, however, he was informed by Goldstein that he wasn't welcome, and that he would be refused entry should he manage to procure a ticket.

As for the show itself, the band again relied on a set comprising of the old standards interspersed with new songs intended for the album. Once again, the show's climax came with 'Paradise City', and as Axl and co. cavorted about the stage, a multitude of vivid images of the Las Vegas strip flashed across the stage screens.

Despite Axl's earlier praise for his old Lafayette buddy, Paul Huge, it seemed that others within the G N' R camp were somewhat less enthused by the guitarist's contributions and the Las Vegas show proved to be his last.

## Second Leg:
## 14 – 26 August, 2002.
## Asia and Europe:
## 22 dates played, 18 cancelled.

On 14 August, 2002, Guns N Roses kick-started their six-date Asia/Europe tour with a show at Hong Kong's Convention and Exhibition Centre – the band's first ever show in China – as part of the Summer Sonic Festival, with former Psychedelic Furs and Ben Folds Five guitarist Richard Fortus having been drafted in as Paul Huge's replacement. Before playing the song 'Chinese Democracy' Axl took time out to explain to the 2,000+ audience the idea behind the title of the forthcoming album, whilst said album's artwork was displayed on a giant screen mounted at the rear of the stage. And as in Vegas at the start of the year, sweeping panoramic views of the neon-lit city outside – as well as China's national flag – flashed across the screens throughout the show.

Following on from Hong Kong, the band flew to Japan, where they played two gigs in Chiba and Osaka on the 17 and 18 August respectively, before then heading to the UK, where they were scheduled to perform two shows. The first of these was on 24 August at the Carling Weekend Leeds Festival staged at the city's Temple Newsham Park, while the second came two days later at London's Docklands Arena. Although it had been nine long years since the last UK G N' R show, Axl kept the expectant 52,000+ Leeds crowd waiting over an hour beyond the allotted start time of 10pm before taking to the stage – his trademark long flowing red hair intricately woven into braided plaits – against a swirling backdrop of flashing lights and screaming skulls. It may have been a different line-up – with *Classic Rock* magazine going so far as to describe the boys as the 'greatest Guns N' Roses tribute band in the world' – but the songs definitely remained the same. And so what if there was no Slash, Duff, Steven or Izzy on stage with Axl, the incumbents present were all proficient enough on their respective instruments to make the old classics sound identical – if not better – than how they'd sounded when first recorded some fifteen years earlier. And if there were any romantics in the crowd yearning for a return to the bad old days of yesteryear, then all they needed to do was close their eyes and it was as if the skulls from the instantly recognisable tattoo adorning Axl's right forearm had magically sprung to life.

Although Axl gave no explanation as to why Guns N' Roses came on stage over an hour later than scheduled, he took affront when the event's organisers began calling for the band to curtail their set at the pre-designated hour. He brought the proceedings to a halt and informed the audience that although he didn't want to get arrested for inciting a riot – and nor did he want anyone else to get hurt or arrested – he reckoned the band still had another good seven or eight songs to play. He also told them – and the officials milling around at the side of the stage – that he "hadn't come all the way to England to be told to go back home by some fucking asshole." Thankfully, common sense prevailed, and the band was allowed to complete their 16-song set.

He also interrupted the London Docklands show, again just before 'Chinese Democracy'. This time, however, was to light-heartedly inform the 12,500 capacity crowd that there seemed to be some concern amongst the band's fans that, as they were repeatedly playing the same five or six new songs, then there couldn't be any other good tracks remaining. "Au contraire, mon frere," he told them with a reflective shake of the head, "We're just playin' the songs we're not considering putting out as singles or anything. So you'll get eighteen songs, and about ten extra tracks. And once the record company feels that has run its course, then you'll get it all over again. And by that time," he added with a chuckle, "I should be done with the third album."

The band then returned to the US for a surprise appearance at the MTV Video Music Awards held at the Radio City Music Hall in New York, where the band treated the gathered ensemble of ticket-holders, celebrities and music executives to a three-song medley of 'Welcome To The Jungle', 'Madagascar' and 'Paradise City'.

Guns N' Roses first US tour since 1993 was due to commence on 22 November, 2002, with a show across the border in Canada, at Vancouver's General Motors Place arena. And although Axl had personally announced to fans via the official G N' R website that the tour was "our tour", and avowed that he and the rest of the band would be there "for better or worse", the event's organisers were forced to cancel the show at the eleventh hour following the singer's failure to appear at the 10,000 seater venue. In fact, Axl wasn't even in the city at the time he and the rest of the band were due to appear owing to his having delayed his departure from Los Angeles to the actual day of the show. An unforeseen delay to his scheduled flight meant that he was still 35,000 feet up in the air, somewhere above Canada when he should have been taking to the stage at 9.30pm. The rest of the group had made it to the venue but there seemed little point in going on without the star attraction, so they remained in the adjoining backstage area drinking beer in celebration of guitarist Robin Finck's birthday. Buckethead later told one bemused reporter that, although he and the rest of the band had been aware Axl's plane had been delayed and he therefore wouldn't make the soundcheck, they had been under the impression that Axl would still arrive in time to do the show.

As to the ensuing riot, the guitarist told that same reporter he'd been left "shocked and dismayed", and that the first he'd known about the show being cancelled came via an announcement over the PA system whilst fellow Gunners Dizzy Reed and Tommy Stinson were being interviewed by MTV's Kurt Loder.

Needless to say, many of the fans gathered outside the venue – having shelled-out $80 for tickets – vented their frustrations by hurling rocks and bottles before then ramming the metal security barriers mounted outside through the glass doors. The Canadian cops – no doubt anxious to avoid a repeat of the St. Louis riot of eleven years earlier – were taking no chances, and waded into the throng with attack dogs, and wielded their batons with wanton abandon. They didn't even let up as the crowd began to disperse, and continued to chase and hit anyone unfortunate enough to stray into their path. One female fan later told a local TV news crew of how she'd feared the cops were going to kill someone. But a police spokeswoman told that same reporter that the crowd had been out of control and described her colleagues' response as "a correct and proper use of force".

As the band was scheduled to appear in Tacoma, Washington, the following night, Axl gave his version of the previous day's events live on air on Seattle's KISW radio. Instead of apologising, however, or even giving an explanation as to why he chose to remain in L.A. until the day of the Vancouver show, he announced that Guns N' Roses fully intended to play the show, and would have done so had the organisers not pulled the plug. He then went on to blame the venue's manager for making – at least in his and the rest of the band's opinion – a premature decision to cancel the show, before informing the listeners that his legal team were looking into the situation. He then – somewhat sarcastically, given what had occurred in his name – brought the ten-minute interview to a close saying he'd better get his ass down to the soundcheck before that night's show was also cancelled. This – as far as he was concerned – was to be the last word on the Vancouver debacle. And although G N' R's management team were subsequently approached by other local radio stations, all such interviews were to be pre-recorded for Axl's approval, as well as having to adhere to a pre-arranged list of questions, none of which touched on the Vancouver show.

Although there was no way of knowing whether the decision to take the tour to out of the way musical backwaters such as Nampa, Idaho, or Moline, Illinois, backfired on the band, or if the Vancouver riot had any significance, certain shows failed to sell out. There were no such problems for the 5 December gig at New York's Madison Square Garden, however, as the entire ticket allotment went within hours of going on sale.

The next stop on the 34-date US tour was to have been Philadelphia's First Union Centre arena the following evening, but the show was cancelled at the last minute following a telephone call to the 14,000-seat venue at around 11pm informing promoters CCE (Clear Channel Entertainment) that an unspecified band member had suddenly been taken ill. By this time, however, the arena was full, and a large number of angry fans vented their frustrations by ripping out the seats and hurling them at the stage. The band's mixing desk was also trashed and authorities – fearing a repeat of the St. Louis riot of eleven years earlier, and the far more recent Vancouver fiasco – called in armed police who managed to restore order without making any arrests. When it later emerged that the 'band member being taken ill' story was bogus, and that the group's no show was due to Axl having remained in New York to watch a basketball game, Philly radio station WMMR announced that unless Axl called in to apologise on air then it intended to implement a three-week boycott of all Guns N' Roses music – including material from the new album should it be released during that time period.

This, however, was the least of the band's problems, for over the next few days subsequent shows in Washington D.C., Albuquerque, Phoenix, Sacramento and San Jose were all cancelled. And when no one from the G N' R management team seemed willing to come forward to explain the reasoning behind the cancellations, anxious CCE promoters warned ticketholders to expect more. And on 11 December their fears were realised when all remaining tour dates were, indeed, cancelled.

## Third Leg:
## 25 May, 2006 – 20 December, 2006.
## Europe and North America:
## 74 dates played, 7 cancelled.

On 12 May, 2006, Guns N' Roses returned to the live arena with the first of four warm-up dates at New York's modest 2,000-capacity Hammerstein Ballroom in preparation for a full European tour due to commence in Spain later that same month.

The Hammerstein shows not only served as preparation for the forthcoming tour, but also provided the band with the opportunity to introduce new guitarist Ron "Bumblefoot" Thal, who'd been drafted in to replace Buckethead. And it was Bumblefoot who got the proceedings underway by stroking the by now instantly recognisable intro to 'Welcome To The Jungle'. Once again the set relied heavily on the old G N' R standards, but the ecstatic New Yorkers treated each

song like a long-lost relative. Axl may have been a few years older – and packing a few extra pounds beneath his black leather shirt – but the New York shows proved he could still deliver when it mattered. Over the course of the four near-identical shows, the group were joined on stage each night by Sebastian Bach, who sang a duet with Axl on 'My Michelle'. When Axl had first announced the New York shows on Eddie Trunk's syndicated radio show one Saturday evening, he had mischievously hinted that his old buddy Izzy might be putting in an appearance at one of the gigs. Needless to say, the Manhattan rumour mill had gone into overdrive, with many fans daring to hope that Izzy would be making a permanent return to the fold. And although such rumours proved unfounded, on the final night, 17 May, and much to the frenzied delight of the 2,000 attendees, a beaming Izzy Stradlin sauntered onto the stage for a 3-song encore of 'Think About You', 'Patience' and 'Nightrain'. The tour brought about another reunion as Del James had been brought in to assist with the logistics.

Although the New York fans had willingly embraced what had essentially been a Guns N' Roses comeback, the city's media was rather less enthusiastic, with the *New York Times* going so far as to question the band's relevance twenty years on from their initial impact. The European and British press were equally harsh, with

*The Times* – when reviewing the band's London Hammersmith Apollo show of 7 June – likening the dreadlocked Axl to a cross between Metallica's James Hetfield and Simply Red's Mick Hucknall. Axl may well have been older, but he seemed to be no wiser, and he once again tested the audience's patience by keeping them waiting. And as it was a midweek show, many disgruntled fans were forced to leave midway through the set in order to catch the last train home.

Three days later, on 10 June, Guns N' Roses returned to Castle Donington to headline the festival where, eighteen years earlier, two fans had tragically died during the band's debut performance. Although they went on stage at the appointed hour, the 59,000 strong crowd was openly hostile from the off and began pelting the stage with plastic water bottles – one of which struck bassist Tommy Stinson on the side of the head. Instead of haranguing the leather and denim-clad audience as many expected, Axl seemed taken aback at the hostile reception, and threatened to curtail the show unless the barracking ceased. Even the introduction of Izzy, who would make similar guest appearances throughout the tour, failed to restore order, and it was later reported that swaths of people were streaming for the exits whilst the band was still on stage. The show was an unmitigated disaster, and – as if one were needed – the coup de grace came courtesy of the one-time G N' R espousing *Kerrang!*, who gave the show 0/5 in a subsequent review.

Next on the agenda were Prague and Warsaw where, yet again, the shows were blighted by the band's tardiness. Even a return to Axl's supposed "favourite city", Paris, failed to stop the rot, and the evening threatened to descend into mayhem when the band still hadn't taken to the stage some two hours after the allotted time. The next appearance, at Zurich's Hallenstadion on 21 June, needed to be hastily rescheduled for 1 July owing to drummer Bryan Mantia returning to the US to be with his wife, who had gone into labour earlier than the doctors had expected. His stand-in, Frank Ferrer, an old friend and musical collaborator of Richard Fortus, flew out to Belgium in time for the band's appearance at the Graspop Festival on 24 June.

Next up was Stockholm on 26 June, where, sometime the following morning, Axl was arrested

by police following an unsavoury incident in the lobby of the Berns Hotel where the band were staying following the show at the Swedish capital's 13,000-capacity Globe Arena. Stockholm Police spokesperson, Tove Hägg, informed the Associated Press that Rose, who was deemed too intoxicated to even be questioned straight away, had returned to the hotel after partying at one of the city's nightclubs until dawn and got into an altercation with hotel staff, proceeding to cause an undisclosed amount of damage to the lobby's fixtures and fittings – including a large decorative wall mirror. When the hotel's security guard – who just happened to be an off-duty cop – tried to intervene, Axl had bitten him on the leg. One of the arresting officers, Fredrik Nylen, told reporters that the rocker [Rose] had behaved so aggressively towards the police that he had to be restrained with handcuffs. Axl himself later commented: "We had a great gig in Stockholm and I am not going to let this incident spoil that. My assistant Beta and I were talking in the lobby of the hotel when security started to give us a hard time. My only concern was to make sure she was okay."

The friction had started at the venue prior to the show when Axl upset the Swedish media by refusing to allow any pictures to be taken during the show unless the photographers were willing to first sign away their copyright to the band's management. Not surprisingly, many of the disgruntled photographers declined the singer's ultimatum and boycotted the show.

Axl's manager Merck Mercuriadis, upon being informed that the Swedish authorities took an extremely dim view to anyone threatening a police officer, hurried out to find a local lawyer. For if Axl were to refute the charges and be found guilty at trial, then he would face up to four years in jail. But as Guns N' Roses were scheduled to appear in Oslo the following evening, Axl reluctantly admitted the charges and was released that same evening after agreeing to pay a fine of 40,000 krona (about $3,000) and a further 10,000 krona ($750) in damages to the security guard. In a subsequent press release, however, Mercuriadis insisted that Axl was innocent, and had only admitted to the charges in order to avoid having to cancel the remainder of the tour. And it seemed the Swedish authorities had threatened the singer with anything between five days and three weeks behind bars without bail if he'd refused to co-operate. Mercuriadis claimed that the authorities were fully aware that millions of dollars were at stake, which made the whole experience tantamount to Axl's being held to ransom.

At the Oslo show Axl couldn't resist having a dig at those same Swedish officials and introduced 'Patience' to the Spektrum crowd as "a good song to sing when you're in jail after being arrested by a cop." Perhaps not surprisingly, he dedicated 'Out Ta Get Me' to the Swedish police, but his mood eventually lightened, and before 'November Rain' he mused: "Well, maybe I am a fucking asshole, but I'm a fucking rock 'n' roll asshole!"

On 2 July, following the rearranged Swiss gig, Guns N' Roses flew on to Holland for a show at Nijmegan's Goffert Park where Izzy joined the band on stage for 'Think About You', 'Patience', 'Nightrain' and perennial encore song 'Paradise City'. After successful appearances in Finland and a second date in Oslo, the band was supposed to then fly to Germany where they were due to play two shows opening for the Rolling Stones on the aging rockers' *A Bigger Bang* world tour, but when those dates were cancelled, owing to Keith Richards having bizarrely injured himself falling out of a coconut tree whilst vacationing on Fiji, the band instead flew on to Malakasa, Greece, where they were booked to appear at the Rockwave Festival, where, once again, Izzy joined the band on stage for the encores.

On 14 July, Guns N' Roses headlined the Bilbao Live Festival with a supporting cast which included The Cult, Blue Oyster Cult, Placebo and Fun Lovin' Criminals. And although the band didn't go on stage until 11.20pm – some 80 minutes later than scheduled – they made amends by playing for over two-and-a-quarter hours.

On 18 July, the group returned to the UK for eight shows, the first of which was at Sheffield's Hallam FM Arena, where Sebastian Bach once again opened the proceedings. Next up was Newcastle's Metro Radio Arena, and, yet again, restless fans were left to their own devices for over an hour before the band finally graced the stage. During the 21 July show at Glasgow's SEC Centre, which had latter-day punksters Towers Of London as opening act, Axl took time out to banter with the audience and mentioned that he himself was half-Scottish. After a meandering jaunt across the length and breadth of Britain with stop-offs in Manchester, Birmingham and Nottingham, the G N' R bandwagon rolled into London on 29 July for the first of two sellout shows at Wembley Arena. Once again, however, the band infuriated its audience by remaining cosseted within their dressing room for a full ninety minutes after the last support act, Bullet For My Valentine, had finished their set. When they did finally put in an appearance, Axl brought the proceedings to a halt to inform the audience that the band was running not one, but two competitions that evening. The first saw a hundred or so lucky punters – whose names were subsequently called out – being invited to join the band within the plush setting of the Cuckoo Club in upmarket Mayfair for an after-hours, intimate semi-acoustic show, while the second – and even more mouth-watering

– prize was an all expenses paid trip out to Devore, California for KROQ's Inland Invasion Concert on 23 September. It was only then that the audience understood why each of them had been asked to supply their name upon entering the venue. And in order to prolong the suspense, Axl introduced Izzy onto the stage for a medley of covers consisting of the Rolling Stones' 'Sway', Rod Stewart's 'Sailing' and the Beatles' 'Back In The USSR', whilst plucking out the names of the lucky winners in-between songs.

Although no one could question Axl's sincerity or generosity, the acoustic show at the Cuckoo Club didn't get underway until 4am, and, as the second Wem-

bley show was scheduled for later that same day, the strain of performing three shows in 48 hours proved too much for him, and Sebastian Bach was forced to take over vocal duties for the encore. Axl had started to feel unwell within a couple of hours of finishing the 75 minute acoustic show and a doctor was hurriedly summoned to the singer's hotel suite at the Mandarin Oriental hotel in Knightsbridge. The doctor diagnosed Axl as suffering from low blood pressure and low blood sugar, and strongly advised hospitalisation. This, of course, would have meant cancelling the second Wembley show, which, in years gone by, perhaps wouldn't have overly concerned Axl. But

this was no longer an option as Sanctuary – having finally lost patience over the spiralling costs of the still unreleased *Chinese Democracy* album – had severed financial support, which, coupled with the fact that the tour hadn't been the financial success everyone had been hoping for – despite playing to over half-a-million people – meant the show would have to go on.

One month later, on 31 August, Axl appeared at that year's MTV Video Music Awards and informed those in attendance, as well as the world-wide television audience, that Guns N' Roses would begin an American tour on 24 October. The band were to begin with several warm-up shows commencing with two consecutive nights at The Joint in Las Vegas on 16 and 17 September, followed by two more at San Francisco's Warfield Theatre on 20 and 21 September, and culminating in the aforementioned KROQ Inland Festival two days later. Immediately following the KROQ show, which was again marred by the band's tardiness, Axl threw a party at his Malibu mansion, where – much to their collective surprise – the assembled guests were treated to twelve or so songs intended for the *Chinese Democracy* album. For once it seemed the rumours of a looming release date appeared to be true (*Rolling Stone* claimed to have been tipped the wink to 21 November) as further Californian shows were rescheduled owing to Axl wanting to remain close to

home in order to put the finishing touches to the album. Needless to say, the record didn't surface on 21 November, and the rescheduled shows were again cancelled.

The 19-date US tour finally got underway on 20 October at the Veterans Memorial Arena in Jacksonville, Florida. The choice of opening venue was rather apt given that Axl was himself a veteran of some 20 years standing, but, although Axl and many of the band's inner circle were confident that the tour would be a resounding success – especially as the Madison Square Garden date on 11 November had again sold out in a matter of hours – the other dates didn't fare quite so well. The harsh and inescapable truth was that by 2006 Guns N' Roses were no longer 'the most dangerous band in the world', and nor were they capable of filling 50,000+ arenas. Axl may have surrounded himself with seasoned musicians who all knew their trade and could nail the riffs and keep the beat, but Messrs Fortus, Finck, Stinson, Pitman, Ferrer and Thal would never truly be able to exorcise the ghosts of Adler, Izzy, Duff and Slash. Those kids who had rushed out to buy *Appetite For Destruction* back in '87 were now parents with kids of their own, and were far more likely to slap on a DVD of their one-time heroes than they were to attend a live show. And the latest generation of teenage rabble-rousers – although happy to snag the old man's dog-eared G N' R albums for an occasional spin – needed musical heroes of their own, and were therefore spending their allowances on Marilyn Manson, Nine Inch Nails and Green Day.

If the sight of row upon row of empty seats at certain venues wasn't disconcerting enough to the band's management, then the subsequent scathing reviews should have been enough to set the alarm bells ringing. The *Boston Herald*'s review of the 8 November show at the nowhere near full DCU Centre in Worcester, Massachusetts, cited Axl's vocals as "mediocre", and the band as an "octet of soulless virtuosos", while Greg Kot of the *Tribune* uncharitably described Axl as the "middle-aged mouthpiece for a bunch of pros doing what pros do on six-figure retainers". J. P. Gorman, who was reviewing the Cleveland show for *cinemablend. com* was even less charitable, and, aside from citing the current line-up as "the most legitimate Guns N' Roses cover band in America today", he advised the band's old-school fans to take the $100 they were intending on using to purchase a ticket and throw it down the nearest sewer and then punch themselves in the stomach. Having suitably recovered, they should then return home, squeeze into their faded denims and tie a bandana about their forehead, listen to 'Paradise City' and cry themselves to sleep remembering the good old days of yesteryear.

Following on from six Canadian dates, the band returned to the US

for a show at Cleveland's Quicken Loans Arena, where Axl took exception to support act Eagles Of Death Metal. Much to bassist Tommy Stinson's vexation – Tommy was friends with EODM, and had recommended them for the tour – Axl informed the bemused crowd that this would be the last time the Pigeons Of Shit Metal would open for Guns N' Roses. Stinson was so incensed that he hurled his bass to the floor and insulted the somewhat bemused Axl, before then storming off stage; although he would sheepishly return to continue with the set after missing four songs.

EODM's singer Jesse Hughes was equally furious at Axl's on-stage character assassination and informed the assorted press that Axl had no right to comment on his band's performance that evening as he wasn't even at the venue when they came off stage. EODM weren't the only casualties on the tour, for by the time of the final date at the Gibson Amphitheatre in Los Angeles on 20 December, Axl had parted company with Merck Mercuriadis owing to the never-ending *Chinese Democracy* saga.

## Fourth Leg:
## 2 June, 2007 – 21 July, 2007.
## Mexico, Australasia and Japan

On 5 June, 2007, the now seemingly rudderless Guns N' Roses arrived at the Palace De Los

Deportes in Mexico City for the third of three sell-out Mexican shows. 14 years had passed since the band had last performed at the 20,000 capacity stadium, which had staged the 1968 Olympics, but unlike their American cousins, the Mexicans cared little about who was standing stage left of Axl. They were here to worship at the G N' R altar, and the two unfortunate local support bands, Nata and Maligno, received extremely short shrift, with the latter band forced to bring their set to an unscheduled halt after 20 minutes due to incessant booing and catcalls.

Indeed, the anticipation had reached fever pitch by the time the lights dimmed at 11.45pm with one over-excited fan rushing from his seat and hurling his beer at Axl as he walked on stage. The crowd held its collective breath fearing and expecting the worst, but Axl, dressed in a custom-made 'charro' (traditional Mexican folk costume), took the incident in his stride and slammed into 'Welcome To The Jungle'. During 'Knockin' On Heaven's Door' another fan rushed forwards and hurled his country's national flag up onto the stage, and the entire stadium erupted as Axl picked it up and draped it across his shoulders. Although new songs such as 'Madagascar', 'I.R.S' and 'The Blues' were courteously received, it was the old classics that the crowd really wanted to hear – particularly the ballads – and the Mexicans sang along to every word of 'Don't Cry', 'Patience'

'November Rain', and Dizzy's piano spotlight solo of the Rolling Stones classic 'Angie'. The band ended their set, and their return to Mexico, with a pyrotechnical and special effects-laden 'Paradise City' which left the jubilant Mexicans baying for more.

The opening Australasian date at the Burswood Dome in Perth – which had Rose Tattoo and Sebastian Bach as opening acts, and surprisingly got underway at the designated hour of 11pm – was unfortunately marred by sound problems, both of the technical and vocal variety. The Burswood is well-known for its poor 'muddy' sound, which kind of defeats the object of staging bands, but Axl was also struggling to reach his heyday best – particularly the high notes – and only sounded anywhere near his old self whilst seated at the piano for 'November Rain'. As was now the custom, the band remained on stage for over two hours, but the fact that it was a Sunday show meant a large number of the audience faced an early start in the morning and the arena was near half empty by the time of the ticker-tape shrouded 'Paradise City' finale.

Following on from two consecutive nights at Sydney's Acer Arena on 23 and 24 June, the band flew on to New Zealand for another three shows, before then heading to Japan, where they were scheduled to play another five gigs starting off with two over consecutive nights at Chiba's Makuhari Messe on 14 and 15

July. Three nights later, Guns N' Roses made a triumphant return to the Nippon Budokan in Tokyo – the band's first appearance there for nigh on two decades – where they were joined on stage by Bubbles (Canadian actor, Mike Smith) from the hit Canadian TV show *Trailer Park Boys,* for a rendition of 'Liquor & Whores'. The final show – or final show to date – of the *Chinese Democracy* tour came in Osaka the following night, but as with London nearly twelve months earlier, the band performed an after hours show at a private club in Osaka. Once again, they were joined by Bubbles, as well as Japanese author Takayoshi Azuma, for a relaxed semi-acoustic sing-a-long to several G N' R numbers such as 'Patience' and 'Used To Love Her', as well as 'Liquor & Whores', Led Zeppelin's 'Whole Lotta Love', Kiss' 'Strutter', Cheap Trick's 'I Want You To Want me' and Tom Jones' 'It's Not Unusual'.

# CIVIL WAR

'Civil War', which originally featured on the 1990 fundraiser album *Nobody's Child,* subsequently appeared as the opening track on *Use Your Illusion II*, and reached #4 on the Billboard Hot 100 when it was released as a single in 1993.

Nobody's Child – or The Romanian Angel project to give it its proper title – was set up by ex-Beatle, George Harrison and his wife Olivia as a means of raising funds for the children left orphaned by Romania's despot leader Nicolae Ceauscscu, who'd recently been overthrown during a military coup. The remorseless dictator, along with his wife Elena, was executed by a three-man firing squad on 25 December, 1989.

Although all five original members of Guns N' Roses were supposedly apolitical, 'Civil War' is a protest song worthy of ranking alongside Dylan's 1962 classic 'Blowin' In The Wind', John Lennon's 'Give Peace A Chance' (1969), and Rage Against The Machine's more up-to-date offering, 'Killing In The Name Of'. Following a snippet of Strother Martin's dialogue from the 1967 movie 'Cool Hand Luke', 'Civil War' is a lament to the seemingly never-ending wastage of human

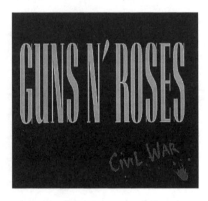

life, and the suffering caused by the civil wars which have stained the pages of history. In September, 1993, at the time of the song's release as a single (the Gunners' thirteenth to date), Duff, who had co-written the lyrics with Slash and Axl, informed Rockline that the idea for the song had basically evolved from a riff the band had been messing about with during soundchecks. His own telling contribution: "Did you wear a black armband / When they shot the man / Who said peace could last forever" had apparently come

from a real-life experience, when, as a four year-old, he'd accompanied his mother on a peace march in 1969 at the height of the Vietnam War. Axl also chips in, with his earliest memory being hearing of Robert F. Kennedy's assassination in the basement kitchen of the Ambassador Hotel in Los Angeles on 5 June, 1968, which goes some way to explaining why the band chose the Ambassador as the setting to shoot the video for 'Patience'.

'Civil War' received its first public airing at Farm Aid IV, which was staged at Indianapolis' Hoosier Dome on 7 April, 1990, when the Gunners performed alongside Elton John, Lou Reed and event co-organisers Willie Nelson, Neil Young and John Cougar Mellencamp. When Axl discovered the fourth benefit concert to raise funds for America's family farmers was to be held in his home state of Indiana, he contacted the organisers and offered the band's services. The show, which marked Dizzy Reed's live debut, would prove to be Steven Adler's last with the band before being ejected owing to his chronic heroin addiction.

## CLARKE, GILBY

Gilby Clarke was a little known, wannabe guitarist eking a living playing in clubs along L.A.'s Sunset Strip when the call came through in November, 1991 offering him the chance to replace Izzy Stradlin in Guns N' Roses.

It was Slash – having been struck by a similarity in style between Gilby and Izzy – who'd made the call, and although Gilby couldn't believe his luck, his elevation from virtual unknown to being in the most happening rock band in the world meant he had to hit the ground running, for Izzy's shock departure came in the midst of G N' R's colossal 28-month *Use Your Illusion* world tour. Having learnt – and rush-rehearsed – some thirty songs in three weeks, Gilby's baptism of fire came on 5 December, 1991 at the Worcester Centrum Centre in Worcester, Massachusetts. Gilby remained with Guns N' Roses for the next three years, and although he didn't actually record any original material with the band, he did appear on '*The Spaghetti Incident?*' as well as the band's *Live Era: '87 - '93'* & *Greatest Hits* albums.

His fall from grace came in March, 1994, shortly before the band was due to enter the studio to record a version of the Rolling Stones classic, 'Sympathy For The Devil' for the *Interview With The Vampire* movie soundtrack, when, with neither consultation, nor explanation, he was replaced by Axl's long-time friend Paul Tobias.

Gilby's first indication that all was not well came when his, by now, customary weekly stipend failed to appear in his bank account. His initial thought was

that it had been an oversight by the Gunners' accountants, and this did indeed appear to be the case when the payments resumed as normal. But when the same oversight occurred several times over the following weeks, he consulted his lawyer Jeffrey Light. Light wrote a letter on behalf of his bemused client to the Gunners' then lawyer Laurie Soriano, requesting that some light be shed on the situation and was summarily informed, in no uncertain terms, that his client's services were no longer required. When the expected royalty check for his involvement on *The Spaghetti Incident?* failed to arrive, however, and still smarting from such shoddy treatment, he instructed Light to initiate legal proceedings. At first, and much to Gilby's dismay, Soriano announced he would fight the action, and attempted to call Gilby's bluff by launching a ridiculous counter lawsuit against the guitarist for having 'misappropriated his name, likeness, photograph, voice and performance'. But, upon realising Gilby was not the bluffing kind and was intent on standing his ground, Soriano dropped the countersuit and agreed to settle out of court, with Gilby receiving an undisclosed sum.

Although Gilby had inexplicably found himself on Axl's shit list, he remained on good terms with the other Gunners, and even appeared on Slash's *It's Five O'Clock Somewhere* solo album. In a bizarre twist, a decade or so on from his unceremonious and acrimonious dismissal from Guns N' Roses, Gilby was brought in to collaborate with Tracii Guns on the album *The Roots of Guns N' Roses*.

Gilby was born in Cleveland, Ohio, on 17 August, 1962, and having spent his formative years jamming with friends in his parents' garage instead of attending school, it came as no surprise to all concerned when, at 17 years of age, he announced to friends and family that he and his trusty six-string were heading to neon-lit Los Angeles to try and make a name for himself in music.

His first paying gig came with a band called Candy, who, judging from their chosen attire on the cover of their one and only album, *'Whatever Happened To Fun?'*, which was released on the PolyGram label in 1984, were a power-pop quartet similar to The Knack circa 1979, or Blondie's perennial backline. Having tired of Candy's pretentious pop-preening, however, Gilby crossed over to the glitzier side of the Strip and joined Kill For Thrills, with whom he penned and recorded most of the songs for the band's two albums *Commercial Suicide* (1988), and *Dynamite From Nightmareland* (1989).

In 1994, shortly after his summary dismissal from the court of King Axl, Gilby released his debut solo album, *Pawnshop Guitars*, much of which was recorded whilst he was still in Guns N' Roses and features contributions from Slash, Duff, Dizzy, Matt and even Axl himself. Twelve months later he released his second solo offering, the *Blooze* EP on Virgin,

and has since gone on to release three more studio records: *The Hangover* (1997); *Rubber* (1998) and *Swag* (2002) as well as a live album, aptly entitled *99 Live* (1999) and a *Best Of* in 2007.

In 2001, Gilby collaborated with ex-Stray Cats – and onetime Brittbanger – Slim Jim Phantom in the band Col. Parker, which resulted in the V2 album *Rock 'N' Roll Music*. He is also an occasional member of the Cathouse houseband, The Starfuckers, as well as the Blues Mafia, which plies its trade down at the legendary Sunset Strip blues hangout, The Baked Potato.

When he wasn't busy gigging with the likes of Nancy Sinatra and Heart, recording, or taking up column inches in *Hot Bike Magazine* where he could be found purring over his Harley Davidson motorbikes, Gilby would be ensconced within his home studio (Redrum Studios). His producing credits thus far include L.A. Guns' 1999 album *Shrinking Violet*, on which he also makes a guest appearance, *Rolling Stone* 'Best Newcomers' award recipients The Bronx's eponymous debut offering in 2003, as well as Girlsplayboys debut album *From Ritual to Romance* (2006).

In 2006, following a solo tour which took in the US and Europe, Gilby teamed up with Mötley Crüe's Tommy Lee, and ex-Metallica bassist Jason Newsted in the supergroup Supernova. Rather than approach a known singer, however, the three recruited Lukas Rossi, the recent winner of the American reality *CBS* TV show Rockstar: Supernova. Unfortunately their choice of name soon met with controversy when a Californian pop-punk trio of the same name filed a federal lawsuit. In September, 2006, San Diego Judge John Houston ruled in favour of the original band and granted their request for a preliminary injunction pending a trial, which forced Messrs. Lee, Clarke, Newsted and Rossi to rename their band Rock Star Supernova. The band's self-titled debut album was released on 21 November, 2006, but by this time, Newsted had been replaced by ex-Black Crows bassist Johnny Colt, owing to his having injured both arms whilst trying to catch a falling bass amp and requiring a lengthy recuperation period following surgery.

As with most reality TV shows, however, Rockstar: Supernova's viewing audience was only interested whilst the show was on air, and were less enthused about parting with $20 to see the band play live – regardless of its stellar backline – while equally poor reviews meant that the album failed to trouble the Billboard 100

## CLINK, MIKE

Mike Clink is a successful producer who first cut his teeth on *Appetite For Destruction*, and went on to produce all five Guns

N' Roses studio albums released to date.

Baltimore-born Clink began his career as an engineer at New York's Record Plant studios on West 44ᵗʰ Street, working alongside the studio's in-house 'soft rock' producer Ron Nevison on recordings by the likes of Jefferson Starship and Heart. The pair had also been responsible for producing Survivor's 1982 'Rocky' anthem, 'Eye Of The Tiger', but what really sold the idea to Guns N' Roses of allowing Clink to oversee their debut was his involvement on UFO's 1977 standout album *Lights Out*.

In 1986, Clink decided to strike out on his own and, having severed the umbilical cord to Nevison, moved out to Los Angeles, where, after several less-than-successful production attempts – including Triumph's *Sport Of Kings* album – he was approached by Tom Zutaut to harness the manic sound of the then up-and-coming Guns N' Roses.

It is well documented that Clink wasn't Geffen's first, or indeed even second or third choice for the task, but Zutaut – perhaps sensing that patience would be a vital attribute – was confident he had found his man. Clink was no doubt aware of Geffen's misgivings over his capabilities – or lack thereof – but he was equally aware of what was required. He knew the Gunners would be after a rawer, harder-edged sound than any of the pop acts which appeared on his production resume, and, more importantly, he knew how to get it. Rather than waste precious studio time twiddling knobs in search of an elusive sound, he simply asked each band member to bring their favourite albums into the studio to give him an idea of what sounds were rocking the band's collective boat.

The success of *Appetite For Destruction*, as well as *GNR Lies*, saw Clink elevated to the top of the production pile. He was invited to work his magic on Metallica's 1988 'breakout' album *And Justice For All*, but things didn't go according to plan and he was replaced by the band's in-house producer Flemming Rasmussen. In 1990, Clink set to work on Guns N' Roses' mammoth *Use Your Illusion* project, but still found time to co-produce Megadeth's mega-selling *Rust In Peace* alongside the thrash-metal band's frontman Dave Mustaine.

In January, 2001, he was invited to mix the live half-time entertainment – as well as cheer on his home state team, and eventual winners, the Baltimore Ravens – at Super Bowl XXXV. The interlude featured performances by Aerosmith, N'Sync, Nelly, Mary J. Blige and Britney Spears. That same year, he was also invited to produce Pure Rubbish's debut album *Glamorous Youth*. At the time the Houston-based rockers were signed to Ozzy Osbourne's Divine Recordings label, but the record has yet to receive an official release.

Although Clink's services have not been called upon by Axl for Chinese Democracy, the producer is still very much in demand. But it isn't only headline acts that he is involved with, for in 2005, he produced The Glitterati's debut eponymously-titled album for Atlantic Records. The band – which at the time was being compared to the early, pre-signed Guns N' Roses – couldn't believe their luck when they heard G N' R's legendary producer was interested in working with them. And in 2006, he not only produced Phoenix-based high-energy rockers Crushed's debut *My Machine*, he also released it on his own No Relief Records label.

Clink may well be out of favour with Axl, and nor was he called upon to produce either of the Velvet Revolver albums, but he hasn't quite severed all connections with Guns N' Roses, since, at the time of writing, he is currently working alongside Matt Sorum to produce Camp Freddy's as yet unnamed debut album.

## COBAIN, KURT

Kurt Cobain, the undisputed Guru of Grunge who single-handedly inspired an entire musical genre in the early-'90s, rose to fame as the frontman with Nirvana before allegedly blowing his brains out with a shotgun on 5 April, 1994.

Cobain incurred Axl's wrath following his comments on both Axl and Guns N' Roses, which appeared in the February, 1993 issue of *The Advocate*. At that particular juncture, Guns N' Roses and Nirvana were the two biggest bands on the planet, and the interviewer was therefore almost obliged to ask Cobain for his opinion of G N' R's music. His response was acerbic to say the least. Having declared that he didn't even want to waste his time thinking about "that band", he went on to dismiss the Gunners as a personal affront to his

musical sensibilities, and branded them "pathetic", as well as "untalented". The interviewer – sensing he was one question away from lifting the lid to Pandora's Box – asked Cobain about his recent spat with Axl at the MTV Video Music Awards on 9 September, 1992.

Guns N' Roses had been booked to perform 'November Rain' live at the awards ceremony while Nirvana would open proceedings with a live version of 'Lithium'. Instead of playing the song as expected, the studio bosses were thrown into a panic when the mischievous Seattleites began playing the opening bars of the then unreleased track 'Rape Me', and only segued into 'Lithium' as the furious set director was about to cut to an unscheduled commercial break. As he was leaving the stage, Cobain is said to have spat on the keys of the piano Axl was shortly due to use. The hostilities didn't end there, however, for when Cobain's wife, Courtney Love, spotted Axl making his way through the backstage dining area, she summoned the singer across to their table to mockingly enquire if he'd consent to being godfather to their daughter, Frances Bean. Although Courtney had no way of knowing it, she had chosen an inopportune moment to deride the irascible Axl, and before either she or Cobain could react, Axl unleashed a torrent of abuse during which he remonstrated with Cobain to "shut his bitch up" before he took him down to the pavement to settle the matter 'mano-a-mano'.

The ill-feeling – if only on Axl's part – came as a result of Cobain having declined Axl's invitation for Nirvana to perform at his 30th birthday bash in February, 1992. This, as far as Axl was concerned, was adding insult to injury, as the Nirvana frontman had also recently spurned an invitation to support Guns N' Roses on the second US leg of their *Use Your Illusion* tour that same year. Given that Nirvana was every music critic's flavour of the month throughout 1991-92, which had in turn resulted in the band's two-year monopoly of the airwaves, it was perhaps understandable why Cobain didn't see any need to be subservient to anybody, let alone Guns N' Roses, a band he secretly despised – secretly until *The Advocate* article hit the newsstands that is. But his having refused to help Axl celebrate thirty years on planet earth was seen as one slight too many.

## COLLINS, TIM

Tim Collins is Aerosmith's long-standing manager, and was invited by Tom Zutaut to manage Guns N' Roses in 1986.

The invite came shortly after Guns N' Roses had signed to Geffen in March, 1986, whereby Collins – who'd succeeded in getting Aerosmith's 'Toxic Twins' Steve Tyler and Joe Perry, and the rest of his charges cleaned up – was invited to a specially arranged G N' R showcase gig at the Roxy. And although Collins was aware of the Gunners' predilections for drink, drugs and debauchery, he nevertheless agreed to attend the show in order to see for himself whether the young upstarts were equal to the task of usurping Aerosmith's crown. Collins was suitably impressed by the band's brash performance, and even went so far as to invite them and Zutaut back to his hotel suite to discuss

the matter further. But although Zutaut was willing to talk shop, the five wayward Gunners were intent on winding down the only way they knew – by getting smashed on whatever was available from Collin's mini-bar. Indeed, such was the post gig rumpus that Collins was forced to seek sanctuary in an adjoining room in order to get some peace and quiet. And if further evidence were needed that he should pass on Zutaut's invitation to manage the group, then it surely came the following morning when he discovered the errant

Gunners had run up a $450 bar tab in his absence and charged it to his room.

# COMA

'Coma', which appears as the final track on *Use Your Illusion I*, and runs at 10 minutes 13 seconds, is the longest song to date written by Guns N' Roses.

The lengthy treatise that is 'Coma', which, according to Slash, who co-wrote the song with Axl, contains 500 chord changes, is believed to be a (semi-auto) biographical account of a drug-induced coma which Axl supposedly endured yet lived to tell the tale. And as a means of backing his not-so-spurious claim, Axl – by way of a thank you – invited Dr. Michael Smolens, the very doctor who'd pulled him back from the brink, into the studio to record a voiceover. And to give the lyric added authenticity – if any were needed – the band added ECG (Electrocardiogram) beeps, and even hired a defibrillator, which under normal circumstances, would be used to restore natural rhythmical contractions following a heart attack. During the press debriefing which followed the recording of the *Use Your Illusion* albums, Axl admitted that the idea for 'Coma' had been dancing around on the periphery of his creative consciousness for the past year, but had finally revealed itself whilst he and the rest of the band were in Rumbo Studios, where the lyric had flowed effortlessly from mind's eye to paper. He also declared the song's final segment, which starts with the line 'Got your mind in submission / Got your life on the line', to be – at least up to that point in time – the best lyric he'd ever written.

Due to its considerable length – not to mention the effect it might have on Axl's voice – Guns N' Roses have only ever performed 'Coma' live on four occasions, all of which occurred during the band's *Use Your Illusion* world tour. The first airing came on 4 June, 1991, when it surprisingly served as the set-opener at the Richfield Coliseum in Richfield, Ohio, as it did again, at the Tokyo Dome on 19 February, 1992 (which subsequently featured on *Live Era '87 – '93)*. The penultimate airing came on 9 April, 1992 at the Rosemont Horizon arena in Rosemont, Illinois, while its final appearance on the Gunners' set list came on 10 April, 1993 at the Omaha Civic Centre in Omaha, Nebraska.

# COOPER, ALICE

Alice Cooper is an American singer-songwriter best known for his outlandish stage performances which feature guillotines, electric chairs and boa constrictors.

Alice Cooper was actually the name of the band in which Alice, born plain old Vincent Damon Furnier, in Detroit, Michigan on 4 February, 1948, served as frontman. Having originally started out in 1965 as The Spiders, the band achieved its finest hour in 1972 with their international hit 'School's Out', which went Top 10 in the US, and #1 in the UK. By 1974, however, Alice's theatrical onstage antics, which involved buckets of fake blood, fencing foils and snakes, meant that he was now the focal point of the show and led to his adopting the name legally before then embarking on a solo career.

By the mid-'80s, despite receiving a Grammy nomination in 1984 in the Best Long Form Music Video category for 'The Nightmare', Alice's brand of 'shock-rock' was no longer in vogue, and he was released by his record label, Warner Brothers, the following year. In 1986, after a year-long hiatus, during which time Alice relocated back to Phoenix, Arizona (where young Vincent had spent his formative years), to dry out, save his ailing marriage and improve his golf swing, the rejuvenated singer announced his return to the main stage with the self-produced album *Constrictor*, which featured the song 'He's Back (The Man Behind The Mask)', which was especially written as the theme song for *Friday the 13th Part VI: Jason Lives*. The following year saw Alice release the rockier-sounding *Raise Your Fist And Yell*, and in time-honoured tradition he invited the then current 'hottest band on the block'

– which happened to be Guns N' Roses – onto the promotional tour. The Gunners were somewhat surprised to receive the call as they were under the impression they'd blown any chance of working with Alice again on account of Axl having failed to turn up for a show opening for the moog-eyed one in Santa Barbara some twelve months earlier. On that occasion, Slash and the equally-disgruntled Izzy, Duff and Steven had been forced to go on without their singer, which, needless to say, didn't make for a great show.

Alice, however, having been in the business long enough to know that, although musicians would come and go, the song would always remain the same, probably saw something of his younger self in the mischievous Gunners and went out of his way to make the band – including Axl – welcome. The tour, which got underway at the Fair Park Coliseum in Dallas, Texas, on 4 December, 1987, may have been on a smaller scale to that which the Gunners had just undertaken opening for Mötley Crüe, but a closer proximity to their audience provided an extra dynamic which was more suited to their style of play. Having spent several weeks on the road with the Crüe, however, had resulted in a sizeable increase to their col-

lective, daily drug and alcohol intake. Indeed, said intake was so off the scale that Alice – himself no stranger to substance abuse and only recently free from 'freebasing' – was overheard expressing his fear that he wouldn't be surprised if one or more of the Gunners finished the tour in a coffin. An untimely death did indeed bring the tour to an unscheduled halt. But it was Alice's father who'd sadly passed away, which resulted in the remaining shows being cancelled. Steven took the news almost as badly as Alice himself, and vented his drink-fuelled frustrations by punching a streetlamp which saw him sidelined for several weeks with a broken hand and resulted in Cinderella's Fred Coury being drafted in as a temporary stand-in for the band's immediate live commitments.

By 1988, Alice's career appeared to be in the doldrums when his latest recording contract with MCA expired. But you can't keep a good man down for long, and the following year Alice – having signed to Epic – was back with a new album *Trash*, which spawned the US Top 10 hit single 'Poison'. In 1990, whilst G N' R were recording the songs destined to appear on the *Use Your Illusion* double albums, someone commented on how much Axl had sounded like Alice on 'The Garden'. Rather than take offence, Axl agreed with the comparison and duly invited Alice, who was conveniently staying in Los Angeles at the time, to record the song as a duet.

Slash returned the favour by making a guest appearance on the title track of Alice's 1991 album, *Hey Stoopid*. But whereas

Guns N' Roses were big enough to withstand the recent Grunge explosion, Alice was not so fortunate, and the album failed to make any significant impact on the charts.

## COURY, FRED

Fred Coury, who is perhaps best known as the drummer for glam metal band Cinderella, served as a temporary stand-in for Steven Adler for four Guns N' Roses shows at the Perkins Palace in Pasadena, California in December, 1987.

Coury, who was born on 20 October, 1966, in Johnson City, New York, was only 5 years-old when he first began expressing himself musically. And although it was the drums which would prove to be his forte, it was the violin which first caught his eye. Following two years studying at the Beirut Conservatory of Music – during which time he gave his first public performance – the 12-year-old musical prodigy decided to try his hand on drums and within the year was providing the

beat for a local band called Sunjammer. His decision to devote all his energies to the drums came in 1980 upon witnessing Kenny Jones in action with The Who at the CNE Stadium in Toronto. Within five short years Coury would return to the CNE with his band Cinderella.

## CULT, THE

The Cult is a British rock band fronted by Jim Morrison acolyte Ian Astbury, whose most successful period came during the mid-80s and early-90s.

The Brixton-based rockers had originally started out in 1981 as Southern Death Cult, taking their name from a 15th century tribe of American Indians from the Mississippi Delta, and made their live debut in Bradford, West Yorkshire, on 29 October that same year. The band remained together for some 16 months, yet released one solitary single: the double A-sided 'Moya', although a compilation album of sorts, which consisted of the two tracks from the single, radio sessions and live recordings, was posthumously released on the indie label Beggars Banquet.

In April, 1983, following the arrival of Manchester-born guitarist – and his future long-time collaborator, Billy Duffy – Astbury truncated the band's name to Death Cult. They released the single 'God's Zoo' that October

before embarking on a short UK tour which was followed by one of Europe. In January, 1984, keen to gain broader appeal and also anxious to distance themselves from the burgeoning UK Goth scene spearheaded by the Sisters of Mercy, Astbury and co. truncated their name further still to simply The Cult, and in April that same year released their debut single 'Spiritwalker', which reached #1 on the UK Indie chart. It was the band's fourth single, 'She Sells Sanctuary', released in March, 1985, which served to propel The Cult into the major league. Not only did it crack the UK Top 20, but also spent a very respectable forty-one weeks on the chart, while the parent album *Love* went on to sell over 2.5 million copies worldwide.

Astbury's introduction to Guns N' Roses came in June, 1987 when he caught one of the band's now legendary Marquee shows and later confessed to Slash that he knew they were going to be huge in the near future. And so, shortly after the release of *Appetite For Destruction*, the Gunners headed out on a six-week tour of North American in support of The Cult, who were promoting their third long-player, *Electric*. And Astbury – who would reportedly spend more time in the Gunners' dressing room during the tour than he did his own – proved such an ardent admirer of Guns N' Roses that it eliminated the usual 'headliner grabbing the glory' bullshit scenario, where the main act's road crew would purposely sabotage the opening act's sound to give their own performance far greater impact. The on-tour camaraderie saw long-standing friendships develop – especially between respective singers and bassists. Indeed, Duff's friendship with his Cult counterpart, Stephen "Haggis" Harris, led to the latter standing in for him during a subsequent G N' R support tour with Iron Maiden. And although much has been made of the parallels between Ian Astbury and his hero Jim Morrison, it was Axl who would emulate the self-styled Lizard King during a show in Atlanta, when he was arrested on stage mid-set by local police for an earlier incident when the highly-volatile frontman attacked a security guard prior to Guns N' Roses taking the stage. The incident no doubt provided Axl with plenty of kudos on the tour bus, but left his bewildered bandmates to carry out an impromptu improvisation whereby Slash and Steven played fifteen and ten minute solos respectively; and provided one of the roadies with his Warholian fifteen minutes of fame upon being deputised as Axl's stand-in.

By Slash's own admission, he and Duff were the major instigators of chaos and mayhem on the tour. One night during the Canadian leg, after yet another bout of drink and debauchery, the guitarist, unable to find his way back to his own hotel, not only passed out on a sofa in the reception of the hotel where The Cult were staying, but humiliated himself further still by wetting himself in his sleep. As none of the hotel's staff appeared willing to assist him, Slash staggered out into the freezing dawn, and may well have caught a chill had it not been for his piss-soaked leather pants serving as an impromptu insulator.

In 1991, maverick director Oliver Stone offered Ian Astbury the role of Jim Morrison in his planned biopic, *The Doors*. Astbury, however, who would later front the reconstituted 21st Century Doors, turned the offer down, having apparently disapproved of the way Morrison would be portrayed in the movie. The role eventually went to Val Kilmer.

## CREW, TODD

Todd Crew was the bassist with L.A. rock band Jetboy, as well as an occasional roadie for his G N' R drug buddies.

Although Jetboy went on to enjoy a modicum of chart success with their 1988 debut album *Feel The Shake*, which featured three songs that subsequently appeared on the soundtrack to *The Burbs* starring Tom Hanks, back in 1987, they – like every other L.A. wannabe band – were left to wallow in G N' R's sizable wake. Todd's friendship with the Gunners, especially Slash, however, meant that his own band could always count on an occasional support slot, as well as being on hand to provide high jinx and light relief whilst out on the road. Although happy to play the fool, Todd was well schooled, and as he was still in possession of the two round

trip tickets to Paris he'd received as a gift from his proud parents upon graduating from college, he and fellow G N' R associate Del James, used them to make the trip to London to watch the Gunners' three Marquee shows.

Later that same year, whilst Slash was in New York oversee-ing the art layout for *Appetite For Destruction*, the guitarist was roused from his slumber at the Milford Plaza on 8<sup>th</sup> Avenue, where he was holed up with porn star Lois Ayres, to discover Todd was in the Big Apple, and apparently in need of a shoul-der to cry on. For not only had he been sacked from Jetboy and had all his equipment confiscated in the process, he had also split up from his long-time girlfriend.

Although it was only seven a.m., the bassist was well the worse for wear. Slash had several impor-tant meetings scheduled for the day ahead, but there was no way he was going to leave his friend alone at such a time and took him to each and every meeting. Trying to lead a dead weight around the busy streets of Manhattan was no mean feat, but somehow Slash managed to get Todd to his first appointment – which happened to be at Geffen's New York offices – where the bassist duly crashed out in reception.

By mid-afternoon, Todd was thankfully beginning to show signs of life, and Slash – with his professional duties at an end – decided an afternoon spent chug-ging a few beers in Central Park would do them both the world of good. Just as they were about to enter the park, however, they ran into three mutual muso acquaintances from L.A., who were on their way to Alphabet City to score heroin and invited Slash and Todd to join them. Todd, although relatively inexperienced in chasing the dragon, was all in favour of getting high to banish his worldly woes, whereas Slash had just weaned himself off the drug and was therefore in no particular hurry to tread that dark path again and instead suggested going for a drink in a nearby bar. Although the others reluctantly agreed, it wasn't long before the conversation again turned to smack. Once again Slash tried to intervene, but having been outvoted, decided to accompany them down to the East Village – if only to keep an eye on Todd.

They managed to score from a mutual acquaintance, and as the heroin wasn't particularly potent, Slash decided it was safe to partake in the illicit wares. After spending a couple of hours holed up in a dingy cinema on Times Square, Slash decided it best to take Todd back to his hotel. He'd been hoping to put his friend to bed to sleep off his drunk, but no sooner had they stepped inside the room when the three L.A. cronies showed up with more friends, more beer, and more drugs. Slash, although pissed off at the unwarranted intrusion, wasn't overly concerned as the heroin was again low grade, and nowhere near strong enough to cause anyone

any lasting harm. During the course of the evening, however, one of the new guys, who happened to be in possession of something a little stronger, surreptitiously slipped some of his stash to the hapless Todd.

Slash only realised something was wrong when Todd collapsed. But instead of helping, the others fled the room and disappeared

into the night leaving the guitarist to do what he could. He managed to drag Todd into the bathroom and began frantically dousing his friend with cold water in an attempt to revive him. But, although Todd briefly regained consciousness, he slipped under again and died in Slash's arms. He was just 21 years old.

Guns N' Roses later dedicated *Live Era '87–'93* to Todd's memory.

# DAWSON, ROSARIO

The African-American actress best known for her roles as Roxane in Oliver Stone's epic *Alexander* (2004), and Gail in Frank Miller's *Sin City* (2005).

You're probably wondering what possible connection Rosario Dawson could have with Guns N' Roses – except that her studded leather and fishnet *Sin City* character Gail wouldn't have looked out of place in one of the band's videos. But it was at her 27th birthday bash on 18 May, 2006, (Rosario's actual birthday fell on the 9th) at a small two-storey club called Plum, located at 124 Ludlow Street on New York's Lower East Side, that the Gunners performed a secret acoustic show (acoustic except for Robin Finck's semi-acoustic Gibson guitar and Dizzy's keyboards).

The unannounced show, which came after G N' R's final concert at the nearby Hammerstein Ballroom, was supposed to be a secret, but word of mouth – which falsely claimed it would be the Gunners' original line-up taking to the stage, or at least a line-up which included Izzy and Matt Sorum – ensured that the 500 capacity club was packed to the rafters. Amongst those jostling for prime vantage points was Rosario's boyfriend, *Sex And The City* star Jason Lewis, her *Sin City* co-star Mickey Rourke, Kid Rock, who had also made a guest appearance at the Hammerstein Ballroom, Lenny Kravitz, Lindsay Lohan, and *24*'s Eric Balfour.

The Plum show was supposed to be a relaxed affair, but trouble seemed to follow Axl around like a bad smell, and the singer had barely stepped through the doors when he found himself embroiled in an altercation with renowned fashion designer Tommy Hilfiger. When asked for his version of events on L.A. radio station KROQ the following day, Axl said he'd been making his way to

a private booth when Hilfiger took objection to his having moved the designer's girlfriend's drink so that it wouldn't get accidentally spilt as he passed. Hilfiger, however, painted a different picture and told a *New York Daily News* reporter that the flare up occurred because Axl was being "rude and obnoxious" towards him. Another reason for the pair's antagonism is said to have been due to Axl having dated Hilfiger's brother's ex-wife, Diana O'Connor, whilst the group was staying in New York.

The band took up positions as best they could on the tiny stage, and as there was a giant movie screen-sized monitor behind them which displayed the lyrics to each song in turn, Axl jokingly introduced the show as the "Karaoke version of Guns N' Roses". The show lasted for over an hour, and the ecstatic crowd whooped and hollered en masse as Axl returned to the stage. This, however, would be no ordinary encore, for after sheepishly admitting to have forgotten to do something because he was "a fuckin' idiot" he called Rosario up onto the stage and led the audience in a raucous rendition of 'Happy Birthday to You'.

Having Guns N' Roses provide the entertainment at her birthday party wasn't Rosario's only link with the band, however. For three years earlier, she starred in the Peter Berg directed, 2003 movie, *The Rundown*, which, when it was released in the UK and Australia, was renamed *Welcome To The Jungle*.

# DICK, NIGEL

Nigel Dick is the English-born music video and film director who directed the Guns N' Roses videos 'Welcome To the Jungle', 'Swect Child O' Mine', 'Paradise City' and 'Patience'.

Nigel Andrew Robertson Dick was born in Catterick, North Yorkshire on 21 March, 1953. Following a private education at the select Gresham's School, Dick trained as an architect, and before deciding to seek fame and fortune in the music business, the Old Greshamian tried his hand at several jobs, including working as an architectural draughtsman, cab driver, motorcycle messenger, waiter, and even served a short spell at the East Anglian Water Authority's Sewage Division.

His first step on the music ladder came in 1978 with Stiff Records, the independent label founded by Dave Robinson which was responsible for kick-starting the English punk scene by signing The Damned, and releasing their debut single 'New Rose' (which Guns N' Roses

would later cover). Dick remained at Stiff for five years before leaving in 1983 to begin a three-year stint as a video director at Phonogram Records, where, amongst others, he directed the Band Aid video for 'Do They Know It's Christmas', which featured the then crème de la crème of the British pop charts including Boy George, George Michael, Duran Duran, Sting and David Bowie.

In 1986, the same year he co-founded Propaganda Films, which went on to become the hottest commercial and video production company in town (he later sold his share of the company to his one-time bosses at Phonogram), Dick headed for the bright lights of Hollywood to direct his first full-length feature film *P. I. Private Investigations*, released the following year and starring Ray Sharkey and Martin Balsam. The film turned a tidy profit upon its sale to MGM and has since gone on to achieve late-night cult status. Since then Dick has written eight screenplays, directed more than a score of films and documentaries, and over three hundred music videos for artists including Guns N' Roses, ex-Beatle Paul McCartney, Oasis, Elton John, Ozzy Osbourne, Ricky Martin, Gloria Estafan, Il Divo and Britney Spears. Dick's talents as a film and video director has earned him three MTV awards, two Billboard Awards and three MVPA awards, a BRIT Award, and in 2000, the MVPA awarded him a Lifetime Achievement Award.

# DONINGTON

Donington Park, located near the Leicestershire village of Donington Castle, has become synonymous with the British heavy metal music scene for having played host to both the Monsters of Rock and Download festivals.

On Saturday, 20 August, 1988, Guns N' Roses made their first appearance at the legendary *Monsters of Rock* festival. Despite *Appetite For Destruction* and 'Sweet Child O' Mine' both sitting pretty at #1 on the US Billboard charts, which effectively made them the biggest rock band in the world, the Gunners were placed a lowly – and somewhat insulting – fifth on the bill behind festival headliners Iron Maiden, Kiss, David Lee Roth and Megadeth, with only event-openers Helloween going on before them.

Donington first came to prominence in the 1930s when it began staging motorcycle races as well as the British Grand Prix in 1937 and 1938. The circuit was closed for the duration of WWII and didn't resume staging races of any kind until 1977. The inaugural *Monsters of Rock* festival had been staged back in 1980, and by 1988 it had become the largest, and therefore the most prestigious, outdoor event in the British rock calendar.

Even without Guns N' Roses, promoter Maurice Jones was expecting a crowd in excess of 90,000, which would not only smash the existing record of 66,500 from four years earlier, when Aussie rockers AC/DC had headlined the event, but also guaranteed a bumper payout for all concerned. The official attendance that day of 97,559 was indeed a festival record (outside sources have put the number at nearer 110,000), and many believe this was due to the Gunners' eleventh-hour inclusion. The fact that 35,000 extra tickets were sold on the day of the festival itself is further evidence that Guns N' Roses' popularity had increased a hundred fold in the ten months since their last visit to England's shores.

The Gunners, having taken time out from supporting Aerosmith on the latter band's *Permanent Vacation* US summer tour, merrily availed themselves of the in-flight privileges afforded to Concorde's Business Class passengers, before then boarding a connecting domestic flight from Heathrow up to the East Midlands. With Axl's voice once again in fine mettle following time out to rid his vocal chords of the painful nodules which had forced the band to pull out midway through a tour supporting headliners Iron Maiden earlier in the year, all five members – particularly Slash, who'd been born and raised in the British Midlands – were looking forward to performing again in the UK.

Indeed, the only dark cloud threatening to spoil the party was of the meteorological variety, and in true keeping with the inclement British weather, the ever-darkening skies opened up the exact moment Helloween took to the stage. The sheeting rain continued unabated throughout the Germanic rockers thirty-minute set, while the accompanying gales were severe enough to tear one of the giant 50 foot side-stage video screens from its moorings, providing a chilling portent of the tragedy waiting to unfold.

By the time Guns N' Roses went on stage at 2pm, with Axl sporting a custom-made white leather G N' R tour motorcycle jacket and matching cowboy boots, the attendance was probably only around 50,000 strong, largely due to the 'Maiden Faithful' purposely choosing to remain in the beer tents and ignore the young pretenders who were intent on appropriating their home-grown heroes' throne. By this time, the rain had – albeit temporarily – subsided, but several hours of near-incessant downpours had transformed the sloping field into a mud-bath. The Gunners' opener 'It's So Easy', was greeted with stilted applause, but the second and third numbers, 'Mr Brownstone', and the slower-tempo version of 'You're Crazy', were enough to crank up the atmosphere several notches. Indeed, it was during the latter song that the first indication of the catastrophe which lay in waiting first reared its ugly head, when a disturbance in the thronged crowd forced the band to an unscheduled halt.

Confusion reigned whilst the venue's hapless security staff attempted to restore order. And after what seemed like an age, normal service was resumed when Slash began stroking the infectious opening riff to 'Paradise City'. It wasn't long before the band was again forced to down tools, with Axl even going so far as to remonstrate with the tightly-massed ranks at the rear who were inadvertently causing some of their leather-clad brethren to be crushed up against the unyielding security barriers, mounted at the front of the stage. His heartfelt plea, however, fell on deaf ears, and like the Danish King, Canute, he failed to stem the tide.

With the situation seemingly under control again, the band launched into a shaky – and somewhat subdued – version of 'Welcome To The Jungle'. But with the slate-grey sky growing darker by the minute the group attempted to calm things down further still with the aptly-named 'Patience', which was receiving its first UK public airing. Next up was 'Sweet Child O' Mine', which understandably received the biggest cheer of the day so far. And Axl returned the crowd's gusto by thanking them for making it their first UK hit. As soon as the song ended the band fled the stage, visibly relieved that the ordeal was over. There was no encore.

Although there was no way of determining just when the tragedy occurred, it wasn't until after the Gunners had left the stage that they learned two fans – 20-year-old Landon Siggers, and 18-year-old Alan Dick – had been trampled to death in the crush. Siggers had been so badly disfigured that he was only identifiable from his tiger and scorpion tattoos. Axl later told reporters that he himself had seen the tragedy unfold: "I saw it go down, right from the stage. I saw these two faces go up, and then go down. They came up again, and went back down, and then didn't come up again." Little could he have known as he left the stage that his parting shot of "Have a good fucking day and don't kill yourselves," would come back to haunt him.

It is impossible to determine whether the two kids Axl saw were indeed Dick and Siggers, simply due to the fact that their mangled bodies were rendered unidentifiable. And if he did see what was unfolding then why didn't he call an immediate halt to the show so that the St. John's Ambulance teams could be brought to the fore? Slash also claimed to have witnessed the tradegy: "It was real scary," he told one journalist from the backstage area immediately following the performance. "It was kids piled on kids, piled on kids, horizontal on the ground. They were unconscious, and more people kept falling on them. We stopped the show a few times and they finally pulled the last couple of people out and I think they were dead. I saw no life in those bodies at all."

Regardless of the fact that West Midlands Police Chief Superintendent, Dennis Clarke, went on record to cite the crowd's behaviour as "otherwise superb" – a statement backed up by the fact his officers made no arrests that day – the following day's Sunday tabloids went overboard with scurrilous, and woefully inaccurate accusations. One of which claimed the stage had collapsed during Guns N' Roses' performance, and that the band had refused to stop playing even after being informed of the fatalities.

The subsequent coroner's inquest sided with the police's findings and recorded an open verdict, concluding that nothing more could have been done by the organisers to guarantee crowd safety.

No matter how much pre-planning is put into such events, no one can predict how an audience – especially one that is pumped up on alcohol, adrenaline and other substances – will react when their idols take to the stage. Blameless the organisers may have been, but Northwest Leicestershire's district council still insisted on placing a restrictive 70,000 crowd capacity on future events. And it would be two years before promoter Maurice Jones was granted another music license.

## DON'T CRY

Alternate versions of the captivating ballad 'Don't Cry' appear on each of the *Use Your Illusion* albums. The song was also Guns N' Roses' eighth single release.

'Don't Cry', which, along with 'November Rain' and 'Estranged', makes up Guns N' Roses' unofficial '*Illusions*' power ballad trilogy, was inspired in part by Del James' short story *Without You*. It was also the first song to be written by the band following the name change from Hollywood Rose to Guns N' Roses.

Legend has it that 'Don't Cry' was written about an unnamed girl Izzy dated shortly after his arrival in Los Angeles. Axl had subsequently succumbed to the girl's charms, but the amorous vocalist was left heartbroken upon discovering his love was unrequited. Axl had apparently been unable to contain himself and had broken down in tears when the girl ended their brief dalliance outside The Roxy. And it was her parting words of "don't cry" which inspired him and Izzy to pen the heartfelt lyric the following evening.

The original version of 'Don't Cry' appears on *Use Your Illusion I*, while the alternate take features on the sister album. There is also a third version of the song which never made it beyond the demo stage, having been recorded during the *Appetite For Destruction* sessions in 1986. It was the second single to be culled from the *Illusion* albums, and earned the Gunners' their fifth US Top 10 hit. The accompanying video – which centres upon Axl and his then girlfriend, and future wife, Erin Everly – is widely regarded as one of Guns N' Roses best, possibly due to it being far more cinematic than any of the band's previous

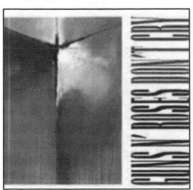

efforts. Although it was the first of the so-called unofficial '*Illusion*' trilogy to be released, there is still much confusion amongst fans as to whether it is the first or second segment of the trilogy. The general consensus, however, is that 'Don't Cry' is indeed the first part, as it shows Axl and his girl having relationship problems, which he subsequently laments in the second and third segments. The video shoot also proved to be an early indication as to the internal problems within the G N' R camp, as Izzy failed to turn up for the filming, which features Slash holding a hand-written card reading: 'Where's Izzy?'

It is also interesting to note Axl's choice of headgear during the video. Firstly, a baseball cap bearing the Nirvana logo can be seen by the side of his leg whilst he lies prostrate on the psychiatrist's couch (the stunning psychiatrist is played by his real-life therapist Suzzy London), which could have been a subliminal dig at Kurt Cobain's refusal to accept Axl's invitation for Nirvana to appear on the second US leg of the *Use Your Illusion* tour. Axl can also be seen wearing a St. Louis Cardinals baseball cap – surely an equally-intentionally veiled reference to the riot at the city's Riverport Amphitheatre on 2 July, which the singer inadvertently sparked following a fracas with a member of the audience.

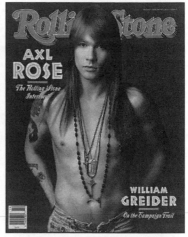

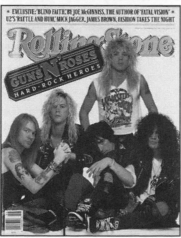

## ESTRANGED

'Estranged', which appears on *Use Your Illusion II*, and was also released as a single in 1994, is the third and final segment of Guns N' Roses' 'unofficial' power-ballad trilogy.

Of the three songs loosely based on Del James' short story '*Without You*', it is 'Estranged' which encapsulates James' tragic tale of a drug-addled, fictional rock star called Mayne, who dreams of 'Elizabeth', a girl of breathtaking beauty and innocent charm. The recurring dream, however, always descends into a nightmare, with the ethereal beauty committing suicide by shooting herself in the head whilst dancing to one of his songs. One only has to read the story and James' depiction of Mayne with his 'long flowing blond locks', 'tattoos', and 'scraggly beard', to know the character is based on Axl. Indeed, James has since admitted the inspiration for '*Without You*' came one night in 1989, when a distraught

Axl poured his heart out to his friend about the miserable state of his stormy relationship with Erin. Several months later, shortly after Del had shown a rough draft of the story to Axl, the singer called him up again one night to tell him the storyline fitted in with a song he'd been working on. Axl initially intended to call the track 'Without You', but by the time the Gunners went into the studio to record the *Use Your Illusion* albums, the song had reverted back to its original title, 'Estranged'.

If it can be said that Del James' short story has commemorated Axl's doomed relationship with Erin Everly to print, then the lovelorn singer's equally disastrous relationship with Stephanie Seymour has been forever immortalised on film. We were first introduced to the gorgeous Victoria's Secrets lingerie model in the promo video for 'Don't Cry', which was simply an extension to her off-camera role as Axl's real-life girlfriend, and again as the blushing (corpse) bride-to-be in the 'November Rain' video. By 1994, however, the couple's tumultuous relationship had come to an end, and so making the 'Estranged' video, with its underlying theme of isolation and abandonment, must have twisted Cupid's arrow further into Axl's tortured soul.

The video, which had a reported budget of \$4 million, opens with a SWAT team – complete with surveillance helicopter – assault on Axl's ivory tower, where the

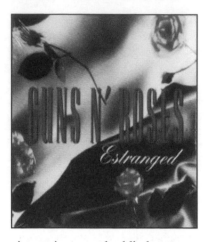

singer is seen huddled atop a wardrobe as the officers carry out a torch-lit search of the seemingly otherwise empty abode. Between snatches of the Gunners performing the song on stage during the *Use Your Illusion* tour, and Slash ripping through the solo on the sidewalk outside the Rainbow Bar & Grill, Axl can be found trawling the deck of a tanker far out to sea, no longer walking quite so proud as once he did. Axl, sporting a 'Charlie Don't Surf' T-Shirt, emblazoned with Charles Manson's murderous black-eyes, seems determined to end his misery and throws himself over the side. Despite Gilby's and Dizzy's best efforts to save him, the singer slips silently beneath the surface surrounded by circling dolphins. While the viewer is left pondering the significance of the dolphins – or indeed whether the clever cetacean creatures will save Axl – Slash emerges from the shimmering depths, Poseidon-like and clasping his six-string tri-

dent... well, I've always said the dude walks on water.

And there was no need to worry about Axl after all. For the cavalry arrives in the form of the SWAT helicopter seen earlier, and all that is lost to the ocean's murky depths is a sneaker bearing Axl's name on the heel to provide a subliminal hint to the pain and anguish he was going through at the time.

## EUROPEAN TOUR, 1987

In late September, 1987 Guns N' Roses undertook their first European tour, which included five UK dates.

The original idea had been for a joint G N' R/Aerosmith tour, but when Aerosmith were forced to pull out at the eleventh hour, it was L.A. glamsters, Faster Pussycat who got the call to pack a flight bag and head down to LAX. The European tour – which was Doug Goldstein's first as G N' R tour manager – got underway on 29 September at Hamburg's Markthalle, where Axl engaged in a little audience participation by alternating verses on 'Knockin' On Heaven's Door' with the kids gathered at the front of the stage. As the band had the luxury of a day off before heading down to Düsseldorf for the second and last German show, they decided to take in the seedy sights of the city's notorious Reeperbahn. Although both bands were staying in the same hotel, their being on tour together didn't necessarily mean the five Gunners were willing to spend time with the guys from Faster Pussycat. The band's frontman, Taime Downe, and most of the Pussycat camp had picked up on the headliners' 'stay away' vibe and sought their own entertainment. So it came as something of a surprise when their drummer, Mark Michals, announced he was going out for a night on the tiles with Axl and co.

Having availed themselves of everything on offer along the Reeperbahn, the five Gunners – with Michals still in tow – returned to their hotel where the Pussycats drummer duly passed out on Duff's bed. Slash was already lying prostrate on his own bed, and so Izzy – sensing an opportunity for a little fun before lights out – launched into a tirade against Michals for having the audacity to crash on Duff's bed. And when Duff's none-too-gentle bedside manner failed to rouse Michals, it was Izzy who mischievously suggested stripping and binding the hapless drummer and dumping him in the elevator. Michals woke up just as the two were about to bundle him into the open elevator, but his pleas for help were quickly stifled with more gaffer tape and he was express-delivered down to reception. The hotel's staff didn't see the funny side in having their nocturnal tranquillity disturbed by a naked American, but reluctantly made the necessary calls to reunite the drummer with his band. Michals was thrown out of the group in 1989 after being arrested in Omaha,

Nebraska, whilst on tour promoting the band's second album, *Wake Me When It's Over,* for naively trying to mail heroin to his hotel room.

Following a show at Amsterdam's Paradiso on 2 October, the tour party made its way via cross-channel ferry to England where, despite largely excellent reviews – not to mention the release of 'Welcome To The Jungle' as a promotional single – *Appetite For Destruction* was struggling in the lower reaches of the album chart. The first of the five regional UK dates was at Newcastle's City Hall on 4 October, which, along with the show at Nottingham's Rock City the following night, was rapturously received. The overly-enthusiastic Nottingham fans were so thrilled to have the Gunners playing in their town they showed their appreciation by attempting to topple the tour bus. The tour's penultimate show, at Bristol's Colston Hall, was another resounding success, and following on from this they headed for London. The final show was at the Hammersmith Odeon, which – thanks to the likes of Judas Priest and Iron Maiden – had come to be regarded as the Mecca of the British Metal scene. There were some metal purists who believed Guns N' Roses were not yet ready to tread the Odeon's illustrious stage, but such was the excitement surrounding the band that the show was a paltry 200 tickets shy of being a complete sell-out, leading to both the band and the music press hailing the tour an unqualified success. This, however, was not strictly true, as poor ticket sales for the 2,000 capacity Manchester Apollo Theatre on 6 October had forced the organisers to cordon off the venue's upstairs balcony.

## EVERLY, ERIN

Erin Invicta Everly is the daughter of Don Everly, who, alongside brother Phil, was one half of the successful early 1960s singing pop duo The Everly Brothers, and actress and one time *Miss Los Angeles Press Club,* Venetia Stevenson.

Erin, who was born on 8 November, 1965, and whose blue-sky eyes, and curly dark tresses provided Axl with the inspiration for Guns N' Roses' biggest-selling single, 'Sweet Child O' Mine', was working as a model for the Wilhelmina Agency in New York when the pair met at a party in her native Los Angeles in 1986. Having fallen for the then unknown Axl's charms, she relocated back to California and moved in with the errant singer shortly thereafter.

At the time, Guns N' Roses was just another wannabe band barely making enough money to survive, and so Erin continued modelling in order to pay the rent on their modest West Hollywood apartment. As the group's career took off, however, instead of assuaging Axl's fiery temper, the demands of being in a happening band only served to heighten the couple's fighting.

On one occasion Axl reportedly dragged a partially-dressed Erin outside onto the street inflicting several unsightly abrasions which forced her to cancel a lucrative lingerie shoot. While on another occasion, Erin's model friend Taryn Portman was concerned enough to call the police out to the couple's apartment, only for Erin to then protect Axl by pretending the call had been a false alarm. And it seems Axl's flare-ups were not confined to behind closed doors, because another of Erin's friends, the independent TV producer Heidi Richman, told *PEOPLE* magazine that she witnessed Axl – who was acting like a "rabid dog" – beating Erin and dragging her by the hair at a mutual friend's barbeque up in the Hollywood Hills.

As with countless other victims of domestic violence, Erin was living in denial and unable to leave the person that was inflicting pain on a daily basis; "I always believed things would get better," she told one reporter. "I thought I could make his [Axl's] early childhood suffering all better." Perhaps the song written in her honour should have been renamed 'Naïve Child O' Mine'.

On 27 April, 1990, by which time Axl had moved out of their apartment and was living in a condo above Sunset Strip, the singer arrived at Erin's door unannounced at 4am and told her that he had a gun stashed in the boot of his car and that he was going to shoot himself unless she agreed to marry him. And so, the following day the

pair drove to Las Vegas and made their vows (one of which was that Axl wouldn't hit Erin ever again) before God, and a low-rent minister, at the city's Cupid Wedding Chapel. Less than a month after the service, however, and with the ink barely dry on marriage certificate C199803, it seemed Axl's feelings for Erin were on the wane, and friends on both sides were left shocked and stunned when he threatened to file for divorce. This was only one of several such threats. But there was little doubt the union was destined for the law courts when, two months later, Axl beat Erin so badly that she was hospitalised. It was while she was recovering in hospital that Axl attempted a reconciliation of sorts by moving Erin's belongings into his condo. But, despite assurances to the contrary, the domestic bliss proved short-lived as Axl – who by this time was an extremely wealthy individual – was refusing to give his wife either cash or a front door key, and also forbade her to see her family and friends, who'd all repeatedly urged her to leave him for good.

In September, 1990, it seemed everything in the garden would turn out rosy after all when Erin discovered she was pregnant. Axl's elation quickly soured, however, and he threw her out of his home and also threatened to take the baby. Erin tragically suffered a miscarriage in her third month, but at the time when she needed her husband most, Axl refused to have anything to do with her and she was forced into selling her jeep in order to cover the medical expenses. It was while Erin was recuperating that Axl trashed his condo, causing an estimated $100,000 damage. The final straw for Erin came in November 1990 when Axl flared up over her having cleaned his CD collection. "I didn't think I could survive mentally any longer, I was dying inside." she told the same reporter. "At the door, I stopped and turned around and told him 'I want you to take a good look at me, because you're never going to see me again', and he never has." And although Axl initially refused to comment on Erin's accusations, he later claimed that if he'd struck Erin then he had done so in self defence. (This is somewhat hard to believe if one stops to consider that, at the time, the waiflike Erin was 5'6" to Axl's 5'9" and weighed in a substantial 41 lbs lighter.)

The marriage was annulled two months later in January, 1991. The annulment came at Axl's behest since, under Californian law, any marriage lasting less than two years can be annulled, which therefore denied Erin any entitlement to a share of his sizeable fortune. That said, however, Axl was not prepared to move on, and constantly tried to renew contact with Erin by sending letters, flowers and even caged birds to her condo in the San Fernando Valley. "One day the phone rang, and it was Axl," she told the reporter. "I moved the next day."

In 1992, Erin had a brief fling with Donovan Leitch, son of '60s troubadour Donovan, and future Camp Freddy vocalist, and the following year began dating the actor David Arquette. Although Arquette reportedly tried to get Erin to talk publicly about her ordeal at Axl's hands, it wasn't until she was subpoenaed by Stephanie Seymour's lawyers in March, 1994 to testify against Axl in the model's own abuse case that she decided to file her multi-million dollar domestic violence law suit against her erstwhile husband. She even went public with harrowing tales of Axl's mental and physical abuse towards her during their turbulent four-year relationship. This, of course, was long before the O.J. Simpson trial brought domestic violence's hitherto unseen dirty washing out into the American public domain, and the two lawsuits were settled out of court with both women supposedly receiving sizable settlements.

Like Axl, Erin also endured a troubled childhood following her parents' separation in 1970 (the couple eventually divorced two years later) when she and her siblings were forced to give up their upscale home in Studio City in favour of a more modest rented affair, as well as bid a fond farewell to the privileges afforded to them at the exclusive Buckley private school following Don Everly's refusal to pay child support. This must have been doubly difficult for Erin as she suffered from dyslexia and was regarded as something of a 'slow learner'. She has since got her life back on track by marrying Jack Portman, and in 1998 she gave birth to their son Easton.

# FARTZ, THE

The Fartz was a Seattle-based hardcore punk band which featured a pre-G N' R Duff McKagan in its line-up.

In truth, The Fartz was just one of several punk bands which Duff played with – this time as the drummer – before making the move from Seattle to Los Angeles. The outspoken, and oft confronta-tional, band's set list consisted of short, sharp two-to-three minute songs, which railed against all the usual suspects of the day: govern-mental and religious corruption, racism, sexism, poverty et al, and, in keeping with punk's penchant for silly names, singer Blaine Cook rechristened himself Blaine Fart, the bassist was Steve Fart, while Duff's replacement on the drum stool was fittingly known as 'Loud Fart'.

The band originally formed in 1981, and the release of their debut vinyl offering, a 7" self-issued EP entitled 'Because This Fuckin' World Stinks', helped establish them as one of Seattle's premiere hardcore Punk bands.

The following year, the Fartz released their debut album *World Full Of Hate* on Dead Kennedys frontman Jello Biafra's Alternative Tentacles label. The album sold moderately well in and around

the Pacific Northwest, even if it was only to the band's small yet devoted following – although having said that, one single attracted enough overseas interest to earn a place in the Top 10 in the *NME*'s alternative chart. Despite this moderate success, vocalist Cook announced his departure, citing the time-honoured excuse of "irreconcilable musical differences". Another reason could have been that by 1982, punk rock, both in the UK and New York, had run to a fast and frenetic conclusion, and wouldn't actually figure again in the US until 1991 with the emergence of Nirvana, and Sonic Youth, by which time the Fartz had gone their separate ways, leaving little more than a lingering smell in their wake.

In 1998, however, and largely due to Duff's association with the band, Alternative Tentacles issued a retrospective album entitled *Because This Fuckin World Still Stinks Compilation*, while a second compilation album, *What's In A Name,* appeared on the same label in 2001.

## FASANO, MIKE

Mike 'The Sack' Fasano is a renowned session drummer who has at one time or another toured and recorded with the likes of Eric Clapton, Warrant, Dad's Porno

Mag, Roxie 77 and Gilby Clarke's post G N' R solo projects.

It was through his association with Gilby Clarke that he guested on G N' R's cover-version of Nazareth's 'Hair Of The Dog' which appeared on *The Spaghetti Incident?* In 1996, Fasano was also credited as a 'band tech' on the liner notes to the Neurotic Outsiders album.

## FASTBACKS, THE

The Fastbacks was yet another Seattle Punk band which, despite enjoying a longevity lasting some twenty-two years and taking them into the new millennium, would have barely registered on the radar had it not been for its having briefly boasted Duff McKagan in the line-up.

The Fastbacks formed way back in 1979 when 18-year-old aspiring songwriter/guitarist Kurt Bloch teamed up with his old high school friends Lulu Gargiulo (guitar/vocals), and aspiring Gaye Advert wannabe, bassist Kim Warnick. And although these three would remain a constant throughout the band's existence, it is believed that anywhere between twelve-to-twenty different sticksmen – including Duff – occupied the drum stool at one time or another; the most famous apart from Duff being Mudhoney's Dan Peters.

# FENDER'S BALLROOM

Fender's Ballroom was L.A.'s legendary punk venue where the pre-signed Guns N' Roses played several chaotic shows in 1986.

During the '80s, the now long-defunct Fender's Ballroom in the L.A. suburb of Long Beach, was what The Roxy was to London in 1977, and CBGBs to New York in the mid-to-late '70s. Indeed, any self-respecting punk or metal band that came to, or spilled out of, Los Angeles was proud to strut their stuff on stage at the one-storey converted car garage which had once belonged to the adjoining five-storey Lafayette Hotel, which in turn was subsequently renovated into luxury condos.

The International Ballroom – as it was previously known – first opened its doors at 521 East 1st Street on Christmas Day, 1956, and at 17,500 square feet was the largest banquet facility west of Chicago. In 1985, its owner, John Fender, announced plans to purchase the Lafayette, which had ceased operating as a hotel in 1967 to be converted into residential apartments, but fell foul of Long Beach's Homeowners Association over none payment of his monthly assessments on the ballroom due to a long-standing dispute. In July the following year, a sports club, also owned by Fender, was closed down as part of a city crackdown on the cocaine rings operating in Long Beach. It was reported that undercover officers had purchased cocaine from five employees working at the Players Sports Club on nearby Linden Avenue. Although Fender narrowly avoided a custodial sentence, and also survived a petition filed by Lafayette's affluent put-upon residents, who'd all long-since tired of the excessive noise

and late-night drunken fights, the writing was on the wall and the ballroom closed its doors later that same year.

Fender's concert promoter, and partner-in-crime, was one-time booking agent Ken Phebus, who, with his bandana, beard, and shades, looked like an extra from *Easy Rider* – a look which Axl himself later adopted. The club may have been a shadow of its former glory by the mid-'80s, but the kids didn't care about the shoddy décor, nor having the local police tease and torment them as they queued up in the adjacent alley, as there was 2,500 square feet of dancefloor to leap about on.

Guns N' Roses made their debut at Fender's on 21 March, 1986, as special guests of one of their idols, Johnny Thunders, the one-time New York Doll who'd hacked off his hair and traded in his lip gloss and sling-backs to form the unrelenting, and highly under-rated Heartbreakers to provide a little Lower East Side swagger to the nascent UK punk scene. The Gunners may have been top dogs on the Strip and packing them in at the Troubadour, Roxy et al, and were days away from signing to Geffen, but they couldn't yet hope to fill the spacious Long Beach venue on their own. The band opened their set with 'Out Ta Get Me' and as Slash picked out the intro to the next song, 'Welcome To The Jungle', a speeding Axl – who boasted of having been awake for the previous 48

hours – challenged the audience to remember the band's name, which he'd happily daubed on the cramped dressing room's graffiti-laden walls before taking to the stage.

The group returned to Fender's eight days later on 29 March – by which time they had indeed put pen to paper with Geffen – this time as special guests for Lords Of The New Church, featuring another of their punk heroes, ex-Dead Boy, Stiv Bators. The Gunners would subsequently pay post-humous homage to both Thunders and Bators on *The Spaghetti Incident?* Indeed, it could be argued that said album was in homage to Fender's Ballroom as much as it was to punk rock, as six of the twelve accredited bands featured on the album performed at the venue at one time or another. L.A.'s premiere punk band, Fear, played there in 1985, as did both The Damned, and the UK Subs.

In November, 1986, the Gunners took time out from recording their debut album to play two shows at Fender's Ballroom. The first, on 15 November, was as special guests for a reconstituted Dead Boys, while the second came six days later opening for Cheap Trick. The Illinois rockers' 1979 record *Live At Budokan* had made them a household name in America, but their latest studio album, *The Doctor,* had recently stalled at #115 on the Billboard 200. The show was a harmonious affair, but in 1988, while the Gunners were in Chicago on tour with Aerosmith, Cheap Trick's Rick Nielson sought to renew his acquaintanceship with the Gunners by inviting the band to his home, where he foolishly challenged Slash – a guy who was downing Jack Daniels as though it was sarsaparilla – to a drinking contest. Needless to say, Slash proved the victor, whereas Nielson proved a sore loser, and drunkenly assaulted the band. The fight was brought to a swift conclusion when Izzy felled the aging rocker with a swift kick to the balls.

## FERRER, FRANK

Frank Ferrer, the highly respected session musician, occasional Psychedelic Furs and one-time Love Split Love drummer, became an official member of the ever-expanding Guns N' Roses fraternity in October, 2006. The

invite came about owing to his having already impressed during his brief tenure with the band when he stood in as an emergency substitute for Bryan Mantia during their European summer tour of that same year.

## FREDDIE MERCURY TRIBUTE CONCERT 1992

The Freddie Mercury Tribute Concert for AIDS Awareness was staged at Wembley Stadium on Easter Monday, 20 April, 1992.

Following the flamboyant Queen frontman's untimely death from AIDS on 24 November, 1991, the three remaining band members, Brian May, Roger Taylor and John Deacon – along with their manager Jim Breach – decided to organise an open-air concert, not only as a means of celebrating Freddie's life and legacy, but also to raise funds for AIDS research. The first the world at large heard about the event came in February, 1992 at the annual BRIT Awards (British Record Industry Trust) ceremony, where May and Taylor announced plans for the Wembley extravaganza. And somewhat unbelievably, although none of the acts that subsequently performed at the show had been finalised by the time the tickets went on sale the following month, all 72,000 sold out in just two hours.

The first half of the show was reserved for bands which openly

admitted to having been influenced by Queen, and first on stage was Metallica, who blasted their way through three tracks from their new eponymously titled album: 'Enter Sandman'; 'Sad But True' and 'Nothing Else Matters'. Next up came Extreme, who treated the crowd to a 'Queen medley' and two of their own songs, 'Love Of My Life' and their recent Billboard #1 hit single, and housewives favourite 'More Than Words'. Sheffield's favourite sons, Def Leppard performed the hits 'Animal', and 'Let's Get Rocked', before inviting Brian May onto the stage to perform 'Now I'm Here' from Queen's *Sheer Heart Attack* album.

Although Guns N' Roses had performed their own sell-out show beneath Wembley's twin towers less than eight months earlier, and were also currently engaged in their mammoth *Use Your Illu-sion* tour, which would see them perform to some seven million people worldwide, they walked out on stage – slotted between the side-splitting spoof rockers Spinal Tap, and Elizabeth Taylor's impassioned AIDS prevention speech – to an estimated televised audience in excess of one billion – and boy did they seize the moment. With Axl sporting a Union Jack emblazoned motorcycle jacket and a T-shirt bearing an image of Jesus Christ above the slogan 'Kill Your Idols', the Gunners blasted into 'Paradise City', which sent the already jubilant Wembley audience into rapture. This was followed with the intro to Alice Cooper's 1975 US hit 'Only Women Bleed', which then segued into an extended version of 'Knockin' On Heaven's Door', which, owing to time restraints (possibly caused by Spinal Tap's set delays) resulted in the audience being denied the pleasure of 'Sweet Child O' Mine'.

The second half of the show featured May, Taylor and Deacon (who has only performed on stage once since that day) performing hits from Queen's extensive back catalogue with guest singers such as aging rockers Roger Daltry, David Bowie and Robert Plant, as well as contemporary solo artists such as George Michael, Annie Lennox, Paul Young and Seal. The occasion provided Axl with the opportunity to fulfil a long-cherished ambition in performing a duet with his idol Elton John. Their stunning rendition of 'Bohemian Rhapsody' proved to be one of the show's highlights, and an ecstatic Axl also performed 'We Will Rock You' with Queen's surviving members. Slash got in on the action too by teaming up with Def Leppard frontman, Joe Elliott, for a seat-shaking version of 'Tie Your Mother Down', before he, Axl and Duff joined Liza Minnelli and the rest of the show's stellar cast for a rip-roaring encore of 'We Are The Champions' to send Freddie off into the hereafter.

For reasons which have never been fully explained, when the concert was released on DVD in April, 2002, to mark the 10th anniversary of the Mercury Phoenix Trust, the entire first half of the show – which included Guns N' Roses' two-song set – wasn't included.

# FORTUS, RICHARD

Richard Fortus is a renowned session guitarist who replaced Paul Tobias in Guns N' Roses in 2002.

G N' R's incumbent rhythm guitarist was born on 17 November, 1966, in St. Louise, Missouri. He first rose to prominence in the Midwest with his band The Eyes, which released the independent album, *Freedom In A Cage*. It was the band's live shows, however, that proved the more popular as their high-voltage set combined original compositions along with Red Hot Chili Peppers and Bauhaus covers. In keeping with their dark image, the group first underwent a name change to Pale Divine, and in order to promote their 1991 album, *Straight To Goodbye,* went out on tour in the US supporting British '80s sax-punksters, Psychedelic Furs, who were due to split immediately after the tour. The Furs were perhaps best known for their 1981 hit, 'Pretty In Pink', which subsequently appeared in the John Hughes 1986 movie of the same name and starring Harry Dean Stanton, James Spader, and Molly Ringwald, as well as being adopted by Cingular Wireless for a TV ad campaign for the Motorola 'Pink Razr' mobile phone.

Fortus called time on Pale Divine to team up with Furs frontman Richard Butler – as well as future G N' R drummer Frank Ferrer – on what was initially intended to be the latter's debut solo album.

RETAILER REVIEW

# THE JELLIFISH:
## FOR ACOUSTIC AND ELECTRIC GUITARISTS ALIKE

### By Richard Fortus, guitarist, Guns N' Roses

I always carry a Jellifish with me. I view it as an essential guitar tool, the same way I view a slide, ebow, or fx pedal. I don't use all of them on every session or live gig, but it does something that nothing else does. If you're a blues purist or typical bone-head rocker, or you play in a cover band and are looking for something to help your strat sound like a Ricky 12 string so you can do "Mr. Tambourine Man," Jellifish isn't for you. But if you are the type of guy who likes to coax new and interesting tones out of your instrument, this is probably the best money under $20 you'll ever spend.

It takes a little bit of time investment to find sounds with the Jellifish. For some, probably longer than others. However, that's the fun of it. In fact, I am *still* finding new and exciting sounds with it. I have used the Jellifish to get bowed-type "sustainy" sounds on electric, plucky "zitherish" sounds on acoustic, and droney "worldly" tones on classic nylon strings. It's really useful for big washes of color with delays and reverbs. If you pluck on higher notes, very close to the bridge, you can obtain very unusual sounds that are like an autoharp crossed with a Turkish oud. The Jellifish can have a beautiful metal-scraping-on-metal sound I love. I initially used the Jellifish mostly on acoustic guitar, but now find myself using it on electrics just as often.

When I first discovered the

Jellifish, I was so excited about it that I bought about 25 of them and gave them out to my buddies who I thought would "get it." Some did, some didn't. It's not for everyone. However, those who did "get it," loved it! It's an inspirational tool. The type of thing you reach for when you are looking for something different. I've based entire cues for films around the Jellifish. Used gently on a steel string acoustic, just delicately strumming the guitar gives an intimate tone

that couldn't be duplicated with anything else.

The people who buy a "Jelli" are the same type of people who are going to buy ebows or Z vex pedals: Creative players who are always searching for new sonic textures. It's not going to help you shred faster or make your tone sound more like Stevie Ray Vaughn. For me, it is simply another color on my palette. It's a niche market, but it will inevitably become an essential tool for the creative guitarist. ℝ

### In Brief: Jellifish
- Jellifish, manufactured by Jellifish International Corp. USA, is not referred to as a pick. It is called a "plectrum effect."
- Considered a tool for "finesse players," Jellifish is not for beginners. According to the company, players need to generally be a "5" on a scale of 1 to 10 to have the dexterity to get the product's full benefits.
- However, the product can be sold to beginners. When asking about the product, you may want to tell customers they are likely to grow into Jellifish. As they get better, the benefits of Jellifish will be enhanced.
- It is designed to be used in conjunction with three biome-chanical plectrum techniques: sweep picking, alternate picking, and circular picking.
- Each picking technique produces a slightly different timbre, and the company has given each different timbre a trademarked name: Chorus! Pluck! and Bow! Chorus! (sweep picking) resembles the sound of a chorus pedal or 12-string guitar. Pluck! (alternate picking) is often compared to the sound of a hammered dulcimer. Bow! (circular picking) produces a bowed instrument effect.

*Richard Fortus of Guns N' Roses is working on the band's long-awaited "Chinese Democracy" album. He also worked on the score for the Activision game "Tony Hawk's Thug 2" and is currently working on the score for an Activision Western video game. Fortus has contributed to the scores of several hit movies, including "Monster," "The Fast and the Furious," and "The Village," and is lending his hand to the forthcoming film named "Swimmers." Fortus also wrote scores for several television commercials and program themes. He has played on N\* Sync's album "Celebrity," a Britney Spears album, and recorded with Ben Folds, Frank Black, BT, Enrique Iglesias, and The Tom Tom Club. Fortus has toured with BT, Iglesias, and the Psychedelic Furs.*

*Editor's note: This marks the fourth Retailer Review, where we spotlight a product and have an end-user review it. This month, Richard Fortus, Guns N' Roses guitarist who recently became a father, reviews Jellifish from Jellifish International Corp. USA. The product is available now with a MSRP of $12.95 and MAP of $9.95.*

As the songs took shape, however, Butler opted to expand the solo project into a new band, Love Spit Love (the name came from a 1991 performance art exhibition in New York which featured three naked couples – of varying sexual orientation – openly engaged in sexual acts). The band's debut, self-titled album, which features Butler's brother, and ex-Psychedelic Furs bassist Tim, was released on Imago Records in August, 1994. The following year, Love Split Love were called upon to record a version of The Smiths' 'How Soon Is Now' for the soundtrack to the 1996 movie, *The Craft* starring Neve Campbell and Skeet Ulrich, which was also released as a single. Warner Bros. would also subsequently utilize the track for its new TV series *Charmed*. The band's second album *Trysome Eatone* was released on Madonna's Maverick label in August, 1997. After touring in support of the record, Love Split Love went into indefinite hiatus, and when the Butler brothers decided to resurrect the Psychedelic Furs, both Fortus and Ferrer went with them as second guitarist and drummer respectively, and appeared on the band's live album *Beautiful Chaos: Greatest Hits Live*.

In 2002, after a stint with Nena of 99 Red Balloons fame, Fortus replaced Paul Tobias in Guns N' Roses, and his flamboyant style, as well as a talent for both rhythm and lead guitar, moved Axl to pay him the ultimate compliment by saying "Richard is the guy that we [Guns N' Roses] were always looking for."

# FREESE, JOSH

Josh Freese is a highly-respected session drummer, percussionist, and songwriter who replaced Matt Sorum as G N' R's resident drummer in 1997.

Although Freese was born in Orlando, Florida on 25 December, 1972, he has lived in Southern California since he was 6 months old. Aside from occupying the Gunners' drum stool for five years, he is also a permanent member of The Vandals, Viva

Death, Devo, and A Perfect Circle. It is perhaps not surprising, given his father was the conductor in the Disneyland Band and his mother was a classically-trained pianist, that young Josh developed an interest in music. He first began playing drums when he was eight-years-old, and by the time he was 12 he was following his father's footsteps by playing professionally in Polo, a Top 40 Disneyland band. By the age of 15, however, he had bid a fond farewell to Mickey, Donald and Goofy et al, and began touring and recording with The Vandals. He has been the permanent drummer with electro-punk outfit Devo since 1995.

His leap to centre stage came in 1997 when he replaced Matt Sorum in Guns N' Roses, signing a two-year contract with the band. He features on the recording of 'Oh My God' for the *End Of Days* movie soundtrack, as well as various bits and pieces – including a supposed co-wrote for the *Chinese Democracy* album's title track – before departing in 2000 to launch A Perfect Circle. That same year, he released a solo album, *The Notorious One Man Orgy* on Kung Fu Records, which includes several tracks from his 1998 six-song EP, *Destroy The Earth As Soon As Possible,* which he released under the somewhat bizarre pseudonym 'Princess'.

Freese has also worked with the likes of The Offspring, appearing on the Californian punksters' 2003 album *Splinter,* and was a member of Sting's touring band for the ex-Police frontman's 2005 Broken Music Tour, which also included an appearance at the Live 8 concert – an experience which Josh later cited as the "greatest show of my life".

Towards the end of 2005, he stepped in as a temporary replacement for Nine Inch Nails drummer, Jerome Dillon for the band's *With Teeth* tour, and also laid down the drum tracks for two songs on the band's *Year Zero* album. He continued to tour with NIN throughout 2006 and early 2007, but took time out to contribute drum tracks for Lost Prophets' third album, *Liberation Transmission*.

# GEFFEN, DAVID

David Lawrence Geffen, the founder of both Asylum Records and Geffen Records, is also a successful movie and theatrical producer.

David Geffen was born into a respectable Jewish family in Brooklyn, New York, on 21 February, 1943. After graduating from New Utrecht High School, he enrolled at the University of Texas in Austin, but dropped out again soon after, and having no desire to follow his older brother Mitchell into law, set his sights on a career in the entertainment industry. Although his first job was as a lowly clerk in the William Morris Agency mailroom, it was the first rung on the ladder to success. Incidentally, one of his co-workers in the mailroom was Elliot Roberts who would later become his business partner.

One of the WMA's pre-requisites, however, was that all its employees provided proof of having graduated college, and so

rather than lose his job, Geffen forged a letter and brazenly handed it in to his bosses. Having risen to the position of agent, Geffen left WMA to set himself up as a personal manager and achieved immediate success with composer and lyricist, Laura Nyro, and folk rockers Crosby, Stills and Nash. It was while he was trying to procure a record deal for the budding singer/songwriter Jackson Browne, however, that Atlantic Records executive Ahmet Ertegün suggested he should perhaps start up his own record label.

In 1970, Geffen did as Ertegün suggested and founded Asylum Records, and after signing Browne to his fledgling label he also procured the services of Californian soft rockers The Eagles, Joni Mitchell, Linda Ronstadt, and Bob Dylan. Asylum's – not to mention Geffen's – reputation quickly grew, and in 1972 Warner Communications acquired the

label and duly merged it with Elektra Records. Geffen was placed in charge of the newly-formed Elektra/Asylum Records but resigned as director three years later after having been told by his doctors – speciously as it turned out – that he had a malignant cancerous cyst. Despite living under the storm cloud of a life-threatening illness, Geffen continued working as Vice-Chairman of Warner Brothers film studios, as well as teaching business studies at Yale University, before retiring in 1980. Upon discovering that the earlier diagnosis was indeed erroneous, Geffen decided to return to work in the music industry and set up Geffen Records.

Today David Geffen is believed to be the richest person within the entertainment industry, with an estimated personal fortune of $4.7 billion.

## GEFFEN RECORDS

Geffen Records, which signed Guns N' Roses back in March, 1986, is owned by the Universal Music Group, and operates as one third of UMG's Interscope-Geffen-A&M label.

Geffen Records was founded in 1980 by former Asylum Records head honcho David Geffen, who had only stepped down as Asylum's CEO after being diagnosed with cancer. Upon being told the life-threatening cyst was, in fact, benign, he sought an immedi-

ate return to the music business by striking a ten-year deal with Warner Bros. Records, to create Geffen Records. The deal saw Warner providing 100% of the required operational funding, and overseeing total distribution of product, while Geffen retained 50% of the profits from sales.

The first artist to sign to Geffen's label was disco diva Donna Summer, with the resultant album *The Wanderer* achieving gold status. Geffen followed on from that success with the release of John Lennon's *Double Fantasy*, which was the former Beatle's first album to contain all-new material in several years. That alone would surely have provided Geffen with a hit record and a healthy profit margin, but this was chillingly ensured when two days following the album's release, a no-mark called Mark Chapman callously gunned Lennon down outside his New York City apartment block.

Geffen went from strength-to-strength during the 1980s and procured music heavyweights such as Elton John, Cher, Peter Gabriel, Joni Mitchell and Neil

'Crazy Horse' Young. It was Geffen's passion for rock music – coupled with an iron-clad guarantee that the band could operate under its own steam without corporate interference – that resulted in the label winning the battle for Guns N' Roses' signatures. When the time came for the Gunners to put pen to paper, David Geffen made a point of being present at the meeting, but failed to recognise the band's top-hatted, droopy-eyed, Jack-slugging guitarist as the polite fresh-faced youngster who had regularly accompanied his father Tony Hudson to these very offices a decade or so earlier. Indeed, the startling revelation only came when Geffen ran into Slash's mother, Ola – whom he knew both socially and professionally – and innocently enquired after her eldest boy.

Acquiring the Gunners, David Coverdale's Whitesnake, and the recently-rehabilitated Aerosmith, led to Geffen creating the subsidiary label DGC (David Geffen Company), which solely focused on alternative rock and became home to Beck, Sonic Youth, Hole, Counting Crows, Teenage Fanclub and the undisputed Kings of Grunge, Nirvana.

In 1990, with the expiration of its agreement with Warner, David Geffen sold the label to MCA Music Entertainment (later renamed Universal Music Group) for a reported $1 billion in cash and stock, and an agreement whereby he would remain its head for five years. Following the sale, Geffen began operating as one of Universal's leading independently managed labels. When David Geffen finally stepped down in 1995, he formed a business partnership with Jeffrey Katzenberg, and Steven Spielberg to form DreamWorks SKG which today is a multi-billion multimedia empire dealing in movies, TV, books and music, with Geffen Records acting as sole distributor for all releases on the subsidiary Dream-Works Records label.

Universal Music Group's acquisition of PolyGram in 1998 saw a corporate reorganisation which resulted in Geffen Records – along with another acquisition, A&M Records – being subsequently merged into Interscope Records. And although Geffen continued to exist as its own imprint, it was dramatically reduced in both size and stature and DGC ceased all operations entirely.

By 2000, despite having been neutered by its corporate UMG master, Geffen continued to prove itself a shrewd operator within the music business. So much so in fact that by 2003, UMG had incorporated MCA Records into Geffen, and although Geffen had always been regarded within the industry as a pop-rock label, its assimilation of MCA provided it with a more diverse roster. It was around this time that Dream-Works Records folded and was also absorbed by Geffen. Geffen's incorporation of MCA and Dream-Works has boosted its status and seen it gain an equal footing with Interscope, which has led to many industry insiders predicting that it may one day become a dominant force again.

# GILMORE, GREG

Greg Gilmore is the Seattle-based drummer who played in Ten Minute Warning with Duff McKagan, and accompanied the future Guns N' Roses bassist to Los Angeles in 1985. He is also the co-founder of the First World Music record label.

Greg was born in France on 3 January, 1962, but relocated to the US with his family while still a toddler and grew up in the Seat-tle area. Like most aspiring Seat-tle musicians in the late '70s and early '80s, Greg was enamoured with punk rock, and played in sev-eral low-rent bands before taking the drum stool with psychedelic punksters, Ten Minute Warning. When his buddy Duff announced he was striking out to make a name for himself in Los Angeles, Greg decided to tag along. The pair rented a cockroach infested apartment in West Hollywood so they could be close to the action and began trawling the 'musicians wanted' section in *Music Connection*, and also attended auditions. When Duff became temporarily involved with Road Crew, Greg

accompanied him to several auditions, but would have quickly realised that Slash and Steven came as a team. He was also on hand when Duff subsequently got involved with Axl and Izzy and one has to wonder why he didn't step up to the plate to replace Rob Gardner in the fledgling G N' R line-up.

With Duff firmly ensconced in Guns N' Roses, there was little to keep Greg in the City of Angels and the drummer began pining for the Pacific Northwest. He returned to Seattle where he flitted from band to band – including a two-gig stint in Jack Endino's Skin Yard – before eventually teaming up with ex Malfunkshun vocalist Andrew Wood, guitarists Bruce Fairweather and Stone Gossard and bassist Jeff Ament (who had all played together in Green River) in the critically acclaimed – yet tragically short-lived – seminal grunge outfit Mother Love Bone. The band's promising career was cut short when Wood – who had a history of drug problems – succumbed to heroin in 1990 just days before the release of the band's debut album *Apple*. Woods' roommate, and Soundgarden frontman, Chris Cornell, approached Gilmore and the others to see if they'd be willing to record two songs with him, written in tribute to Woods. The two-song project evolved into an entire album and was released under the name Temple Of The Dog, which they'd lifted from one of Woods'

songs. Once the project was completed, however, Cornell returned to Soundgarden, and while Greg was yet again left to twiddle his sticks, Gossard and Ament went on to enjoy worldwide fame with Eddie Veder's Pearl Jam.

In the early '90s, Greg again teamed up with Jack Endino, who, when he wasn't performing or releasing his own solo efforts, was a much sought-after engineer and producer who had produced Nirvana's Subpop debut, *Bleach*. And although Greg continues to collaborate with a wide variety of artists, including Steve Fisk, Doghead and Radio Chongqing, he will surely always be known as the drummer who could have been.

# GLOVER, MARTIN

Martin 'Youth' Glover is a South African-born producer drafted in to work on *Chinese Democracy*.

Glover first came to prominence as bassist in the British post-punk band Killing Joke who enjoyed a modicum of success in the late-70s and early-'80s with hits such as 'Wardance', 'Requiem', and 'Follow My Leaders'. Following his departure from Killing Joke, he set up the independent label Butterfly Records which has produced hits for the likes of Paul McCartney, Tom Jones, and Maria McKee, while his work as co-producer on The Verve's *Urban*

*Hymns* earned him a Producer of the Year Award in 1998.

# GNR LIES

*GNR Lies*, the second Guns N' Roses album, released in the US in November 1988, and the following month in the UK, has gone on to sell over 12million copies worldwide.

The track-listing is as follows: *Reckless Life* (3:20); *Nice Boys (Don't Play Rock 'N' Roll)* (3:02); *Move To The City* (3:42); *Mama Kin* (3:57); *Patience* (5:56); *Used To Love Her* (3:13); *You're Crazy* (4:10); *One In A Million* (6:10) LP, CD, Cassette – Geffen Records, 1988.

With *Appetite For Destruction* still riding high at #3 on the Billboard 200, and shifting units by the wagon-load, Geffen were naturally keen to keep the momentum going and decided upon a mini-album to satiate the fans' hunger for new product – as well as help keep Guns N' Roses in the public eye – while the band got on with writing and recording songs for the highly-important follow-up album.

As well as the four songs featured on the *'Live?!*@ Like A Suicide'* EP, the mini-album contained the original slow-tempo version of 'You're Crazy' and three brand-new acoustic numbers. 'Patience' was Izzy's lament to his lost love, Angela Nicoletti, 'Used To Love Her', a tongue-in-cheek misogynistic ditty on uxoricide (murdering one's wife) which would come back to haunt the band some five years later when the song bizarrely featured in the Florida vs. Justin Barber murder trial, while the final track, 'One In A Million', would prove even more controversial. These three new songs had been written and recorded in a single afternoon session at Rumbo Studios which Mike Clink would later describe as "one of those magical rock 'n' roll history moments." Several other songs, such as Duff's 'Cornshucker', and 'Crash Diet', were also recorded during the sessions, but failed to make the album's final track-listing.

With the *'Live?!*@ A Suicide'* EP, a much sought-after item amongst Guns N' Roses fans – and commanding a hefty price on the black market – it made sense to re-release these songs, and with regard to why the previously-released 'You're Crazy' also featured on the new album, the band issued the following explanation on the album cover: YOU'RE CRAZY: A song originally written acoustically right after the band was signed to Geffen Records only to be trans-

formed in rehearsal, and live, into the version heard on *Appetite For Destruction*. Now it's been taken back to its original pace, though it has remained electric. None of which has been done for better or worse… only for the sake of something to do. (We do what we want.)

Still smarting over the British tabloid press' scaremongering headlines and trashy tales of drink, drugs and debauchery that greeted the band's first visit to London the previous year – not to mention the totally undeserved blame heaped upon them over the Donington tragedy of four months earlier – the Gunners extracted

their revenge, albeit tongue-in-cheek, by issuing the eight-track album housed in a foldout sleeve, parodying those same newspapers' front pages. To accompany the names of the four new acoustic songs and vacuous headlines such as

'MAN SUES EX-WIFE: "SHE TOOK MY SPERM WITHOUT PERMISSION", 'SUE'S TOES SHOT OFF BY SNATCH GANG', and 'SEX, SEX, SEX IS THE SECRET BEHIND HER $6 MILLION FACE',

black and white images of all five Gunners feature on the eye-grabbing front page, dated 6 December, 1988, which *The Sun*, *Daily Mirror*, *Daily Sport*, and their ilk would have been proud of. Axl is shown slumped against a wall looking suitably mean and moody, while a louche Slash, clutching a bottle of whatever, peers out from beneath his corkscrew curls in a 'Guns N' Roses Picture Exclusive'. The photo of a be-shaded Izzy, shown nonchalantly strumming a guitar, accompanies yet another farcical headline 'Elephant Gives Birth To Midget', while the blonds in the band, Duff and Steven (who is also sporting shades), both stare out from the front page like teen idols from *19*, *Honey*, or *My Guy*.

The equally inane inside sleeve features the obligatory page three blonde accompanying risqué headlines such as

'GAY VICAR IN GANGBANG HORROR', 'POP KILLED SEX BEAST', 'HEIR TO THE THRONE CAUGHT WITH TROUSERS DOWN IN LURID LUST PIT', AND 'DINKY DEN IN THE PEN'.

The latter refers to the fictional TV soap character Den Watts, the decidedly-dodgy womanising pub landlord played to perfection by cabbie killer-cum-actor Leslie Grantham in the *BBC*'s then relatively new flagship soap opera, *Eastenders*.

The front cover also features the album's original title

*GUNS N' ROSES: LIES! THE SEX, THE DRUGS, THE VIOLENCE, THE SHOCKING TRUTH*,

but Al Coury, who was head of Geffen's promotions team, foresaw the logistical headaches that a lengthy title would undoubtedly bring when trying to promote the album, and Geffen therefore opted for the truncated – and far snappier sounding – *GNR Lies*. Despite the controversy and negativity in certain quarters regarding 'One In A Million', the new album was soon flying off the shelves as rapidly as its predecessor, and the champagne corks were popping over at Geffen Records when the Gunners became the first band since the Beatles some fifteen years earlier to have two albums sitting pretty in the Top 5 of the Billboard 100.

# GOLDSTEIN, DOUG

Doug Goldstein replaced Alan Niven as Guns N' Roses manager in 1991 and remained in charge of the band until 2003.

Goldstein, who started out as a humble security guard, was brought in to assist Alan Niven in managing the Gunners with duties no more taxing than wet-nursing the individual band members, and overseeing the occasional trip to rehab. But his being more personable, and even-tempered than the brusque Niven, paved the way to his being elevated to the managerial hot seat, following Niven's dismissal in May, 1991. He then,

at the behest of Axl and on behalf of Guns N' Roses, set up his own management company, BFD (Big Fuckin' Deal).

Suddenly finding himself the man with his hand at the G N' R tiller must have been a dream come true for an ambitious ladder-climber such as Goldstein, but although Guns N' Roses currently had two double-albums being mixed ready for release, and about to undertake the largest tour in rock 'n' roll history, the crux of the matter was that Guns N' Roses had already reached their peak. And with the megalomaniacal Axl now able to hold the rest of the band to ransom – as he had shown by instigating Alan Niven's dismissal – Goldstein was manager in name only. And little could the puppet gen-

eral have imagined as the G N' R bandwagon rolled into East Troy, Wisconsin, for the opening shows of the *Use Your Illusion* tour, that he would be nothing more than a helpless bystander watching on from the wings, as the Gunners' incumbent line-up would be whittled down one by one, until only Axl remained.

Loyalty, however, was obviously Goldstein's watchword. And instead of taking flight as many other managers would surely have done, he stoically remained at Axl's side, permanently on hand to clean up after – or carry the can for – his master, as he was called upon to do in November 2001, following the cancellation of an already rearranged European tour. In a press release, which bordered on the ridiculous, Goldstein firstly apologised to the fans for yet another delay to the *Chinese Democracy* album, before going on to admit culpability for having – in his words –jumped the gun in arranging the European tour in order to promote said album, which Axl later admitted to only having found out about whilst perusing the internet.

By the summer of 2003, however, Goldstein had finally reached the end of his tormented tether, and instead of accepting the lofty position of Co-President of Sanctuary Music Management, which was offered to him when the British-based company took control of both Guns N' Roses, and the band's back-catalogue, he opted to sell Sanctuary his management contract for a rumoured $8 million and headed off to play golf under the Hawaiian sun.

# GREATEST HITS

*Greatest Hits* is the name of Guns N' Roses' compilation album, released in 2004.

The album's track-listing is as follows:

*Welcome To The Jungle; Sweet Child O' Mine; Patience; Paradise City; Knockin' On Heaven's Door; Civil War; You Could Be Mine; Don't Cry; November Rain; Live And Let Die; Yesterdays; Ain't It Fun; Since I Don't Have You; Sympathy For The Devil* – Geffen Records, 2004.

The *Greatest Hits* album was released with little or no fanfare on 15 March, 2004. Yet despite a total lack of promotion from either Axl, or any of the band's erstwhile members, within a month of going on sale it had sold over 3 million copies worldwide and claimed the number one spot in the UK as well as nine other European countries, while upon its release in the US one week later, it quickly shifted 1.8 million copies and soared to #3 on the Billboard Hot 100. *Greatest Hits* went on to sell a massive 3 million copies in the US, and remained on the Billboard 200 for 138 weeks, making it the band's second-longest charting album in the US, behind *Appetite For Destruction.*

Although Greatest Hits packages are usually seen as a band's final hurrah before the respective members embark on solo careers or more likely gracefully disappear off into the sunset, by 2004 Guns N' Roses was still a viable asset, with a new album supposedly on the cusp of release. The idea to release a Greatest Hits record was first mooted in August, 2003 by Axl's Interscope paymasters, who were anxious to recoup some of the eight-figure investment it had thus far poured into *Chinese Democracy.* Axl, however, was equally anxious that any new G N' R product shouldn't denigrate what he was doing with the band's new album and instructed Sanctuary to block the release. Sanctuary managed to persuade Interscope to hold back on the idea by dangling the *Chinese Democracy* carrot and insisting it would be in the shops in time for the Christmas market. When Christmas came and went with no sign of the finished record, however, Interscope finally lost patience and in February, 2004 wrote to inform Axl that the company was no longer prepared to continue funding *Chinese Democracy*, and that it was now his obligation to fund and complete the project.

# H'

## HAMILTON, VICKY

Vicky Hamilton was Guns N' Roses' unofficial manager from their early days through to their signing to Geffen records in March, 1986.

There are conflicting versions relating to the extent of Vicky Hamilton's involvement with Guns N' Roses. She, herself, claims to have first hooked up with Axl and Izzy whilst she was working as a booking agent with Silverlining Entertainment, and they were both involved with Hollywood Rose. Axl had approached Vicky – who was also a successful club promoter – in the hope that she could do for his band what she had already achieved with Mötley Crüe and Poison, in getting both bands much-needed publicity and exposure. This in turn had led to her becoming Guns N' Roses' unofficial manager/benefactor, which has a certain amount of credence, in that she moved the boys – and their equipment – into her modest apartment. She also fed them, washed their clothes, booked their shows, and touted the band to record companies. The latter claim is backed up by Slash, who stated in a subsequent interview that there was no record

label interest prior to Vicky's involvement. After the release of *Appetite For Destruction*, however, and with Vicky no longer around, Axl chose to paint a very different picture. "Vicky basically had a monopoly on booking bands at The Roxy and The Whisky," he told one reporter. "We needed those gigs, and we also needed a place to live. She offered us help and said she'd get us $25,000, money we desperately needed for the proper equipment so we could start getting close to the sound we

wanted. But she never managed the band, we – Slash, Izzy, Steven, Duff and me – *we* managed the band."

Although the expression 'Hell hath no fury like a woman scorned' is actually a misquote from William Congreve's 17th century tragedy *The Mourning Bride*, every man understands the malevolence contained within, and Vicky, upon discovering there was no financial proviso for her within the Geffen contract, invoked each and every

nuance of the age-old expression and sued the band for $1 million. Part of this, she claimed, was owed to her for "out-of-pocket expenses", while the rest was what she felt she was owed for her efforts. Needless to say, the band viewed things somewhat differently and initially refused to even acknowledge her existence – let alone her contribution. The sorry saga was eventually settled out of court with Vicky receiving $30,000, half of which was paid by the band, and the remainder by Geffen.

## HELL TOUR

The 'Hell Tour' is the name Guns N' Roses gave to their first tour excursion in June, 1985.

The so-called 'Hell Tour' may have proved to be a logistical and sanity-threatening nightmare, but it was also pivotal in scrving to bond the newly-constituted Guns N' Roses into a cohesive working unit. It was Duff, being the outsider, so to speak, and eager to make an impression, who was responsible for booking the mini tour, which consisted of several dates across three states: California, Oregon and his home state, Washington.

The idea was to get out of Los Angeles and temporarily leave behind the misery of their day-to-day penny-pinching existence, but disaster struck when the transportation – their buddy, Danny's dilapidated green Oldsmobile – broke down outside of Fresno, some 200 miles from Los Angeles. Most musicians might have cursed their luck – not to mention the vehicle's owner – before clambering aboard a Greyhound Bus to take them back into the city. But Axl, Izzy, Duff, Slash and Steven were made of sterner stuff, and, still dressed in their rock 'n' roll finery, handed over their meagre cash supply to Danny to purchase the necessary spare automobile parts, grabbed their guitars from the trunk, and set off along the baking asphalt with eyes peeled and thumbs extended. And those thumbs would remain extended for several hours, without so much as a state patrol car stopping by, before a speed freak – and we're not talking miles-an-hour here – pulled his truck over to the side of the road. Although the boys were happy to avail themselves of the miscreant's sulphate stash, they were less enamoured with the guy's body odour, and his seemingly endless supply of road stories were enough to put an insomniac to sleep. Having bailed out at the first available truck stop, they spent several hours kicking dust before being taken pity on by two hippie chicks, who kindly delivered them to the outskirts of Portland – feeding them hash brownies along the way – where Duff's friends were waiting to give them the bad news that Danny and his Oldsmobile were heading back to L.A.

Having already missed three of the proposed shows, the Gunners arrived in a windswept Seattle with but a few hours to spare before they were due on stage at the city's aptly-named Rock Theatre. The former cinema, located on an industrial wharf at the corner of 5th & Jackson, actually contained two separate venues, and the Gunners took to the stage in the Gorilla Gardens while local heroes, No Means No were playing in the adjoining room. Their tardy arrival meant they'd had no time to promote the show, and it was only thanks to Duff calling in a favour from Lulu Gargiulo, the singer/guitarist with Seattle's premier punk band The Fastbacks – with whom he'd once played – that they were able to borrow some amplifiers and a drum kit. The band's late arrival and the rounding up of borrowed equipment, resulted in their putting in a rushed and shoddy performance in front of an apathetic audience. And the venue's equally disinterested owner was only willing to hand over $100 of the pre-arranged $150. The Gunners, however, refused to be downhearted by their inauspicious start, and it is a measure of their new-found tenacity that they were able to slap the face of adversity and fulfil their outstanding commitments with subsequent shows in Portland, and Eugene, Oregon, for which they received payment in beer and burgers. And thanks to another of Duff's connections, they were able to make it back to Los Angeles.

## HOLLYWOOD ROSE

Hollywood Rose was the pre-Guns N' Roses band which featured Axl Rose and Izzy Stradlin in its line-up.

Although Guns N' Roses went on to become a musical institution, it is only thanks to the emergence of the 15-track album *The Roots of Guns N' Roses* in 2004, that we can finally pass judgement on the rough and ready delights of Hollywood Rose. The fact that the album contains three previously unreleased tracks meant that it would certainly appeal to G N' R fans, but, that said, it is something of a rip-off as it only contains five songs in total, which are then replicated twice over. The original five demos are 'Killing Time', 'Anything Goes', 'Rocker', 'Shadow Of Your Love', and 'Reckless Life' with the remaining ten tracks being Gilby Clarke and Fred Coury remixes.

'Anything Goes', and 'Reckless Life' would – albeit with alternative lyrics – subsequently appear on *Appetite For Destruction* and *GNR Lies* respectively. 'Rocker' and 'Killing Time' were, perhaps not surprisingly, consigned to the trash can, while 'Shadow Of Your Love' survived long enough to feature on early G N' R set lists as well as in the recording studio. Steven Adler has since gone on record to say the latter track was his particular favourite song during the recording of *Appetite* and was disappointed that it didn't make it to the final mix. In 1998, the band's original guitarist, Chris Weber, launched a second lawsuit against Axl (the first was back in 1991) for not receiving a writing credit for 'Shadow Of Your Love' and 'Back Off Bitch', which he claimed to have co-written before sloping off into obscurity. Doug Goldstein responded by informing the *L.A. Daily News* that Axl and Izzy both venomously denied Weber had any involvement in either song – one of which was apparently written before Axl and Weber had even met. Weber, however, was supposedly in possession of a video tape of Hollywood Rose performing the song, and had sent a copy to Axl. But Geffen's Bryn Bridenthal appeared on MTV News and openly dismissed the guitarist's claims as nothing more than a nuisance suit. "Whenever a band sells millions of records," he told the reporter, "you can count on frivolous pub-

lishing lawsuits following right behind."

For an interesting, and highly informative, history of Hollywood Rose, I recommend checking out the band's drummer, Johnny Kreis' website www.laserfire.com, where he reveals that he was playing in a Hollywood-based outfit called Shire when he was first approached by Izzy with a view to laying down the drum tracks for some demos he was working on with Axl (who just happened to be crashing in Shire's garage rehearsal space at the time). Although a quarter century has since passed, Kreis remembers his initial encounter with Izzy with total clarity. Not because of Axl's and Izzy's subsequent success in Guns N' Roses, but rather due to Izzy's proffered method of payment – a six-pack of Budweiser and a medium-sized pizza. Izzy and Axl had booked a day's recording at the Angry Samoans

Studio in West Hollywood, and Kreis was happy to oblige, as doing a spot of 'moonlighting' for other bands was a common occurrence amongst L.A.'s rock fraternity. And as this was light years away from Axl's fixation for perfection, there was no need for Kreis to learn the songs' arrangements as there were none. In fact Axl's sole pre-requisite of Kreis was that he "play really fast, and pound away with a blues feel."

This, of course, was what Kreis did best, and he obviously did it with aplomb, for his display prompted Axl and Izzy to prise him away from Shire to join Hollywood Rose. The accompanying photos on Kreis' website show a wild-haired Axl sporting the obligatory biker jacket with bare chest underneath, while Izzy adopts a sedate 'Ronnie Wood' look, of open-necked white shirt with the sleeves rolled up above the elbows. Indeed, the band's garish image – a hybrid of punk and glam metal – bewildered audiences at The Troubadour, Gazzarras, and Madame Wong's alike. Kreis is still in possession of the original demo tape – a sample of which can be heard on his site – but with 1985 fast approaching, it was a case of 'New Year, New Start' as far as Axl and Izzy were concerned and they called time on Hollywood Rose with one final performance in San Pedro, California, on 31 December, 1984.

# HOON, SHANNON

Richard Shannon Hoon, the late frontman with the band Blind Melon, provided backing vocals on several tracks that appear on the *Use Your Illusion* albums.

Shannon was a native of Lafayette, Indiana, who, like Axl and Izzy before him, relocated to Los Angeles in search of rock 'n' roll stardom. Despite having shown great promise at football, as well as being an excellent athlete, immediately after graduating from McCutcheon High School in 1985, Shannon turned his back on sports in favour of music, and joined a local band called Styff Kytten. But, also like Axl and Izzy, he soon realised his rock 'n' roll aspirations were never going to be fulfilled in Lafayette, and so, armed with an acoustic guitar and a few bucks in his pocket, he clambered aboard a Greyhound bus bound for L.A. He had only been in the

city but a short time when he was approached at a party by future Blind Melon bassist Brad Smith, and guitarist Rogers Stevens, who were both sufficiently impressed with his vocal talents to invite him to join their number. After recruiting guitarist Christopher Thorn and drummer Glen Graham, the five-piece outfit decided upon the name Blind Melon, and, in 1991 – on the back of their self-produced four-track demo – they signed a $500,000 contract with Capitol Records.

The band's eponymous debut album, which was produced by Pearl Jam's Rick Parashar, was released the following year. But, despite garnering favourable reviews, the record initially failed to make much of an impact, and it wasn't until they began touring, supporting the likes of Ozzy Osbourne, Soundgarden, and Guns N' Roses, that their stone finally began to roll. Their 1993 album, *No Rain*, which features the hit single of the same name, achieved multi-platinum status. As the band's success increased, however, so did the five musicians' drug intake, with Shannon being the main offender. The world appeared to be their proverbial oyster, but the band was making headlines for all the wrong reasons. In 1993, whilst on tour to promote the new record, Shannon's behaviour became more and more erratic. In Vancouver he was arrested and charged with indecent exposure after strip-

ping naked onstage and urinating on fans, and at Woodstock '94 the following year – where he took to the stage wearing his girlfriend's dress – he ended the band's set by hurling a set of conga drums into the crowd. That same year he went on a drug-crazed rampage at the *Billboard Music Awards* and attacked a security guard.

In 1995, Shannon became a father, but time which should have been spent with his new-born daughter, was instead spent in rehab. Thanks to considerable pressure from the powers-that-be at Capitol Records, who were anxious for the band to get out on the road to promote their new album *Soup*, Shannon was able to negotiate an early release from his detoxification programme; but only on the stipulation that his counsellor accompany the band on the tour. Temptation soon reared its ugly head, however, and the counsellor was dismissed less than a month into the tour. And once free from restraint, Shannon's drug intake escalated beyond all control.

Following a particularly shambolic show in Houston on 20 October, 1995, Blind Melon headed for New Orleans, Louisiana, where they were scheduled to appear that evening. Shannon had spent the night berating his fellow band members and binging on cocaine before passing out on the tour bus. When one of the roadies – sent to summon him for the pre-requisite soundcheck – failed to rouse the singer, an ambulance was duly summoned, but the 28-year-old Shannon had breathed his last and was pronounced dead at the scene. The coroner's report cited the cause of death as 'accidental cocaine overdose'.

# IRON MAIDEN

Iron Maiden, whose career has spanned over three decades to date, are arguably the most successful exponents of the NWOBHM (New Wave of British Heavy Metal).

On 13 May, 1988, at the Moncton Coliseum in Moncton, Canada, Guns N' Roses opened for Iron Maiden on the North American leg of the British rockers' tour to promote their latest album, *Seventh Son of a Seventh Son*. At the time, Maiden, who had enjoyed worldwide success with albums such as *Killers* (1981), *The Number of The Beast* (1982), and *Powerslave* (1984), had been together in one form or another for thirteen years, having been formed on Christmas Day, 1975 by the band's incumbent bassist, Steve Harris. Indeed, Harris is the sole survivor from the band's festive founding line-up, although long-standing rhythm guitarist Dave Murray was recruited early on, in 1976. According to the band's *Early Days* DVD, their original vocalist Paul Day was sacked due to a lack

of stage charisma, but his replacement, Dennis Wilcock – who took to the stage daubed in face paint similar to that worn by his heroes KISS – also failed to bring about a reversal of the band's fortunes, and this led to Harris temporarily calling time on the project. A chance meeting in the bassist's Leytonstone local, however, led to Paul Di'Anno being invited to take the microphone.

Despite having a full compliment and a loyal – if somewhat local – fanbase, the future did not bode well for Iron Maiden. The band didn't actually record any material until New Year's Eve 1978. But, when three songs from this session were subsequently released as the 'Soundhouse Tapes' EP the following November, all 5,000 copies of the initial pressing – which were only available via mail order – sold out in less than a week. This brought them to the attention of the majors, and before the year was out Iron Maiden had signed to EMI.

Maiden's debut single, 'Running Free', which was culled from their eponymous debut album, reached a respectable #34 on the UK singles chart, while the album itself – which was released on 14 April, 1980, and featured their 'monster from the grave' mascot, Eddie, on the cover – reached #4 on the UK album chart. The follow-up record, *Killers*, brought them serious attention from across the Atlantic, but by this time Di'Anno's propensity for cocaine was affecting his performances and so he was replaced by ex-Samson vocalist

Bruce Dickinson. The decision proved an astute one when the band's third album, *The Number Of The Beast,* went to #1 on the UK chart, and also achieved Top 10 status in several other countries around the world.

By 1988, however, and despite still enjoying god-like status in Europe – particularly the UK where *Seventh Son Of A Seventh Son* had gone to #1 on the album chart – the British rockers' American appeal appeared to be on the wane as the album stalled at #12. Their slip in the rock ratings was due to the emergence of Mötley Crüe and Guns N' Roses, so rather than risk losing face – not to mention thousands of dollars in revenue – Maiden's manager Rod Smallwood swallowed his pride and called his G N' R counterpart, Alan Niven.

Although inviting rock's hottest property onto the tour proved a shrewd move on Smallwood's part, as it guaranteed an immediate return to playing sell-out shows, it has been suggested in some quarters that there were those within the G N' R camp who viewed the move as something of a backward step. The indignation was supposedly due to the cocksure Gunners believing that the renewed interest in the Maiden tour was solely down to their coming on board. It has also been suggested that Duff was so disillusioned at playing second fiddle to the supposedly 'second rate' British band that he absconded midway through the tour to marry long-term girlfriend Mandy Brixx, leaving his Cult buddy, Haggis, to stand in for him. Yet, while such tales undoubtedly gave Guns N' Roses muchos kudos amongst their West Hollywood peers – and elevated them higher up rock's dog-eat-dog food chain – neither one quite rings true.

My two best mates, renowned punk rock writer and fledgling director, Alan Parker, and Paul Young have both suffered with

callused knees through their having worshipped at Eddie's altar, whereas my flag has always been firmly planted in the Gunners' corner, which is why I readily accepted such nepotistic tales to be fact. Paul's fixation with all things Maiden came back in the late-80s, and early-90s, which, owing to us living in the same house at the time – as well as playing in a band together – gave us ample opportunity to disagree. And boy, did we disagree. He even spurned the chance to see the Gunners play Wembley Stadium in August '91 in favour of a new tattoo. But I persevered with my crusade until he finally saw the light. Alan, however, remains impervious to my reasoning. And I can't really blame him, given that, at the time of writing, he is living out his fantasies by interviewing Bruce, Steve, Nicko, et al, for Mick Wall's forthcoming official Iron Maiden biography, *No Holds Barred* (Mainstream).

Although it's true that shortly after the Gunners joined Maiden on tour *Appetite For Destruction* achieved platinum status, the British rockers' latest offering had also accrued – or was well on its way to accruing – the necessary one million sales to merit a platinum disc. And while *Seventh Son Of A Seventh Son* only reached #12 on the Billboard chart, there were several other gold and platinum discs mounted on Rod Smallwood's office wall, which at that point in time, served as pointed reminders as to which band held the greater standing within America's mainstream rock fraternity. And it is also highly unlikely that Duff chose to bail out before the show at Calgary's Olympic Saddledome on 27 May on a drunken, spur-of-the-moment whim to get hitched. According to Danny Sugarman, in his excellent book *The Days Of Guns N' Roses: Appetite For Destruction*, Duff was well aware of the impending wedding date as Mandy had been planning the ceremony for several weeks, and that Duff, upon realising that the tour wasn't going to be rescheduled on his behalf, called on Haggis to serve as a one-off gig stand-in.

Further rumours of unrest began to circulate when L.A. Guns were called in as a last-minute replacement for Guns N' Roses for the first of two consecutive shows at Irvine Meadows, California, on 8 June, due to problems with Axl's voice. And the rumour mill went into overdrive the following night when it was announced the Gunners would be leaving the tour owing to their singer's inability to perform. There were those, however, who refused to accept the official explanation and insisted that the real reason was the singer's resentment at having to open for a band he now perceived to be of a lesser standing than his own. Their argument fell flat, however, when subsequent G N' R shows in Japan and Australia were also cancelled.

## IT'S ALRIGHT

'It's Alright' is a Black Sabbath song that Guns N' Roses performed live on occasion during the *Use Your Illusion* tour, and features on *Live Era '87 – '93*.

'It's Alright' appears on Black Sabbath's 1976 album *Technical Ecstasy,* which, unlike the Brummie rockers' previous doom and darkness records, contains songs about drug dealing, prostitution

**BLACK SABBATH**

**TECHNICAL ECSTASY**

and transvestites. And, as these true-to-life subjects were in keeping with the everyday lives of Axl, Slash and co., it was therefore a perfect choice of cover song for the Gunners. Sabbath's attempt to break away from their trademark sinister sound by experimenting with keyboards, synthesisers and orchestration, however, was not appreciated by their fickle fans, and the album was something of a commercial failure.

Black Sabbath's version was actually sung by the band's drummer, Bill Ward, owing to singer Ozzy Osbourne having temporarily gone A.W.O.L. during the recording sessions. Indeed, the absence of Ozzy's vocals on the track meant that many people initially failed to recognise it as a Black Sabbath song. By the following year, Ozzy's spiralling drug problems saw him stop turning up for rehearsals altogether, and, although he returned to the fold in time for the recording of the band's follow-up album, *Never say Die*, he was eventually asked to leave in 1979.

# J'

## JAMES, DEL

Del James, who was born Adelberto V Mirando on 5 February, 1964 (sharing his birthday with Duff) is a respected musician, writer and journalist, whose fictional short story, *Without You* was the inspiration behind Guns N' Roses' 'unofficial power-ballad trilogy'.

James, a long-time friend of Axl Rose, and one-time resident of North Gardner Street, was born in Rochelle, in upstate New York, but relocated to Los Angeles in 1985. Within days of his arrival in Hollywood, he was befriended by West Arkeen, as well as Axl and the other members of the, then, unsigned Guns N' Roses. His friendship with the band led to his directing several of their videos, and it was a short story of his entitled *Without You*, (one of a collection of horror stories that appeared in his book *The Language Of Fear*), that proved the inspiration behind G N' R's so-called 'unofficial power-ballad trilogy' of 'Don't Cry', 'November Rain' and 'Estranged'. He also co-wrote 'The Garden', and 'Yesterdays' with Arkeen, which feature on *Use Your Illusion I & II* respectively. His songwriting talents have also been utilized by Testament, TNT, and The Almighty, and aside from penning songs and ghost stories, James is a respected journalist, and even served as senior editor at the now defunct RIP Magazine, which, at the time, was dedicated to championing L.A.'s metal scene.

James still lives in southern California and, unlike many of those that have entered Axl's circle, his friendship with the G N' R frontman has survived to the present day and he is actively involved with the band's current line-up.

# JOHN, ELTON

Elton John, or Sir Elton 'Hercules' John CBE, to give him his proper title, whose five-time Grammy Award-winning career to date has spanned four decades, was born Reginald Kenneth Dwight in Pinner, Middlesex on 24 March, 1947. In April, 1992 he and Axl Rose performed a duet of the Queen classic 'Bohemian Rhapsody' at the Freddie Mercury Tribute Concert.

According to Mick Wall's unauthorised *W. Axl Rose* biography, not only had the young and highly-impressionable Bill Bailey held Elton John in the highest esteem, the future G N' R frontman has also cited the bespectacled pianist as having been a major influence on his own songwriting style. Indeed, during an interview recorded back when the journalist was on speaking terms with Axl, the singer had chosen 'Benny And The Jets', from Elton's 1973 double album, *Goodbye Yellow Brick Road*, as one of the songs which helped form his musical taste; so to appear on the Wembley stage with his idol must have been a dream come true.

It appeared the appreciation was mutual, for when Guns N' Roses – and particularly Axl – came under fire over the lyrical content of 'One In A Million', Elton sent flowers along with a message of defiance urging Axl not to let 'the bastards grind him down' to the band's dressing room on the first night of their four-date stint opening for the Rolling Stones at the Los Angeles Coliseum in October, 1989. And the friendship was still going strong in 1994 when Axl put in an appearance – his last one in public for six years as it turned out – at the Rock 'N' Roll Hall of Fame induction ceremony, where Elton was one of that year's inductees.

In April, 2005, Elton and Axl became label mates when the Sanctuary Group acquired 100% of the share capital in Elton's management company, Twenty First Artists, for a reported $16 million, which also resulted in Elton acquiring Merck Mercuriadis as his manager. Although Elton was keen to work with Merck, owing to his having learnt his craft at the feet of Sanctuary's founders, Rod Smallwood and Andy Taylor, his fiscal antennae told him all was not well at Sanctuary and he therefore insisted on having the

label audited before putting pen to paper. Despite thinking nothing of spending £293,000 over an 18 month period on flowers, Elton was not one to see money – especially his own – being wasted. So when it came to light that Sanctuary were footing the bill while his old buddy Axl Rose was living the Manhattan high life instead of putting the finishing touches to *Chinese Democracy*, he was none too impressed. It is said that Axl – along with his sizable entourage – had taken over an entire floor at the mega-bucks-per-night Trump Tower Hotel, where the singer spent the long balmy summer evenings quaffing champagne with his celebrity friends.

Word has it – said word being supplied by an ex-Sanctuary employee, who naturally wishes to remain anonymous – that even Sanctuary's management team were stunned at the number of digits listed beside the $ sign on Axl's hotel bill; and with precious little product to show for their investment. Rather than risk upsetting Elton, Axl and his free-loading entourage were summarily dispatched back to Los Angeles on the first available flight.

## JOHN, ROBERT

Robert John is a Los Angeles-based photographer who was Guns N' Roses' official lensman from 1985 – 1993.

Robert John was born in Birmingham, Alabama on 10 November, 1961, but moved out to California with his parents when he was just three-years-old. His formative years were spent behind the wheel of his souped-up car, but his dreams of a racing career were cruelly cut short following an injury to his back.

Having opted for a much safer career in photography, John began trawling the clubs along Sunset Strip snapping away at up-and-

coming unsigned bands, including L.A. Guns, London and Hollywood Rose. And his having kept a finger firmly affixed to West Hollywood's rhythmic pulse, as well as a friendship with Izzy Stradlin, meant he was in the perfect position to capture the emergence of Guns N' Roses. After shooting one of the band's earliest Troubadour shows on 20 September, 1985, he accompanied the Gunners to Reseda the following month for a gig at Chuck Landis' Country Club on 18 October. The band were obviously keen to see the results of John's labours, and, having been warned by Izzy that Axl was a hard taskmaster, he elected to show the photographs on his slide projector. His work received Axl's seal of approval and he was then invited to do a group photo session that, in turn, led to his becoming the band's exclusive lensman when they later signed to Geffen in 1986. A book of his photographs: *Guns N' Roses:* *The Photographic History*, which includes a foreword by Axl Rose, and chronicles the band's rags-to-riches career, from their humble beginnings in West Hollywood through to world domination on the *Use Your Illusion* tour and everything else in-between, was published in 1993, and was subsequently used as the title for a BBC documentary. His close association with Guns N' Roses also led to his making cameo appearances in several of the band's videos.

A decade on from his publication, however, John was forced to take legal action against his old buddy, Axl, over the singer's refusal to honour an earlier contract in which he had agreed to pay the photographer $80,000 for photos – of which there were hundreds – he'd taken of the band over an eight year period since 1985. Axl had apparently been in possession of said photos for several months by the time of the legal wrangling in May, 2003, and had shown no inclination whatsoever of either stumping up the cash, or returning the photos.

Today Robert John is a highly sought-after photographer whose twenty-five-year-to-date portfolio reads like a 'Who's Who' of rock, and, as well as Guns N' Roses, has seen him capture Alice Cooper, Ozzy Osbourne, Elton John, Rolling Stones, Aerosmith, Faith No More, Marilyn Manson, Motorhead, Sepultura and Jane's Addiction in his lens. His photography and artwork has also graced numerous album covers and liner sleeves, not to mention the front pages of every self-respecting music magazine, including *Rolling Stone*, *Kerrang!*, *Metal Hammer* and *RIP*.

## JONES, STEVE

Steve Jones was – and still is on occasion – the guitarist with the Sex Pistols, and was a one-time member of the now defunct supergroup Neurotic Outsiders alongside Duff McKagan and Matt Sorum.

Stephen Phillip Jones was born in Shepherd's Bush, London on 3 September, 1955, but relocated to nearby Hammersmith when his father – an amateur boxer named Don Jarvis – fled the family home. His mother remarried and the family returned to Shepherd's Bush, but young Steve didn't get on with his stepfather, who looked upon him as little more

than excess baggage. Like the teenage Axl in Lafayette, Steve was always knee-deep in trouble with the local authorities. He even spent three months incarcerated in Ashford Remand Centre, which, although robbing him of his freedom, did at least provide him with three square meals a day – a luxury seldom seen at home. Today, Steve will happily admit that the Sex Pistols saved him from a life of crime and the consequences that would surely have followed.

It was whilst he was at the Christopher Wren School on Shepherd's Bush's run-down Wormholt Estate that he met his future partner-in-crime, Paul Cook, and another wayward youth called Warwick "Wally" Nightingale who owned a guitar and encouraged his fellow truants to form a band. With this aim in mind, Steve began channelling his thieving into acquiring musical equipment, including an entire backline – complete with top-of-the-range microphones – from the Hammersmith Odeon where David Bowie was engaged on the final night of his Ziggy Stardust farewell tour.

Having procured the services of a manager, the svengali-like Malcolm McLaren, who gave the band its name, as well as a charismatic singer in the form of Johnny Rotten, the Sex Pistols began playing low-key dates at colleges, strip clubs, prisons and anywhere else that might have them. Although the band was showing promise and had attracted a small nucleus of disenfranchised kids – who would subsequently go off and form their own bands, which, in effect, kick-started the UK punk movement – it is fair to say that the Sex Pistols might never have expanded their horizons beyond London had it not been for Steve's four-letter verbal spat with Today host Bill Grundy on 1 December, 1976.

When the Sex Pistols imploded in San Francisco in January, 1978, Steve, although barely able to read and write, possessed enough 'street smarts' to know Malcolm was still holding the Pistols purse-strings. And with this in mind, he and Cook agreed to continue working with McLaren on his cinematic opus, *The Great Rock 'N' Roll Swindle*, which, although by and large a complete fabrication of the Sex Pistols story, did at least provide Steve with a regular stipend and a Top 10 single in 1979 with 'Silly Thing'. A one-off collaboration with Thin Lizzy front-man Phil Lynott, under the guise of the Greedy Bastards, resulted in a surprise Christmas hit which saw Steve clowning around on *Top Of The Pops*. By this time, Steve and Paul had put together The Professionals, but as with most bands, the sum of the individual parts was never going to be greater than the whole. Although the singles 'Just Another Dream' and '1-2-3' sold reasonably well, the parent album, *I Didn't See It Coming* was shelved indefinitely by Virgin, and when Cook was involved in a serious car crash midway through the band's US tour, they decided to call it a day. In 1981, following on from his cinematic debut in the *Swindle*, Steve, along with Paul Cook, the Clash's Paul Simonon and *Scum* star Ray Winston, appeared in the Lou Adler directed movie *Ladies And Gentlemen The Fabulous Stains*, in which they played a fictional band called The Looters. The movie more or less disap-

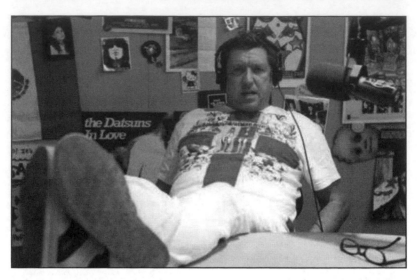

peared without trace, but bootleg copies can be found if you know where to look, and it's well worth a watch, if only to behold Ray Winston's 'Johnny Strummer' performance.

In 1982, by which time Steve was residing in Los Angeles, sporting a shaggy mane, and nurturing a heroin habit, he formed Chequered Past with Michael Des Barres (the British-born singer and actor best known for having once been married to uber groupie, Pamela Des Barres), but the band only released one self-titled album before breaking up in 1985. In 1986, John Lydon (he had long-since reverted to using his original name) successfully sued his erstwhile manager, and Steve – along with Cook – was savvy enough to know which way the wind was blowing and readily sided with Lydon. The result was that all monies that had been frozen seven years earlier, at the time of the original lawsuit,

returned to the surviving members, with Sid's mother, Anne Beverley, being made executor for her late son's estate.

In 1987, Steve released his first solo album, *Mercy,* on the MCA label, but it consisted entirely of dreary, ballad-esque love songs, and quickly sank without trace. His second solo offering, however, the hard-rocking *Fire And Gasoline*, saw a return to form and Steve became something of a celebrity amongst the wannabe rockers plying their trade in West Hollywood. A mutual admiration society between Steve and Guns N' Roses led to numerous on-stage get-togethers, as well as a collaboration with Duff and Matt (along with Duran Duran's bassist, John Taylor) with the Neurotic Outsiders. The project was never intended as a lasting venture, but things took a serious turn when Madonna's Maverick label offered the band an album deal. Although the ensuing record, released in

1995, garnered mainly positive reviews, Duff and Matt were still contracted to G N' R, and Steve would also find himself fully occupied elsewhere.

In 1996, the reconstituted Sex Pistols – including original bassist, Glen Matlock – announced a world tour, for which Steve reportedly pocketed an estimated £1 million, and meant he would no longer have to suffer the humiliation of opening for acts the Sex Pistols had helped inspire.

Today, although happy to strap on his trusty Les Paul to play the odd Sex Pistols show, including five November, 2007 sell-out shows at London's Brixton Academy, Steve has found fame as the host of *Jonesy's Jukebox:* a two-hour daily show between 12-2pm on L.A.'s Indie 103.1 FM, which sees him play an eclectic range of songs from his personal CD collection. Steve can also be found showing off his not-so-silky soccer skills for Hollywood United, a team of ex-pats which, on occasion, includes former Wales international, and Leeds United midfielder turned actor Vinnie Jones, and his one-time *Fabulous Stains* co-star, Ray Winston.

# JU-JU HOUNDS, THE

The Ju-Ju Hounds was the name of Izzy Stradlin's short-lived project following his departure from Guns N' Roses in 1991.

Although Izzy had long since lost interest in G N' R's musical direction, and had also tired of Axl's histrionics, he still wanted to make music – and much to Axl's consternation, he even hired ex-G N' R manager, Alan Niven to oversee his business affairs. Armed with a clutch of basic eight-track demos, Izzy recruited long-time friend and ex-Broken Dreams bassist, Jimmy Ashhurst to help knock the songs into shape. Jimmy, in turn, invited drummer Charlie "Chalo" Quintana onto the project, and ex-Georgia Satellites lead guitarist, Rick Richards completed the line-up of what became the Ju-Ju Hounds.

The resultant album, *Izzy Stradlin and the Ju-Ju Hounds* – which one critic cynically cited as being the best Rolling Stones album since *Tattoo You* – was recorded at New York's Sterling Sound studios between February and July, 1992, and was released on the Geffen label on 12 October that same year. And such was Izzy's high profile that MTV paid a visit to the band's Chicago studio and filmed the guys putting the finishing touches to the album; the crew was also treated to a new song entitled 'Got Away', which subsequently appeared as the 'b-side' on their debut single, 'Shuffle It All'. As was to be expected, given Izzy's passion for stripped down, gutsy, punk-edged honky-tonk blues, the album's 10 tracks comprises of catchy, mid-tempo rockers such as 'Somebody Knockin', and 'Train Tracks', as well as bluesy ballads like the excellent 'How Will It Go' and 'Come On Now Inside' which were far removed from Guns N' Roses' post-*Appetite* multi-layered epics. The record also features a souped-up cover of Frederick "Toots" Hibbert and the Maytals' 1969 reggae hit, 'Pressure Drop' as a subliminal nod to The Clash, who had also covered the track in 1979. Incidentally, reggae toaster Mikey Dread, who worked and recorded with the Clash, most

the loneliness of constantly being out on the road, received moderate airplay, it failed to trouble the Billboard 100. By and large, the majority of the critics were enthusiastic about the album, but certain scribes couldn't help having a dig at Izzy's supposedly never-ending genuflection at the Stones shrine. Such comparisons were perhaps inevitable, especially as Ronnie Wood makes a guest appearance on his own song, 'Take A Look At The Guy', and one-time Stones session man, Nicky Hop-

notably on 'Rockers Galore... UK Tour' which appeared as the b-side on the Clash's 1980 hit, 'Bankrobber', provided backing vocals on the Ju-Ju Hounds version of 'Pressure Drop'. Unfortunately for Izzy, however, the media machine was far more interested in the on-going tour shenanigans of his former bandmates than what he was doing. And, although the single 'Shuffle It All', Izzy's melancholic take on

kins laid down the piano track on 'Come On Now Inside', but Izzy remained unfazed. Indeed, he not only admitted his musical debt to the Rolling Stones, but also paid homage to the blues legends that had influenced the Stones' early sound such as Muddy Waters, Willie Dixon and Howlin' Wolf.

Somewhat surprisingly, given his supposed aversion to touring, Izzy chose to take the Ju-Ju Hounds out on the road. What was even more surprising was his decision to do so before the album was released, which meant that many of those gathered inside Chicago's Avalon theatre to witness the band's stage debut on 22 September, 1991 were unfamiliar with most of the original material, with the possible exception of the three tracks on the recently-released 'Pressure Drop' EP. By way of compensation, the band supplemented their 17-song set with several covers, including The Surfaris' 'Wipe Out', Howlin' Wolf's 'Highway 49' and Bo Diddley's 'Pills', as well as a ripping version of 'Goodnight Tonight' which had featured in Guns N' Roses' early live repertoire.

The Ju-Ju Hounds then embarked on a promotional tour taking in the US, Europe and Japan, where, on 19 September, 1992 – almost one year to the day from their Chicago debut – the band played its last ever show, at Tokyo's Shibuya Koukaido arena. Immediately following the tour, they returned to the US and headed back into the studio to supposedly begin work on songs for the follow-up album. Although several tracks were indeed recorded, they would never see the light of day, for, according to Chalo Quintana, Izzy called a time out during the recording to go out for cigarettes, and never returned. Quintana, Ashhurst and Richards, realising there was little future for the Ju-Ju Hounds without Izzy Stradlin, slapped the padlock on the studio door and went their separate ways.

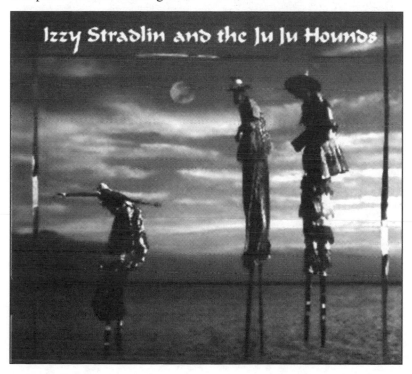

Izzy Stradlin and the Ju Ju Hounds

# K'

## KNOCKIN' ON HEAVEN'S DOOR

'Knockin' On Heaven's Door' is the classic Bob Dylan song which has been covered and recorded by a plethora of artists, including Guns N' Roses, who released it as a single in 1992.

Guns N' Roses' first-known performance of 'Knockin' On Heaven's Door' came at the soundcheck to their first-ever UK show, at the Marquee in London on 19 June, 1987. The band also performed the song during the show, and what better way to introduce themselves as the 'new gunslingers in town' than with a rockin' cover of Dylan's haunting classic, which first appeared on the soundtrack to Sam Peckinpah's 1973 homage to the Wild West outlaw William Bonney, *Pat Garrett & Billy the Kid,* starring James Coburn and Kris Kristofferson (Dylan also appears in the movie, playing the

role of 'Alias', a minor member of Billy's gang).

Despite the movie's failure at the box office, which was probably due to the American public's disenchantment with the stalemate over in Vietnam rather than the movie itself, 'Knockin On Heaven's Door' has stood the test of time, and to date has been covered by over 150 bands and solo artists, including The Grateful Dead, Aerosmith, Bon Jovi, Eric Clapton, Television and U2. Perhaps the most bizarre interpretation of Dylan's masterpiece came on 20 September, 1976 on the first night of the now legendary 100 Club Punk Festival, where the fledgling line-up of Siouxsie and the Banshees (which included future Sex Pistol, Sid Vicious on drums) proceeded to eviscerate the song during their 20 minute stage debut. Without doubt, the most harrowing and heartfelt recording of 'Knockin' On Heaven's Door' came in December, 1996 when a revised version of the song was released in memory of the seventeen victims of the Dunblane Massacre. Nine months earlier, on 13 March, the world had been stunned to learn that an unemployed local resident called Thomas Hamilton had casually strolled into Dunblane Primary School's small gymnasium armed with two 9mm Browning HP pistols, two Smith and Wesson .357 revolvers and over 700 cartridges, and callously gunned down 16 schoolchildren aged between five and six years-old, and their teacher Gwen Mayor who had grown up but a few short miles from my home town of Accrington. Local musician, Ted Christopher – with Dylan's consent – wrote an additional verse for the recording, which included the brothers and sisters of the victims singing on the chorus, and featured Dire Straits frontman, Marc Knopfler, on guitar. The single went to #1 in the UK with all proceeds going to various children's charities.

The Marquee crowd's enthused response to the Gunners' souped-up version of Dylan's acoustic, four-chord classic – which can be heard on the 12" version of 'Welcome To The Jungle' – led to the band adopting the song into their set, where it quickly became something of a mainstay and still features in G N' R's 2007 live shows. The band originally recorded the song for the 1991 movie, *Days Of Thunder,* starring Tom Cruise and Nicole Kidman, and subsequently released it as a single the following year.

## KOSTABI, MARK

Mark Kostabi is the American artist and composer who designed the sleeve cover for the *Use Your Illusion* albums.

Kostabi, who is of Estonian descent, was born in Los Angeles in 1962, and raised in Whittier, California. After graduating from the Californian State University in 1982, he moved to New York City, where he soon became a prominent and respected figure amongst the city's East Village art community. Within five years his work was being exhibited in art galleries throughout America, as well as Japan, West Germany, Holland and Australia. In 1988, in a move which garnered extensive press coverage both at home and abroad, he founded 'Kostabi World', which serves as a platform for up-and-coming artists as well as ideas people.

In 1991, Kostabi's adaptation of Renaissance artist Raphael's (Raphael Sanzio: 1483 – 1520) fresco,

*The School of Athens* (which can be found in the Vatican City's Apostolic Palace) was chosen by Axl as the artwork for the cover of the *Use Your Illusion* albums. Kostabi had edited the original fresco by focusing on just two of the ancient Greek philosophers. And, although the philosophers in question – a young boyish-looking individual (whom Kostabi has made the more prominent of the two) is sat cross-legged putting his thoughts to paper, while the other (a much older man) leans over the boy, seemingly lost in thought – are unnamed, in the original they are close in proximity to Plotinus (205 – 270 ad), who is widely regarded as the father of Neo-Platonism, a philosophical system dominant in European thinking until the 13th century.

By the late-90s, Kostabi had stretched his wings and was dividing his time between New York and Rome, where his talents were also greatly appreciated. In 2005, he began producing a weekly cable TV show called *Name That Painting,* which invites art critics and celebrities such as John Lennon's one-time lover, Mai Pang and author Victor Bockris, to compete against each other to complete the titles to his paintings for cash prizes. In 1995, Kostabi was called upon by the Ramones to design the cover for their final studio album, *Adios Amigos*.

# LAFAYETTE

Lafayette, which has the distinction of being the 215th largest metropolitan area within the United States, is a city in Tippecanoe County, Indiana, lying some 63 miles northwest of the state capital, Indianapolis.

Axl and Izzy's hometown of Lafayette was named after Marie-Joseph-Paul-Yves-Roch-Gilbert du Motier, Marquis de Lafayette, 1757 – 1834, the famous French general and statesman, who fought alongside the American colonists during the War of Independence. The site upon which Lafayette stands was originally inhabited by a tribe of Miami Indians known as the Quiatenon, and the name 'Tippecanoe' is derived from the Indian word, Kethtippecanoogi – their name for the 'Succor Fish People'. In 1811 Tippecanoe lent its name to the battle fought on 6 November of that year, between the then Governor – and future US President – William Henry Harrison, and the legendary Indian chief, Tecumseh.

Today, as with most of Indiana, Lafayette's economy is dependant on the agricultural, manufacturing and transportation industries, but when the town was first platted in 1825 by river trader William Rigby, it was a vital shipping centre on the Wabash River, which, within six months, had become the local seat for the newly-formed Tippecanoe County. Its regional prominence was further cemented

with the opening of the Wabash and Eerie Canal in the 1840s, and further still with the expansion of the railroads a decade later. In 1717, the French established Fort Quiatenon on the Wabash River, some three miles south of present day Lafayette. The fort quickly became a trading centre for fur trappers, merchants and the Quiatenon Indians, and today the locals celebrate their heritage with an annual re-enactment and festival known as The Feast of the Hunter's Moon.

Lafayette can also lay claim to being the site of the first official US air-mail delivery service. On 17 August, 1859, local business-man John Wise set off from the city's courthouse grounds in a hot-air balloon, with a cargo of mail destined for New York. Although adverse weather conditions forced Wise to abandon his flight before he'd even cleared the state line, resulting in the mail making the rest of the inaugural journey by train, in 1959 the US Postal Service celebrated the centennial of Wise's flight by issuing a 7¢ air-mail commemorative stamp.

## L.A. GUNS

L.A. Guns is a Los Angeles-based rock band which once featured Axl Rose and Izzy Stradlin in its line-up.

L.A. Guns was formed in the early '80's and in its original incarnation the line-up consisted of guitarist Tracii Guns (born Tracy Ulrich on 20 January, 1966), singer Michael Jagosz, Danish-born bassist Ole Beich (who died in mysterious circumstances in 1991, supposedly drowning in Copenhagen's St. Jorgen's Lake), and drummer Rob Gardner. In 1984, whilst Jagosz was in jail ruminating over the foolishness of sending cocaine through the US Mail, Axl took temporary charge of vocal duties in L.A Guns before handing the microphone back to Jagosz to concentrate on Hollywood Rose, once the latter was again breathing free air. Although Hollywood Rose would be in direct competition with L.A. Guns, Axl and Tracii remained friends, and it was this friendship which eventually led to their joining forces to form Guns N' Roses in 1985 (other names considered at the time of the collaboration were AIDS and Heads of Amazon). One has to wonder how Izzy, Duff or Rob Gardner could have believed there was room in the band for two egocentric frontmen such as Axl and Guns. As we now know, this line-up only

lasted for one show – at L.A.'s Radio City on 11 April – before Guns and Gardner were replaced by Slash and Steven Adler.

Although his pride had taken a hit, Tracii was now doubly determined to succeed and quickly set about putting another band together. He would, however, have to do so without Rob Gardner, who rode off into the sunset seemingly content to become a footnote in the history of Guns N' Roses. For the new L.A. Guns line-up, Tracii recruited ex-Mau Maus drummer, Paul Mars Black on vocals, future Cramps drummer Nicky "Beat" Alexander, ex-Faster Pussycat guitarist Mick Cripps, who

subsequently switched to bass, and ex-Dogs D'Amour frontman, Rob Stoddard on rhythm guitar and backing vocals. But by the time of the release of the band's eponymous debut album in 1988, Black had departed, to be replaced by ex-Girl frontman, Phil Lewis, Cripps had reverted back to guitar following Stoddard's departure, and ex-Faster Pussycat bassist Kelly Nickels was brought in on bass. During the subsequent promotional tour Nicky Alexander left, to be replaced by ex-W.A.S.P. drummer Steve Riley.

The following year saw L.A. Guns reach the apex of their career with the release of their second album, *Cocked & Loaded*, containing the haunting radio and video hit single 'The Ballad Of Jayne', which helped the parent album accrue sales in excess of 500,000 as well as earning the band their first gold record. And although their third album, *Hollywood Vampires*, released in 1991, failed to live up to the success of its predecessor, it did, however, spawn the moderate hit singles 'Kiss My Love Goodbye', and 'It's Over Now'. But any despondency the band might have been feeling was dispelled with the news that their debut album had eventually achieved gold status. 1994 promised to be another good year for L.A. Guns, but the on-going friction between Steve Riley and Phil Lewis led to the drummer's dismissal shortly after the release of their fourth album, *Vicious*

*Circle*. Although Riley subsequently returned to the fold for the album's promotional tour, *Vicious Circle* failed to shift the prerequisite number of units and Polydor pulled the plug and dropped L.A Guns from their roster, which resulted in both Lewis and Cripps announcing their departures.

In July, 1995, with new recruits, vocalist Chris Van Dahl and guitarist Johnny Crypt, L.A Guns headed into the recording studio to begin work on their fifth album, *American Hardcore*. But less than six months into the sessions, Kelly Nickels announced his departure, and rather than risk interminable delays searching for a replacement, Crypt simply stepped in to fulfil both bass and guitaring duties. Yet, despite heavy touring in support of the new record, *American Hardcore* failed to trouble the Billboard 100. Van Dahl paid the ultimate price for the calamity, and Tracii approached Phil Lewis in the hope that returning their former frontman would bring about a reversal in the band's fortunes. Lewis, however, refused, and so Tracii brought in singer Ralph Saenz, who appeared on the six-track *Wasted* EP, released in September, 1998. By the time of their sixth album *Shrinking Violet*, released in June, 1999 and produced by Gilby Clarke (who also appears on the track 'Dreamtime'), Saenz had been replaced by ex-Love/Hate frontman Jizzy Pearl. Cypt also jumped ship upon learning Tracii had again been in negotiations with Lewis to mull over a 'greatest hits' album and promotional tour.

This time Lewis had proved receptive, and following the release of the greatest hits album: *Greatest Hits and Black Beauties,* L.A. Guns' classic line-up of Tracii Guns, Steve Riley, Phil Lewis, Kelly Nickels and Mick Cripps embarked on a full-blown tour of the US, and their triumphant homecoming show at the Key Club on Sunset Strip on 7 October, 1999, was recorded for the ensuing live album, *Live: A Night On The Strip*. Any hopes the band's fans may have had about the reconstituted line-up becoming permanent were dashed when Cripps and Nickels proved reluctant to commit to further tours. In August, 2000, with new guitarist Brett Muscat and a bassist going by the name of Muddy, L.A. Guns went into the studio to re-record their second album, suitably re-titled: *Cocked & Re-Loaded.* Their seventh studio record, *Waking The Dead* (2000), however, would prove to be Tracii's

final hurrah with the band which bore his name, as he'd accepted Nikki Sixx's invitation to join the Crüe bassist's side project, Brides of Destruction.

L.A. Guns decided to carry on, and with replacement guitarist, Canadian-born Stacey Blades, went into the studio to record the album *Rip the Covers,* which – like Guns N' Roses' *The Spaghetti Incident?* – consisted entirely of cover-versions. Unlike G N' R, however, L.A. Guns' offering was warmly received, and their follow-up album, *Tales From The Strip*, was hailed a critical success on both sides of the Atlantic. By this time, the Brides of Destruction had self-destructed, following a less-than-enthusiastic response to the band's second album that saw Tracii slip away to concentrate on his own solo project: the Tracii Guns Band. As the line-up included ex-L.A. Gunners Paul Black and Nicky Alexander, as well as Tracii's son Jeremy – and with Tracii still owning a 50% stake in the name – it was decided the band would go out as L.A. Guns – despite the fact that the original L.A Guns was still active.

## LIVE AND LET DIE

'Live And Let Die', written by Paul and Linda McCartney as the theme tune to the 1973 James Bond movie of the same name, was recorded by Guns N' Roses and appeared on *Use Your Illusion I*. It was also released as a single in 1991.

Although 'Live And Let Die' earned Paul McCartney a second Academy Award nomination for Best Original Song (the ex-Beatle unfortunately lost out to Barbara Streisand's 'The Way We Were'), it seemed a strange choice of cover song for a rock band at the time enjoying its status as 'the most dangerous band in the world'. Axl told Headbanger's Ball presenter, Vanessa Warwick that the idea to cover the song came about whilst watching a video rental of the movie late one night, shortly before the Gunners were due to go into the studio to begin work on the new album(s). He also told Vanessa that he'd grabbed up the phone and – as this was before keyboardist Dizzy joined the band – beseeched Slash to get out his guitar and find the requisite notes to match Linda McCartney's discordant piano at the song's bridge. The top-hatted one duly obliged, and having added the song to the set-list for their forthcoming world tour, the band gave its first performance of 'Live And Let Die' at San Francisco's Warfield Theatre on 9 May, 1991.

The promo video accompanying the single upon its release – other than opening with home-movie footage of a behatted Axl, aged three or four years old, poised at the doorway of the Bailey homestead in downtown Lafayette, clutching a toy gun – was otherwise pretty

standard fare, showing snippets of the band on stage at various live shows from the *Use Your Illusion* tour to date, interspersed with floating photos of each band member taken when they were kids. In 1997 the Gunners version of the song featured in the John Cusack and Minnie Driver movie *Grosse Point Blank.*

## LIVE ERA '87 – '93

Live Era '87 – '93 is the sole official live album to be released by Guns N' Roses.

The track-listing for the 2xLP, 2xCD disc set is as follows: Disc 1: *Nightrain; Mr. Brownstone; It's So Easy; Welcome To The Jungle; Dust 'N' Bones; My Michelle; You're Crazy; Used To Love Her; Patience; It's Alright; November Rain.* Disc 2: *Out Ta Get Me; Pretty Tied Up; Yesterdays; Move To The City; You Could Be Mine; Rocket Queen; Sweet Child O' Mine; Knockin' On Heaven's*

*Door; Don't Cry; Paradise City* – Geffen Records, 1999.

By the time *Live Era '87 – '93* was released on 23 November, 1999, Axl Rose was the sole surviving member of Guns N' Roses, and the band had ceased to exist in anything but name. Somewhat surprisingly, given that the liner fuse matters, the album's artwork comprises entirely of posters and flyers advertising shows – some of which date back to Hollywood Rose – for the mid-to-late '80s at the Troubadour, Whisky A Go-Go, Radio City and the Roxy; even the dates and locations of the individual tracks are missing. The track

notes boast the 22 songs contained on the double-CD were 'recorded across the universe between 1987 and 1993', are widely accepted as only coming from mixing desk recordings taken during the band's *Use Your Illusion* world tour of 1991 – '93. And to further confuse selection is equally puzzling as 'Civil War' and 'Live And Let Die', which were not only both released as singles, but were also tour perennials, are omitted in favour of 'Pretty Tied Up' and 'Move To The City'. And another conundrum is why 'Coma' only appears as a 'bonus track' on the vinyl edition and the Japanese CD.

Despite being a testament to the Gunners in their heyday, the majority of the band's fans had long-since become disillusioned with the prolonged inactivity – as well as Axl's 'hirings and firings', and the album limped into the US Billboard at a lowly #45. It didn't make much further headway in the coming months and, despite all but one of the tracks – the cover of Black Sabbath's 'It's Alright' – having appeared on albums which had gone multi-platinum, the live offering failed even to accrue the requisite 500,000 sales to achieve gold status – a humiliation which would have been unthinkable five years earlier.

The majority of the production duties fell to Slash, who recruited one-time Faith No More producer, Andy Wallace to help him remix the individual tracks. Duff also popped into the studio to lend a hand, whereas Axl – other than publicly humiliating Matt Sorum by having the drummer who featured on all the tracks listed as an 'additional musician' – had little to do with the project and only communicated with Slash through their respective managers. There was one last sting in the tail regarding the *Live Era* album when G N' R's management launched a $400,000 lawsuit against Slash and Duff for representation the company supposedly carried out on the duo's behalf.

# LIVE?!*@ LIKE A SUICIDE

The 4-track 'Live?!*@ Like A Suicide' EP was Guns N' Roses debut vinyl offering when it was released on 24 December, 1986.

The tracks featured are: *Reckless Life* (3:20); *Nice Boys (Don't Play Rock 'N' Roll)* (3:02); *Move To The City* (3:42); *Mama Kin* (3:57) – Uzi Suicide 1986.

The idea to release the 10,000 limited edition EP came from Geffen, who saw it not only as a stop-gap offering to satisfy Guns N' Roses' burgeoning L.A. fanbase, but also as a means of capitalising on the rapidly-increasing momentum surrounding the band. The Gunners' self-produced EP features four songs – two original compositions, as well as two cover-versions – from the Gunners' set list at the time, which hadn't been selected for inclusion on the forthcoming debut album. The original compositions were 'Reckless Life', written by Izzy, Duff and Slash, and 'Move To The City', penned by Izzy, Del James and Chris Weber, while the covers were Aerosmith's 'Mama Kin', which features on the Boston rockers' 1973 self-titled debut album, and Rose Tattoo's 'Nice Boys (Don't Play Rock 'N' Roll)', which appears on the Australian band's 1978 eponymously-titled debut long-player.

Following a roadie's bellowed introduction of "hey fuckers, suck on Guns N' Fuckin' Roses!", Steven Adler opens the Gunners' four-song sonic salvo with the machine gun drum intro to 'Reckless Life', and within a heartbeat Slash's raging power chords have grabbed the listener by the balls. It is perhaps fitting that 'Reckless Life' was chosen as the opening track as it also opened the proceedings at many of the band's early shows, while the other original song, 'Move To the City' – Izzy, Weber and James' tri-angular verdict on making the transition from their respective hometowns to the sprawling metropolis of Los Angeles – survived through to the *Use Your Illusion* world tour and also appeared on *Live Era '87 – '93'*. Although the inclusion of the lesser-known 'Nice Boys' largely went unnoticed, the rock cognoscenti quickly seized on 'Mama Kin' and openly compared Guns N' Roses to a 1970s-era Aerosmith. If the critics were hoping to somehow diminish the Gunners' flame with such comparisons then they were in for a surprise. For the band readily took any mention of themselves and Aerosmith within the same sentence as a huge compliment.

Crediting Axl and co. with having self-produced the record is something of a misnomer as all they actually did was cull the four selected songs from the mixing desk tape of their appearance at The Roxy back in January, and then re-record them with the added audience backing. Given that the EP was released on the band's own Uzi Suicide label with no advertising and very little in the way of promotion – and therefore relied heavily on word of mouth – it was a testament to the band's popularity that all 10,000 copies sold within four weeks of the release date. The EP's glossy sleeve features a close-up stage shot of Axl and Duff accompanied by the title and an early band logo designed by Slash.

Geffen, as a means of combating the EP's spiralling price on the black market, later included all four tracks on G N' R's second album *GNR Lies*.

# LOADED

Loaded was Duff's first post G N' R band and featured ex-Plexi guitarist Michael Barragan, ex-Black Flag rhythm guitarist Dez Cadena and ex-Reverend Horton Heat drummer Patrick "Taz" Bentley.

The idea to get out on the road again with a full band rather than take the solo option and trade on his name, came about due to Geffen's announcement that his second solo album, *Beautiful Diseas*, was to be shelved indefinitely, following its merger with Universal. Having spent the previous eighteen months working solidly, six days a week, at his home studio in L.A. on the album, only to one day receive a telephone call telling him that his efforts had been wasted, would have broken many a musician's willpower to carry on. But Duff was made of sterner stuff, and having regrouped

and recharged his energies, he put Loaded together and the band hit the road in May, 1999 for a one-month West Coast tour. In keeping with Duff's musical roots, Loaded played at a fast and furious pace with a punk edge, which certainly went down well with their audiences. In fact, the reaction was so overwhelming that immediately after the tour the band headed back into the studio to work on songs for their debut album *Dark Days*, which was released later that year. The group also recorded a live album, *Episode 1999: Live*, which was only available through their website.

# LONDON

London was a Los Angeles-based glam rock band which featured a pre-Guns N' Roses Slash (albeit briefly), and Izzy Stradlin in its line-up.

Although bearing the same name as the short-lived British punk band featuring future Culture Club drummer Jon Moss, London was an American glam-metal group which, in 1985, included both Izzy Stradlin and Slash in its line-up. Indeed, the 'feeder' band also boasted future Mötley Crüe bassist Nikki Sixx, and soon-to-be W.A.S.P. frontman Blackie Lawless in its original line-up. A song co-written by Sixx and Lawless called 'Public Enemy No. 1', whilst still with London, would subsequently appear on Mötley Crüe's debut album, *Too Fast for Love*.

London was formed in 1978 by Blackie Lawless (born Steven Edward Duren on 4 September, 1956 in New York), and ex-Tear Garden guitarist Lizzy Grey, with Nikki Sixx and drummer Dane

Rage joining shortly thereafter. By the following year, however, Lawless had departed to form W.A.S.P, but London regrouped and aside from bringing in vocalist Henry Valentine, the band looked to bolster its sound with the addition of keyboardist John St. John. Valentine's tenure with the band proved short-lived, and he was replaced by ex-Mott frontman, Nigel Benjamin. The band plodded on aimlessly without making any significant headway, which resulted in Sixx and Benjamin calling time. And although Lawless briefly returned to the fold replacing Sixx on bass, the momentum had been lost and the band disintegrated.

This, however, was not the last the world would hear of London, for in 1984, Lizzie Grey – hoping to cash in on the resurgence of

glam metal in West Hollywood – put together a new band consisting of ex-Ruby Slippers drummer, Michael Itson, English-born vocalist John Ward, and Donny Cameron on bass. And having decided to recruit a second guitarist, the band placed an ad in *Music Connection*. The successful candidate was one Saul Hudson – more commonly known as Slash. Slash's residency proved extremely brief and the guitarist left London within a few weeks of his joining to form Road Crew with his buddy Steven Adler. Slash's replacement – although neither guitarist was aware of each other at the time – was none other than Izzy Stradlin.

By the following year, however, Itson, Ward and Cameron had all departed for pastures new to be replaced by the exotic-sounding vocalist Nadir D'Priest (Antonio Nadir), drummer Bobby Marks and bassist Brian West. Grey was in the process of booking the band some shows when the newly installed rhythm section of West and Marks quit to form their own band. And although Grey brought in future Cinderella sticksman, Fred Coury, Izzy announced his own departure, to team up with his old Lafayette buddy, Axl, in Hollywood Rose.

Despite London's line-up seemingly in a never-ending state of flux, the band did at least manage to record their debut album, *Non Stop Rock* for Shrapnel Records. Izzy's replacement was Frankie Jones, but the rehearsal room's revolving door was set in motion again when Coury quit shortly after the album's release. His temporary replacement, Wailin' Jennings Morgan, was in turn replaced by Derek Shea, who stuck around long enough to provide the chops for the band's second album, *Don't Cry Wolf*, produced by legendary American producer Kim Fowley. By 1988, however, after ten years, two albums, a surfeit of ex-members, and very little to show for a decade of constant upheaval, the last of London's founding fathers, Lizzy Grey, finally called it a day.

Despite Grey's departure, London struggled on for another two years, and even released a third album, *Playa Del Rock* in 1990, by which time the band had been re-branded D'Priest. The change in name did, briefly, bring about a reversal in fortune when the accompanying video for the salaciously-titled single 'Ride You Through The Night' was flavour of the month at MTV. Any hopes that this would act as a springboard to kick-start their career sadly proved short-lived, and the band called it a day in 1991.

This, however, was not the end of London's story, for in the summer of 2006 reports began circulating on the Hollywood grapevine that D'Priest had put a new band together, trading under the name 'D'Priest's New London' and had gone into the studio to record demos intended for a new album.

## McKAGAN, DUFF

Duff McKagan was Guns N' Roses' bassist for twelve years before leaving the band in 1997. He is currently a member of Velvet Revolver.

Michael "Duff" 'Rose' McKagan was born on 5 February, 1965 in Seattle, Washington. The McKagan household was constantly filled with music of one description or another and he and his seven siblings were encouraged by their father, Elmer – who had once sung in a barbershop quartet – to take up an instrument. Duff chose the guitar, and also taught himself drums. But by the time he was 19-years-old, and having tired of aimlessly drifting from one forgettable local band to another, he packed his belongings into the trunk of his battered cherry-red Chevy Nova and – with buddy Greg Gilmour for company – headed down the coast to Los Angeles. As with Steven Adler, Duff quickly realised guitarists were as common as palm trees in L.A.'s sprawling metropolis. But, rather than devoting all his energies to the drums, the savvy blond, realising bassists were in short supply, opted for that instrument instead.

The fact that he was both tall and lean – like his punk heroes Sid Vicious and Paul Simonon – meant he already had certain, key characteristics required of any budding bassist, and having adopted Vicious' swagger – not to mention his trademark padlock and chain – he set out in search of some action. He didn't have to wait long. Having responded to a 'bassist wanted' ad in *Music Connection*, later that same day he headed along to Cantor's Deli to meet up with potential band mates, and future G N' R buddies, Slash and Steven Adler. The meeting didn't exactly go as planned though, since Slash and Steven were both slightly inebriated, and Duff's choice of attire, which included combat boots and a full-length, red and black leather trench coat – despite the eighty-

degree heat outside – caused Slash's current squeeze, Yvonne, to enquire if he was gay.

Having established his sexual orientation, and his bass-playing credentials, Duff teamed up with Slash and Steven in the latter two's band, Road Crew. It was during their brief time together that the trio wrote several tunes, one of which would later resurface as 'Rocket Queen'. Although Slash and Duff were totally committed to the cause, Steven's work ethic apparently left a lot to be desired. And so when Slash announced he was breaking up the band to try his luck elsewhere, Duff fell in with Izzy Stradlin – who happened to be living across the street from him – and became the bassist in Hollywood Rose, which in turn led to his becoming involved with Guns N' Roses – a commitment which would last for thirteen years.

His commitment to long-time girlfriend Mandy Brixx, whom he married on 28 May, 1988, however, wasn't quite as long-lived and the couple divorced in 1990. His second attempt at matrimonial bliss, this time to Playboy 'Playmate', Linda Johnson, came in September, 1992, but the marriage lasted just three years and they divorced in September, 1995. When it came to tying the knot, it was definitely a case of third time lucky for Duff as he is still very much attached to his third wife, Susan, the model and swimwear designer whom he married on 28 August, 1999. The couple have two daughters: ten-year-old Grace, and seven-year-old Mai Marie, named after his mother Alice Marie, who succumbed to Parkinson's disease in April, 1999. Duff's father, Elmer "Mac" McKagan sadly passed away on 18 July, 2007.

Duff's adventures during his tenure with Guns N' Roses are documented elsewhere in this book, but the years of fast-living and hard-drinking inevitably took their toll. In early 1994, just a few weeks shy of his 30th birthday, Duff's pancreas actually burst. His agony was such that it rendered him unable to even reach the telephone, despite it being on the night table next to his bed. The bassist might well have died had it not been for the timely interven-tion of a visiting friend who duly drove Duff to the nearest hospital, where he was pumped full of morphine to counter the pain, given a dose of Librium to help with his chronic DTs, and rushed into theatre for emergency surgery. The surgery was successful, but the medical team warned him that if he didn't quit drinking he'd be dead before he reached 30. Needless to say, Duff hasn't touched a drop of alcohol since.

It is a measure of Duff's loyalty that he stood by Axl as the original G N' R line-up disintegrated all around him, but he finally called it a day upon realising the band had become a dictatorship and no longer had anything to do with what he, Slash, Izzy and Steven had helped create. Having collaborated with Slash on the guitarist's side project, Snakepit, as well as teaming up with ex-Sex Pistol, Steve Jones and Duran Duran's John Taylor in the Neurotic Outsiders, Duff began work on his second solo record, *Beautiful Disease*. His debut solo album, the punk-edged *Believe In Me*, which was released 1993, had received favourable reviews, but owing to the on-going merger between Geffen and Interscope, the second was destined never to see the light of day; to add insult to injury, Duff was also dropped from the label.

Although financially secure, Duff was still itching to make music and went out on the road with his band Loaded, which resulted in the live album, *Episode 1999: Live*. He would subsequently put together another version of the band in 2001 and recorded the studio album, *Dark Days*. In between these junctures, he teamed up with Izzy to help out on the guitarist's third solo album, *Ride On*. And in 2000, Duff formed Mad For Racket – also known as The Racketeers – with ex-MC5 guitarist, Wayne Kramer and one-time Damned guitarist, Brian James. In 2002, he got together with Slash and Matt Sorum to form Velvet Revolver. To date, the band has released two studio albums.

# MANTIA, BRYAN

Bryan 'Brain' Mantia is a contemporary rock drummer who joined Guns N' Roses in 2000 and played every live show with the band until taking a temporary leave of absence in June, 2006 to spend time with his wife and baby daughter.

Mantia, who was born in the South Bay city of Cupertino, California, in 1964, didn't actually start playing drums until the age of 16. And it was whilst he was studiously applying himself to his new vocation in the high school band that he received the nickname 'Brain' due to his supposed obsession with the complex Anthony Cirone book, *Portraits in Rhythm*. Following on from high school, Mantia continued to

perfect his technique at the Percussion Institute of Technology in Los Angeles. In the mid-80s he joined his first band, a San Francisco Bay Area funk-rock outfit called Limbomaniacs, who came and went before the decade was out without causing much of a ripple. The outfit reformed in 1990 and released the album *Stinky Grooves* before sliding into insignificance.

Following on from that particular venture, Mantia honed his skills further by playing with a variety of bands before then co-forming funk-experimental outfit, Praxis with Parliament Funkadelic stalwarts Bootsy Collins and Bernie Worrell. Also included in the Praxis line-up were record producer Bill Laswell and a pre-Guns N' Roses Buckethead, upon whose insistence Mantia would subsequently be invited to join G N' R. Indeed, Mantia worked with Buckethead both in and outside of Praxis – including two of the masked guitarist's solo albums, *Colma, Giant Robot* and *Monsters*

*and Robots.* Praxis' most notable releases during their time together were *Transmutation (Mutatis Mutandis)* (1992), *Metatron* (1996), and *Warszawa* (1999).

The late '90s also saw Mantia reunited with funk-metal act, Primus, having briefly been a member of the band in 1989, before being forced to vacate the drum stool owing to a broken foot. His second outing proved infinitely more satisfying than first time around, and not only did he tour extensively with the trio, he also recorded three albums in successive years: the *Brown Album* in 1997, *Rhinoplasty* in 1998 and *Antipop* in 1999. During that same period he also recorded *Songs of Love and Hate* with the band Godflesh, and the new millennium saw him collaborate in a side-project called No Forcefield with Primus guitarist Larry LaLonde, which resulted in two more long-players: *Lee's Oriental Massage* in 2000, and *God Is*

*An Excuse* released the following year.

Although he had already established himself as a major player, Mantia's 'big break' came in 2000 when he was invited – largely at the behest of Buckethead – to replace Josh Freese in Guns N' Roses. He was a member of the line-up for the band's sporadic outings throughout 2001 and 2002, and also laid down drum tracks for *Chinese Democracy*. When Guns N' Roses re-emerged from enforced hibernation in June, 2006, it was Mantia who provided the beat at four warm-up shows in New York City before then accompanying the band on a summer tour of Europe. On 21 June of that year, however, Mantia announced he would be taking an official temporary leave of absence from the band to spend time with his wife in expectation of the arrival of their baby daughter, who was born a fortnight later on 4 July. And although his stand-in, Frank

Ferrer was subsequently promoted to full time member of Guns N' Roses – which fuelled speculation that Mantia's paternity leave had been extended indefinitely – G N' R's management has stated that both drummers are official band members.

# MARTIN, STROTHER

An American actor whose tagline "What we got here is failure to communicate…" lifted from the 1967 movie, 'Cool Hand Luke', appears at the beginning of 'Civil War'.

Strother Martin Jr. was born on 26 March, 1919, in Kokomo, Indiana, the youngest of three children to Strother Douglas and Ethel Dunlap Martin. Shortly after Strother's birth, the Martin family relocated to San Antonio, Texas, but their tenure in the Lone Star State proved short-lived and they returned to their native Indiana, setting up home in Indianapolis before moving to Cloverdale when Strother was in his teens. Having proved his prowess as a swimmer by winning the National Junior Springboard Diving Championship aged 17, which earned him the nickname "T-Bone" because of his diving style, and a scholarship on the diving team at the University of Michigan, Strother went on to serve as a swimming instructor in the US Navy during WWII and it was only his failure to secure a higher placing than

'3rd' in the adult diving championships which denied him a place in America's 1948 Olympic team.

Having decided to try his hand at acting, Strother headed out to California where his swimming proficiency earned him several bit parts in movies such as *The Damned Don't Cry*, and *The Asphalt Jungle*, and led to his becoming swimming coach to Charlie Chaplin's children and Marion Davies, a leading Hollywood actress and long-time lover of newspaper magnate William Randolph Hearst. It was through his television work for Sam Peckinpah – a relationship which developed into a lifelong friendship – that Strother landed significant roles in the John Wayne classics, *The Sons Of Katie Elder* in 1965 and *True Grit* in 1969, as well as Peckinpah's own 1969 classic western, *The Wild Bunch,* which made him one of the best known faces in Hollywood. In 1967 he appeared alongside Paul Newman for the first time as 'Captain' in Stuart Rosenberg's *Cool Hand Luke*. His association with Newman led to roles in *Butch*

*Cassidy and the Sundance Kid* in 1969, and *Slapshot* in 1977.

Strother appeared to be at the height of his career when, on 1 August, 1980, he died as the result of a sudden heart attack whilst at his home in Thousand Oaks, California.

## MARQUEE CLUB

The Marquee Club, which was located at 165 Oxford Street when it first opened its doors in 1958, is one of London's most famous music venues. In June, 1987, by which time the club had long-since relocated to its best-known site, 90 Wardour Street, Guns N' Roses made their UK live debut.

The Gunners were booked to play three shows, the first being Friday 19 June, and although *Appetite For Destruction* was still a month or so away from release, word-of-mouth amongst London's rock cognoscenti ensured that a queue was forming along Wardour Street by noon. The album may not have been available but Geffen hedged their bets by releasing 'It's So Easy'/'Mr. Brownstone' as a double A-sided single the previous Monday.

The Marquee shows also happened to be the band's first live appearances outside of America – and their burgeoning hedonistic reputation had well and truly preceded them. Britain's tabloids, never ones to miss out on an opportunity to jump on the character assassination bandwagon, went out of their way to exacerbate the situation by declaring the Gunners, prior to their arrival in the English capital, to be "even nastier than the Beastie Boys". The *Daily Star*, although happy to assure the UK's Volkswagen owners that singer, Axl Rose, had no interest in stealing car logos, he did have an "endearing

habit of butchering small dogs – particularly poodles". This was clearly nothing more than an editor's whimsical attempt to generate distrust and loathing amongst the adult population of a country which is, at heart, a nation of dog lovers, and, of course, it counted for nought amongst the teenagers and twenty-somethings which made up the Gunners' rapidly increasing UK fanbase.

Needless to say, the band's two-week stay in London was not without incident. Slash, thrilled to be following in the footsteps of many of his musical heroes by playing the Marquee, got rat-arsed in the pubs of Soho, and also made a nuisance of himself at the launch party to celebrate the release of *Hearts of Fire*; a new movie starring Bob Dylan, Rupert Everett and Ian Dury. And Axl almost got himself arrested the night before the opening date following a fracas with the security staff at Tower Records in Piccadilly.

The capacity Friday-night Marquee crowd, although not expecting to see a wild-cyed Axl hunched in front of the drum riser chowing down on a poodle, were perhaps expecting something larger than life. And when Guns N' Roses were revealed to be mere mortals – albeit extremely talented mortals – they unleashed a hail of gob and plastic beer glasses towards the stage. When the barrage showed little sign of abating, Axl was forced to call a halt to the proceedings and challenge

the hecklers directly. Although this – along with a threat to leave the stage – did persuade many of those present to desist their puerile antics, there were still a certain number who were intent on spoiling the night for all concerned, in turn leading to the band receiving lukewarm reviews in the music press. The second show came the following Monday ($22^{nd}$), and being a Monday meant the venue was relatively free of show-off power-drinkers, and was therefore of a much higher calibre. It was the third and final gig on Sunday 28 June, however, that would prove to be the high point of their visit to London. Axl, sporting a 'Fuck Dancing, Let's Fuck' T-shirt, got the proceedings underway by dedicating the opening song, 'Out Ta Get Me' to the critics languishing in the shadows at the back. Relaxed and finally able to get down to what they did best, the band treated the Marquee crowd to a blistering set and finished off the show with white-hot, finger-searing versions of AC/DC's 'Whole Lotta Rosie' and 'Knockin' On Heaven's Door', which received its first public airing that night and subsequently appeared as a bonus track on the 12" version of the Gunners' second single, 'Welcome To The Jungle'.

## MAYNARD, SHARON

Sharon Tanemura Maynard is a professional psychic who first entered Axl's world in 1992 during Guns N' Roses' *Use Your Illusion* world tour and has remained in close contact with the singer ever since.

Canadian-born Maynard, along with husband Elliott (who also received a thank you credit on the *Use Your Illusion* liner notes), is also the head of a non-profit organisation called the Arcos Cielos Corp (which translates from Spanish as 'Sky Arcs') which continues to operate out of Sedona, Arizona, an area noted for its 'unique combination of spectacular natural beauty, sunny climate, and peaceful solitude.' Today the corporation's website states that it was created for the development of New Paradigms in Science, Education, Fine Arts, Global Ecology, Human Potential Development, and Future-Science Technology.

Maynard, through her Japanese cultural background, claimed to be skilled at bridging Eastern and Western viewpoints and integrating them into programmes for new ways of thinking and effective action. She also held an ARCT Degree from the Toronto Royal Conservatory of Music, but Axl was more interested in her special aptitude for channelling past lives, and her knowledge on the power of crystals, than her ability to recognise a catchy riff, fill or hook line. The singer even went so far as to arrange a private backstage area for Maynard and her entourage of assistants, and before one of the Tokyo Dome shows, the good doctor insisted on collating information about magnetic and atomic power sources that would be in existence whilst the band was on stage. The rest of the group and crew were somewhat less enthralled by the diminutive, middle-aged woman in their midst and quickly dubbed her 'Yoda', after the aged, green goblin-esque mystic from the *Star Wars* movies. They could poke fun all they wanted behind Axl's back, but everybody – no matter where they stood in the G N' R food chain – was forced to sign confidentiality agreements forbidding them from commenting publicly on any aspect of the tour without Axl's permission.

Axl's trust in Maynard is all encompassing, and the psychic continues to be a major presence in his life, and it is customary procedure for her to vet all potential G N' R employees by examining photographs of each respective candidate, as well as their spouse and offspring (if applicable), to weed out those with bad auras which might taint the singer's life.

# MERCURIADIS, MERCK

Merck Mercuriadis was the Sanctuary Group's North American CEO (Chief Executive Officer) when he took over from Doug Goldstein as Guns N' Roses manager in 2003.

As with the latter stages of his predecessor, Goldstein's reign, Merck's managerial duties largely dealt with pandering to Axl's whims rather than overseeing Guns N' Roses per se. And as there wasn't much going on in terms of either touring or recording, he remained in the shadows, and only came out onto the parapet to defend his client. As he did in March, 2005 when he sent an 'all guns blazing' open letter to the New York Times over the paper's

article in which it dubbed *Chinese Democracy* "probably the most expensive recording never released". Merck was aware of the article, having been contacted several days earlier by *Times* staffer Jeff Leeds, and had told the reporter in no uncertain terms that he couldn't go ahead with his so-called 'investigative story', as he hadn't spoken with either himself, Axl, or anyone else connected with Guns N' Roses. After lambasting both the *New York Times* and Leeds for their spurious invective, he finished off the letter by informing the paper's readers that Axl wasn't interested in fame, money, popularity or what the *New York Times* – or indeed any other newspaper – thought of him, and that the singer's sole interest was in making *Chinese Democracy* the best album possible.

So it is ironic that Merck's fall from grace in December, 2006 should come following what he later insisted was nothing more

than a 'tongue-in-cheek' comment made back in October about the possibility that *Chinese Democracy* "just might appear on one of the [then] thirteen remaining Tuesdays" (Tuesday being the official album release day in the US). On 15 December, in response to Axl's open letter posted on the G N' R website the previous day, in which the singer lambasted his erstwhile manager for making such flippant remarks, Merck posted his own letter to give his side of the story. He defended his "thirteen Tuesdays" comment, but, while he declared Axl to be a "true artist", and "one of the greatest vocalists of all time", he laid the blame for the shambolic summer tour – and album's latest setback – squarely at the singer's door: 'The reality is that all of this year's touring was planned and agreed between Axl and myself, with a view to the album being in the stores before 31 December. We had planned the tour in February, just after Axl's [44th] birthday and we were supposed to finish the album in May, before it [the tour] started'.

Indeed, recording engineers were despatched to New York before the tour started, where, according to Mercuriadis, 'they waited for over a month for the muse [Axl] to come but she never arrived.' Sessions were then set up in London for August, following the G N' R shows at Wembley Arena, but again, Axl failed to show, at which point it was decided to postpone the proposed Labour Day dates so that the band could return to Los Angeles to work on the final two or three days of recording that needed to be completed. Once again, however, Axl failed to put in an appearance. Mercuriadis concluded his missive by expressing his disappointment at Axl's own letter, before then declaring that, not only did the new Guns N' Roses line-up "kick shit out of the old", but that when *Chinese Democracy* did finally hit the streets, it would be "one of the best albums ever made".

## METALLICA

In 1992, thrash metal pioneers Metallica, who have gone on to sell over 90 million albums worldwide, famously took time out from their own *Wherever We May Roam* tour to co-headline the 26-date third leg of Guns N' Roses' *Use Your Illusion* world tour.

When plans for a Guns N' Roses/ Metallica duel headline US tour were first unveiled by Slash and Metallica's Danish-born drummer, Lars Ulrich at a press conference in May, 1992, their respective bands had recently shared the same stage at the Freddie Mercury Tribute Concert. Like Guns N' Roses, Metallica hailed from Los Angeles, where they formed in 1981, and boasted a line-up forged courtesy of the 'musicians wanted' section in the local classifieds. The band's debut album *Kill 'Em All*, released in 1983 on

the Megaforce label, sold three million copies, yet failed to trouble the charts, stalling at #120 on the Billboard 200. By the time of their follow-up, *Ride The Lightning* in 1984, they had signed to Elektra Records. Although the album sold in excess of five million copies, it too failed to crack the US Top 100. As with so many bands, it was the third record that was to prove pivotal. Even though *Master Of Puppets*, released in 1986, only sold around one million copies more than its predecessor, it broke the Billboard Top 40 barrier, peaking at #29.

On 27 September, 1986, in the midst of the *Damage Inc* tour, tragedy struck when bassist Cliff Burton was killed when the band's tour bus skidded from the ice-covered road near the town of Ljungby, Sweden. The surviving members seriously considered calling it a day, but, having received the blessing of Burton's family, they decided to carry on and, as a means of testing out their newly-constructed studio – as well as the bass prowess of new recruit, Jason Newsted – recorded 'The $5.98 EP: Garage Days Re-Revisited', which consists entirely of covers. In August 1988, the same month *Appetite For Destruction* claimed the coveted #1 spot in the US, Metallica released their Grammy nominated album *...And Justice For All*, which slammed into the Billboard Top 10, selling eight million copies in the process. Despite narrowly missing out on the Grammy Award for the newly-created Best Hard Rock/ Metal Performance category, (having been pipped at the post by the decidedly non-Rock/Metal exponents, Jethro Tull), the band went away to lick their wounds and write new material for their 1991, eponymously-titled fifth album which they co-produced with Bob Rock. *Metallica* – or the *Black Album* as it's more commonly known – brought the band their first US #1, and sold a staggering 15 million copies worldwide. Their following three studio albums: *Load* (1996), *ReLoad* (1997), and *St. Anger* (2003) all followed suit by reaching #1 on the Billboard 100, selling five million, three million, and two million copies respectively.

The Guns N' Roses/Metallica co-headline, sell-out tour got underway at the RFK Stadium in Washington D.C on 7 June, 1992. And with both bands at the height of their fame – as well as at the top of their game – the tour promised to live up to the hype. The tickets for the shows could have been sold three times over, and although both promoters and fans were drooling at the prospect of future collaborations between the two biggest rock bands of their generation, the backslapping inter-band bonhomie, which had begun backstage at Donington four years earlier, soon began to deteriorate. One of the key factors leading to the breakdown was Axl's woeful timekeeping. Metallica were renowned throughout the industry for their strong work ethic and were concerned about Axl's shoddy timekeeping. Indeed Metallica's equally hard-working management team was so concerned over Axl's seemingly total disregard for time schedules, they summoned their G N' R counterparts to a meeting where it was decided their band would go on first. Slash and Duff were both painfully aware that Axl's petulance was poisoning the atmosphere backstage, but sought solace in vodka. Matters finally came to a head at Montreal's Olympic Stadium on 8 August, where an onstage pyrotechnical fault left Metallica's James Hetfield with third degree burns, forcing the band to abandon the stage midway through their set.

Upon hearing of the tragedy, Slash, Gilby, Duff and Matt called an impromptu meeting to work out how best to extend their own set so as to make up for Metallica having to curtail theirs. But Axl not only failed to appear at the meeting, he didn't even show up at the venue until some ninety minutes after Guns N' Roses were supposed to go on. Almost four hours had passed since Hetfield's injury before Guns N' Roses took to the stage, but ninety minutes into the set Axl stunned his fellow Gunners, and audience alike, by storming off because he wasn't happy with the monitors. While the Canadians could appreciate Metallica's reason for curtailing their set, certain sections of the crowd felt they'd been short-changed by W. Axl Rose, and vented their frustration by running amok in the surrounding streets. The rioters vandalised and set fire to cars, and looted nearby stores before the authorities finally brought the mob under control.

Although Guns N' Roses couldn't be held directly responsible for Hetfield's mishap in Montreal, the Metallica frontman obviously felt aggrieved, and let his feelings towards Axl be known in the band's documentary: *A year And A half In the Life Of Metallica Part 2,* which was released later that same year. Hetfield had somehow gotten hold of the Gunners' tour rider, which he proceeded to read out in a derisive tone: "Horrible truths," he sneered into the camera. "The piddly wants and needs of certain folks on the road. Axl 'Pose's' dressing room requirements – absolutely no substitutions. One cup of cubed ham, it's got to be cubed so it can get down his little neck!" he snarled, before further deriding Axl's demand for assorted Pringle chips, so he could "grease his hair back". But the culinary coup de grace came with the 'honey', which, Hetfield declared, adopting a mock falsetto to mimic Axl, "makes him SING LIKE THIS!" And after lambasting Axl one last time over his request for Dom Perignon champagne, he tossed the rider sheet into the air before stamping it into the ground.

## MOBY

Moby, who was born Richard Melville Hall, in Harlem, New York, and received his literary nickname in honour of his great-great-great-great uncle Herman Melville – the nineteenth century novelist best known for his 1851 seafaring fable, *Moby Dick* – was one of several renowned producers brought in to oversee production on *Chinese Democracy*.

Aside from producing, Moby is a successful singer/songwriter in his own right, and his groundbreaking 1999 album, *Play* sold over nine million copies worldwide (it was groundbreaking in the sense that it was the first album in history to have all the tracks commercially licensed). Although it was undoubtedly his avante garde approach to music that led to him being invited to oversee the production on *Chinese Democracy*, Moby's occupancy of the production chair proved both ineffective and transitory – largely due to his inability to fathom Axl's way of working. "I found it difficult to chart a linear development of the songs they were working on," he later recalled. "They would work on something; it would be a sketch for a while. And then they'd put it aside and go back to it later." Having his motives questioned – even by a producer of Moby's stature – was still dissention in the racks as far as the irascible Axl was concerned; and one more name was added to the project's already sizeable list of ex-producers.

## MONROE, MICHAEL

Michael Monroe, born Matti Fagerholm on 17 June, 1962 in Helsinki, Finland, is the former frontman for the L.A. rock band, Hanoi Rocks.

Following the demise of Hanoi Rocks in 1985, which was principally due to the untimely death of the band's drummer Razzle (born Nicholas Dingley), who was killed in a car crash the previous December (Mötley Crüe's Vince Neil was at the wheel at the time of the accident), Monroe opted for a solo career and went on to record eight albums. His 1989 offering, *Not Fakin' It* features a duet with Axl Rose on the song 'Death, Jail or Rock 'N' Roll', which – owing to G N' R's popularity – ensured the accompanying video received many an airing on primetime MTV. He also recorded a version of Steppenwolf's 1968 classic, 'Magic Carpet Ride' with Slash for the 1993 movie *Coneheads,*

starring Dan Aykroyd and Jane Curtin.

Monroe also guested on G N' R's *Use Your Illusion I,* providing saxophone and harmonica on 'Bad Obsession', as well as backing vocals on the cover-version, 'Ain't It Fun', which would subsequently appear on *The Spaghetti Incident?*.

In 2002, Monroe reformed Hanoi Rocks with fellow original member, guitarist Andy McCoy. The following year he released his final solo album, *Whatcha Want?*

## MR. BROWNSTONE

'Mr. Brownstone' – coupled with 'It's So Easy' as a double A-side – was Guns N' Roses' debut UK single when it was released on 15 June, 1987. Both songs were set to feature on the soon-to-be-released *Appetite For Destruction,* but Geffen Records decided to rush-release the single in order to coincide with the band's debut UK appearances at London's Marquee Club.

"I used to do a little but a little wouldn't do/So the little got more and more/I just keep tryin' ta get a little better/Said a little better than before." So sang Axl, but as the term 'Brownstone' is American street-slang for heroin, the song would perhaps have had greater resonance if Izzy or Slash had undertaken vocal duties. For, although Axl had openly admitted to experimenting with heroin, he

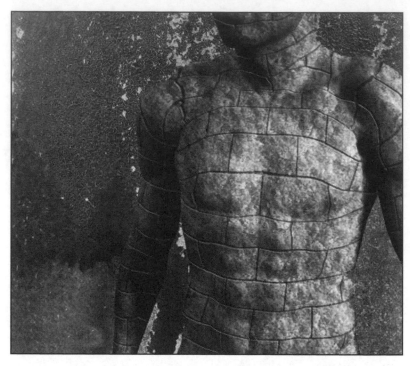

On 18 October, 1989, at the Los Angeles Coliseum, where Guns N' Roses were supporting veteran rockers, the Rolling Stones on the American leg of the latter band's *Steel Wheels* tour, Axl brought the set to an unscheduled halt and stunned the audience by informing them that this would be the last Guns N' Roses show unless certain people in the band started getting their shit together. "I'm sick and tired," he told the hushed crowd, "of too many people in this organisation dancing with Mr. Brownstone."

The only thing which appears to spread faster than the proverbial wildfire, is word of mouth. And although Guns N' Roses had finished their allotted set the previous night, those fans making

had done so whilst in total control of his faculties and never, at any time, did he allow his penchant for the drug to get out of control. And nor would he have considered himself an addict, whilst Izzy and Slash – with whom, as well as Steven Adler, he had co-written the tune – were all liberal users; a disturbing dalliance which was threatening to compromise their on-stage performances – something which wasn't going to be tolerated by Axl. Although it was no secret that heroin was rife in the G N' R camp, it was he – as the band's frontman, and unofficial spokesperson – who often found himself in the firing line over the group's supposed glamorisation of hard drug use.

their way to the Coliseum for the second of the four scheduled L.A. shows must have been pondering what would happen should Axl carry out his threat – if indeed he hadn't done so already. Those fears quickly evaporated into the ether when the Gunners took to the stage on cue, but before a note was played, a rather sheepish-looking Slash – purposely sporting a Betty Ford Clinic T-shirt for the occasion – stepped up to the microphone and delivered an anti-drug speech, during which he name-checked Elvis, Janis Joplin and Led Zeppelin drummer, John Bonham, whose own lives had been cut short through drug abuse. The guitarist then went on to explain how, as a kid, he'd stood in this very arena and watched bands such as the Rolling Stones, Aerosmith, and Van Halen, whilst dreaming of being up on stage. The previous night he had indeed realised his dream, only to have woken in the morning with little or no recollection of the show. He finished off by telling the audience that no one in the band advocated the use of heroin. And that Guns N' Roses wouldn't be one of those weak bands that fell apart because of it.

Whether Slash was speaking only for himself, or on behalf of Izzy and Steven, no one was quite sure. But his decision to stop chasing the dragon wasn't so much an epiphany, but rather due to his having overheard Axl's conversation with David Lee Roth back-

stage the previous night, when the singer bemoaned the fact that three out of the four musicians in Guns N' Roses had been smacked out of their gourds for the opening show, and yet everyone thought he was the junkie. Whatever the reasoning behind Slash's impromptu anti-drug sermon, it served to dispel the black cloud hanging over the band, and he and Axl embraced before launching into 'Patience'.

## MUSIC CONNECTION

*Music Connection*, the bi-weekly trade magazine proudly devoted to bridging the gap between 'the street and the elite' and which in 2007, celebrated three decades of catering to the Californian rock community, played a significant role in the Guns N' Roses story.

The 'musicians' bible' is located, as it was back then, at 16130 Ventura Boulevard, Encino, California, and contains the largest free classified ads section available in any publication in the USA, and – as with the thousands of other aspiring rock 'n' roll wannabes that clambered aboard a Greyhound bus bound for Los Angeles – Izzy, Axl and Duff would have made *Music Connection* their first purchase upon arrival in L.A.

Today, the magazine's features editor proudly boasts that it wasn't only the future Gunners trio who found each other – as well as L.A. residents, Slash and

Steven – through perusing the *MC* classifieds, but it had also helped Mötley Crüe, Joan Jett & The Blackhearts and Billy Idol find like-minded musicians to complete their respective bands. *Music Connection*'s standing within the L.A. rock community means that it has always been hip to what was happening on Sunset Strip, and the magazine began championing Guns N' Roses almost from the band's conception. And in July, 1987, *Music Connection* took the bold – and unprecedented – step of putting the then unsigned band on their front cover. This, however, proved to be an extremely prescient piece of journalism, for by the time the magazine hit newsstands, bookstores, and 7-Elevens across the Golden State, the band had signed to Geffen Records. Indeed, a perusal of the magazine's website today reveals a 'Superstar Covers' section which informs the

reader that *Music Connection* was also the first publication in the world to feature Sebastian Bach's Skid Row, Poison, The Offspring, Nirvana, Madonna, and Alanis Morissette, on their front cover.

# MY MICHELLE

'My Michelle', which features on *Appetite For Destruction*, was written by Axl and Izzy and received its first documented public airing at The Roxy in Los Angeles on 18 January, 1986.

'My Michelle', which was arguably the best Guns N' Roses song never to be released as a single, was Axl's homage to an old flame – and old high school acquaintance of Slash and Steven's – called Michelle Young. As Michelle herself later testified, she and Axl were driving to a gig one night when Elton John's 'Your Song' came on the radio. The tender ballad, which, incidentally, features string arrangements by Paul Buckmaster who would subsequently work on *Chinese Democracy* with Axl, had originally featured on the bespectacled crooner's 1970 eponymously-titled second album.

The song was a mutual favourite, and Michelle – albeit tongue-in-cheek – expressed a desire to have someone write such a beautiful song about her. Axl duly took note and went off to put pen to paper. But instead of presenting the band with a saccharine-sweet ditty that,

in his own words, "didn't really touch any basis of reality", he delivered an honest, true-to-life vignette of Michelle's then troubled and drug-addled existence. The song's opening lines: 'Your daddy works in porno/Now your mummy's not around/She used to love her heroin/But now she's underground', were as candid as they were accomplished. It was no secret in and around West Hollywood that Michelle's dad distributed porn movies for a living, while her free-spirited mother had indeed tragically succumbed to a drugs overdose several years earlier.

Axl has subsequently stated that the rest of the band – particularly Slash and Steven – were critical of the lines, believing that poor little Michelle would 'freak out' at having her dirty laundry aired in public. The unexpected animosity served to put doubts in the singer's mind and he spent several weeks deliberating over whether to show her the finished lyric. He needn't have worried, however, as Michelle – who received a 'thank you' on *Appetite For Destruction*'s liner notes, as well as making a fleeting cameo appearance in the 'Welcome To The Jungle' video – was delighted that her one-time lover hadn't tried to mask the darker and seedier aspects of her life, and happily told all and sundry that she was the song's subject matter.

# NAVARRO, DAVE

Dave Navarro, the ex-Jane's Addiction and Red Hot Chili Peppers guitarist, played on the Guns N' Roses song, 'Oh My God' that appears on the soundtrack to the Arnold Schwarzenegger movie, *End Of Days*.

This, however, wasn't the guitarist's first involvement with Guns N' Roses, for when Izzy announced he was quitting the band back in August, 1991, Navarro, who was born on 7 June, 1967 in Santa Monica, California, was top of Axl's list to replace his old friend. Slash, on the other hand, although appreciative of Navarro's ability, was rather less enthused at the idea and believed that in order to keep the dynamic, the band needed a guitarist that played in a similar style to Izzy; his also being aware of Navarro's heroin addiction at the time was another issue. But Axl refused to budge on the subject and so Slash finally relented and invited Navarro – who had just become

a free agent following the demise of Jane's Addiction – down to the Gunners' rehearsal studio. Come the day of the meeting, however, it was a case of 'no show Navarro', which happened not once, but on three separate occasions. Axl, however, was still convinced he was his man, and after speaking with Navarro, convinced Slash of his commitment and persuaded him to arrange another meeting. But when Navarro again failed to show Slash washed his hands of the proposal and instead went in search of the guy he'd originally thought of: Gilby Clarke.

Slash's feelings towards Navarro obviously mellowed during the intervening years, for both he and Duff were guests at the guitarist's wedding to Baywatch Babe, Carmen Elektra in 2003. The tardy guitarist was also invited to join Velvet Revolver in 2004, but due to his aversion to touring he declined the offer.

# NEIL, VINCE

Vince Neil, the singer with legendary L.A. hellraisers, Mötley Crüe, famously challenged Axl Rose to a fight live on primetime MTV in 1990.

The trouble between the two frontmen started when Vince's second wife, Sharise, a former mud wrestler, whom he married in April, 1988, began showing a little too much interest in Izzy during their first year of wedlock. And although Izzy spurned Sharise's advances, word got back to Vince, who naturally took affront. But rather than blame Sharise – which might have brought unwanted attention to his supposed failure to keep his wife of less than twelve months in line – he instead chose to take umbrage with Izzy. Vince's opportunity to gain revenge – and also save face – came at that year's MTV awards ceremony, where he apparently emerged from the backstage darkness and smacked an unsuspecting Izzy – who had just walked off stage after he and Axl had jammed with Tom Petty – in the mouth, splitting his lip. As Izzy was fully focused on fighting his drink and drug demons, he had no particular interest in squaring up to Vince, whereas the volatile and quick-tempered Axl chased the Crüe singer along the corridor. But when Vince wheeled round with "fists pumping with blood", Axl apparently lost his appetite for confrontation and merely ordered Vince to stay the fuck away from

his band, before heading off to rejoin Izzy and a rather bemused Tom Petty.

This, however, was not the end of the matter, for Vince was later quoted in a magazine saying "I just punched that dick [Izzy] and broke his nose. Anybody who beats up on a woman [Sharise] deserves to get the shit kicked out of them". By way of an explanation for his actions he claimed his unprovoked assault on Izzy was in retribution for his having supposedly struck Sharise sometime the previous year. Axl was steaming when he read Vince's comments and summoned respected English rock journo Mick Wall, who at the time was working for *Kerrang!* Magazine, to his West Hollywood apartment in early January, 1990 to give his version of what really went down at the awards ceremony. Apparently Petty's security team had pounced on Vince and asked Izzy if he wanted to press charges. Izzy had been content to mock Vince by likening the Crüe frontman's punching power to that of a girl, and so Petty's security guys had let Vince go free.

Axl was livid over Vince's comments, and informed the totally bewildered Wall that Vince was in sore need of a "good ass-whippin'", and that he was just the guy to do it. He also told Mick that he wanted to "smash his [Vince's] plastic face in", which was a sarcastic reference to the recent, and very hush-hush cosmetic surgery the Crüe singer had supposedly had. He went on to say that unless Vince was willing to admit in public he'd been lying, as well as apologise to *Kerrang!* and its readers, then he was willing to face him anytime, anywhere, with "guns, knives, or fists".

Mick returned to the UK the following day, and although he knew he was in possession of some pretty inflammatory dialogue, which was certain to feature on the front cover of the next available issue of *Kerrang!*, he was savvy enough to call Axl to see whether the singer was willing to stand by his comments before sending the interview to his copy editor. Axl, fully aware that Mick was recording the conversation, confirmed that although he might not have necessarily made those exact same comments, he was still prepared to stand by them. When Mick asked him what he might do should Vince decide to take him up on his offer, Axl replied that while he didn't really have time to worry about going after Vince, if the Crüe singer wanted to come after him then he would happily "clean up the floor with the motherfucker".

Needless to say, when Vince got wind of Axl's comments he was not best pleased, and picked up the gauntlet by openly challenging Axl to a good old fashioned square up, which – should Axl prove willing – could be broadcast live on MTV. Axl has since publicly denied ever having made the comments, which was effectively calling Mick Wall a liar – and this was the journalist who had been championing Guns N' Roses since witnessing their Manchester Apollo show in October, 1987! However, in Mötley Crüe's official 'eye-opening' autobiography, *The Dirt: Confessions of the World's Most Notorious Rock Band*, published by HarperCollins in 2001, Vince says that a 'meeting', albeit one off-camera, was indeed arranged between the two singers' respective intermediaries, only for Axl to subsequently "chicken out". This was a shame as far as Vince was concerned, as the offer for Axl to go toe-to-toe with him still stood ten years on. "The only thing," he says in *The Dirt*, "that would have given me more pleasure than a number one record was breaking Axl Rose's nose".

Vincent Neil Wharton was born on 8 February, 1961, in Los Angeles, California, to itinerant parents of Italian descent who moved around Southern California from town to town before finally settling in nearby Compton. Apart from growing up suffering – albeit unknowingly – from a mild form of dyslexia, which led to his getting into fights with his fellow pupils, and subsequently being thrown out of school, the teenage Vince had to learn to become street smart at an early age as life in Compton was not without its dangers. He soon learned it was safer to run with a crowd than try to go it alone, although this resulted in

his having his lower face slashed by a rival gang member.

Vince's passion for rock 'n' roll led to his trying out as singer for a succession of aspiring bands at Royal Oak High School in Covina, California – several of which included friend and future Crüe collaborator Tommy Lee. Indeed, it was Tommy's friendship with Vince that proved instrumental in the latter's decision to join Mötley Crüe in 1981. Crüe guitarist Mick Mars had caught Vince strutting his stuff on stage with his band Rock Candy at the Starwood Club in West Hollywood, and having been suitably impressed, offered Vince the gig. Vince, believing that his own band was going places, initially declined the invitation, but quickly underwent a change of heart upon realising that each of his fellow band members were all involved in outside projects.

Although Mötley Crüe have gone on to sell over 45 million albums worldwide, their debut,

self-produced offering in 1981, *Too Fast For Love,* shifted less than 20,000 units. On signing to Elektra Records the following year, however, it was decided the album should be given a makeover. Despite Queen's producer, Roy Thomas Baker, being drafted in, the remixed version fared little better when it was re-released on 20 August, 1982. But the band's second album, *Shout At the Devil,* which was released in September, 1983 and contained a cover of The Beatles' 'Helter Skelter', found a far more receptive audience and reached #17 on the US Billboard 100. Suddenly the Crüe's penchant for hedonism and taking to the stage dressed in women's clothing and heavy make-up was in vogue with America's teenagers. And the arrival of the new music medium, MTV the following year propelled the video-friendly band into the major league.

By the time of their third album, *Theatre Of pain*, which reached #6 on the US album chart and includes a cover of Brownsville Station's 1973 hit, 'Smokin' In The Boys Room', which provided Mötley Crüe with their first US Top 20 single, Vince had been charged and found guilty of DUI (Driving whilst Under the Influence), and vehicular manslaughter. It was during one of the band's now legendary parties that Vince foolishly volunteered to go out for more booze. Sitting beside Vince in the passenger seat of the singer's 72 De Tomaso Pantera sports car that fateful night was his friend and Hanoi Rocks' drummer, Nicholas "Razzle" Dingley. Razzle was killed when Vince lost control of his Pantera and smashed at high speed into an oncoming car, one of the passengers of which was left with permanent brain damage. Vince was subsequently sentenced to 30 days in jail (of which he only actually served 18), and ordered to pay $2.5 million dollars in damages.

Mötley Crüe's fourth album, *Girls, Girls, Girls,* shot to #2 on the Billboard 200 shortly after its release in May, 1987, effectively making the pouting, leather-clad bad boys one of the biggest bands on the planet. And although the word on Sunset Strip was that Guns N' Roses were looking to usurp the Crüe and steal their glam crown, when it came time to go out on the road for a full US tour to promote the album, they happily invited their rivals along for the ride. It was during the tour with G N' R that bassist Nikki Sixx – after partying hard with Slash and Steven Adler – suffered a near-fatal heroin overdose. Sixx's heart reportedly stopped beating for two minutes, which saw him being declared legally dead during the ride to the hospital, before he was eventually revived with two adrenaline shots to the heart. Rather than amend his wild ways, the bassist wrote the song 'Kickstart My Heart', which subsequently appeared on the band's 1989 album, *Dr. Feelgood.* This record would go one better then its predecessor by claiming the coveted #1 spot on the US Billboard 200, as well as earning the backcombed boys a second Top 20 US single. The planned '87 European tour was pulled by the band's management team who feared one or more of the band members would be coming home in a body bag.

By the early 1990's, however, Mötley Crüe's appeal appeared to be on the wane. Guns N' Roses may have still dominated the world stage, but the advent of Grunge had rendered every other metal band near obsolete. And although the Crüe's 1994 eponymously-titled fifth album reached

#7 in the US album chart, it was still viewed as something of a commercial failure by the men in suits over at Elektra. One reason for this 'failure' could have been Vince's departure from the band in February, 1992 to concentrate on a solo career. And although his replacement, ex-Angora frontman John Corabi, remained with Mötley Crüe for five years, he was never truly accepted by the fans.

In 1995, by which time Vince had divorced Sharise and married former Playboy centrefold Heidi Mark, the singer was left devastated when his daughter Skylar succumbed to cancer. He and ex-wife Sharise launched a successful lawsuit against the company Rocketdyne for having dumped cancer-causing chemicals near the couple's Simi Valley home. Vince and Heidi divorced in 2001, and two years later Vince tied the knot for the third time when he married Lia Gerardini.

In 1997, following a reconciliatory meeting, Vince rejoined Mötley Crüe and headed into the studio to record their sixth album, *Generation Swine*. Although the record – which proved to be their last for Elektra – fared better than *Mötley Crüe*, and reached a respectable #4 on the Billboard 200, it too was viewed as a commercial failure by the label and led to a mutually agreed parting of the ways in 1998. The band's future was thrown into further confusion the following year when Tommy Lee left to pursue a solo career. He was replaced by Ozzy Osbourne's drummer Randy Castillo, who provided the beat on the band's June, 2000 album, *New Tattoo*, which sold less than 150,000 copies and stalled at an embarrassing #41 on the US album chart. When Castillo tragically died of cancer in 2002 and Mick Mars had been diagnosed with a degenerative back condi-

tion called Anchylosis, the Crüe went into temporary hiatus. Nikki Sixx went off to form Brides of Destruction, while Vince performed solo shows – albeit ones with a set-list comprising mainly of Mötley Crüe hits.

If there were any doubts regarding the Crüe's true standing in American rock 'n' roll folklore they were blown away with the release of *The Dirt* in 2001. The band's hilarious – yet oft-harrowing – autobiography spent ten weeks on the *New York Times* best-seller list, which led many fans to believe it was only a matter of time before the band buried their differences and got back together. Another three years would pass, however, before the highly-anticipated reunion of the Crüe's original line-up came to pass. In 2004, the same year Vince appeared on TV in a one-hour special called *Remaking Vince Neil*, Nikki Sixx announced that he and Vince had returned to the studio to work on new material. And in February, 2005, the reconstituted Crüe kick-started their reunion by releasing the compilation album *Red, White and Crue*, which features many of the band members' particular favourites, as well as three new tracks. The album reached #6 on the Billboard 100, and has since gone on to sell over one million copies and achieve platinum status. The group also embarked on an extensive worldwide tour in support of the album, duly dubbed the *Carnival of Sins* tour.

Aside from Mötley Crüe's now trademark onstage props, such as Harleys, and flame-bursting pyrotechnics, the shows featured a variety of circus acts including semi-naked female acrobats, fire-breathers and midgets.

By September, 2007, however, the old frictions had resurfaced, and Tommy Lee left the band as a result of a lawsuit which the other three members brought against his manager, Carl Stubner for having contracted the drummer to appear on reality TV shows which they claimed had harmed their bad boy image.

Although still very committed to Mötley Crüe, Vince continues to perform with his solo band, and at the time of writing he is working on a solo album with his in-house guitarist, Dana Strum, as well as his autobiography with UK writer Alan Parker, which is due for publication in 2009.

## NEUROTIC OUTSIDERS

The Neurotic Outsiders, or the Neurotic Boy Outsiders as they were originally called, was an L.A. supergroup of sorts featuring Duff McKagan and Matt Sorum, along with ex-Sex Pistol Steve Jones and Duran Duran's John Taylor.

The initial catalyst for what would become the Neurotic Outsiders came on 28 June, 1995, when Matt and Duff, together with Jones and Taylor, performed a supposedly one-off benefit show at the Viper Room in aid of a mutual friend who was suffering from cancer. As Duff tended to play guitar on non-G N' R projects, Matt offered the gig to Taylor, as he'd been impressed with the Duran Duran bassist's playing on his own side-project, The Power Station, and Duff knew Steve – who'd also recently collaborated with Taylor on the latter's solo album – from mountain biking together in the Hollywood Hills. Having decided upon the name Kings Of Chaos, and with just one rehearsal – which took place on the afternoon of the show itself – the ad hoc combo treated the packed, celebrity-studded audience to a set consisting of cover-versions such as Roxy Music's 'Virginia Plain' and The Clash's 'Janie Jones'.

Although the set didn't include any Guns N' Roses songs, they did run through Duran Duran's debut single, 'Planet Earth' and the Sex Pistols' 'Pretty Vacant', as well as The Stooges' 'No Fun'(which also featured as the B-side to the Pistols' 'Pretty Vacant' single back in 1977). With Guns N' Roses in temporary hiatus while Axl plotted the band's next move, and with Steve and John having plenty of spare time on their hands, the four decided to run with the ball and announced further shows at the Viper Rooms, where they were often joined on stage by the likes of ex-Stray Cat frontman Brian Setzer, Billy Idol and Simon Le Bon.

Buoyed by favourable reviews – as well a positive response from their audiences – the band began playing further afield. In October '95 they undertook a three-date mini-tour of the Eastern seaboard, playing New York, Philadelphia and Boston. By this time, however, they had undergone a name change to the Neurotic Boy Outsiders, before truncating the name – possibly on account of their having a combined age of 142 – to the snappier-sounding Neurotic Outsiders.

The band kicked off 1996 with a show in Tucson, Arizona, on 4

January, where, aside from the punk and Duranie covers, they performed several original numbers, including 'Nasty Ho', 'Jerk', 'Story Of My Life' and 'Revolution', which would all subsequently appear on their eponymously-titled album released on Madonna's Maverick label later that same year. These songs had largely been culled from Steve and John's solo vaults, which – at least in the case of Steve's offerings – proved a double-edged sword. For although they were solid, rockin' tunes with the guitarist's trademark chugging power chords and Sex Pistolian licks, a limited vocabulary meant Steve's lyrics were often sub-standard 'moon in June' rhyming couplets relating to the male and female genitalia. Fortunately for all concerned, a command of the English vernacular has never been a pre-requisite in rock 'n' roll, and 1996 could have been the Neurotics' year – and may well have seen Duff and Matt leave Guns N' Roses sooner than they eventually did – had it not been for the Sex Pistols' long-awaited and much-vaunted reunion, which saw Steve preoccupied elsewhere for much of the time.

Indeed, a show at the Luxor in Cologne, Germany, on 28 September, which was one of several staged during Steve's month-long break from the Pistols' tour, would prove to be their last live performance for three years; although Steve did collaborate with Duff and Matt to record a version of Alice Cooper's 'Elated' for the Alice Cooper tribute album, *Humanary Stew*, released in early 1999.

In April, 1999, by which time both Duff and Matt had left Guns N' Roses, the Neurotics briefly reunited for a month-long Monday night residency at the Viper Rooms. For the final show, on Monday, 26 April, they were joined on stage by The Cult's Ian Astbury and Billy Duffy, and Mel "Sporty Spice" Chisholm, who happened to be in town recording her solo album. This, however, was not the last we would hear from the Neurotics, as they reunited for a one-off show supporting Camp Freddy at the Avalon Theatre in Los Angeles on 7 December, 2006.

As an amusing aside, let me tell you about my one and only encounter with John 'Duranie' Taylor. It came at EMI's former Manchester Square HQ way back in January, 1981, whilst I was serving in my unpaid capacity as a roadie for the Blackburn-based power-pop combo, The Stiffs, who at the time were signed to the label. Well, when I say roadie, what I actually mean is that me and my mates humped a few amps around in return for a free ride and free admission. As the band had a few hours to kill before playing the Marquee later that evening, they decided to call in at EMI to see their A&R man. Coincidently, the Angelic Upstarts – the second generation Geordie punk band that Duff came close to joining some four years later – were also in attendance that afternoon. And if my memory serves, they were having problems keeping hold of their drummers back then.

As roadies – especially lowly amp-luggers – are rarely privy to a record company's machinations, I was handed a plastic carrier bag and given free rein to carry out a little post-Christmas shopping – talk about being given the keys to the sweet shop! Well, there I was merrily helping myself to white label test pressings and promo singles – the old-fashioned variety with the large 'A' stamped in the middle – when I spotted five lads, all trying to look suitably surly, emerging from a side office identical to the one in which the Stiffs were still holding court. One of the secretaries from the typing pool – having decided to curtail my ram-raid on the label's extensive record library – invited us all to join her and her colleagues on their afternoon tea-break. The lads in question appeared friendly enough, and upon discovering they hailed from Birmingham and that their band was called Duran Duran (there was nary a frilly shirt, nor eye-liner in sight, I hasten to add), I set about cajoling them into letting me listen to what I honestly believed was their demo tape.

Now there can be no denying that Duran Duran have written some decent pop tunes in their time, but I can honestly say I didn't hear anything special that particular afternoon. So, as the Stiffs had completed their dealings and were ready to head off for their Soho soundcheck, I jokingly told the Duranies not to give up their day jobs, and to get their arses along to the Marquee to hear some decent music. You can imagine my chagrin, then, as I sat watching them performing their debut single, 'Planet Earth' on *Top Of The Tops* less than a month later.

Well, I certainly backed the wrong horse that day…

## NIVEN, ALAN

Alan Niven served as Guns N' Roses' manager from August, 1986, through to May, 1991.

When Tom Zutaut first approached Niven, the abrasive, blues-loving New Zealander was running his own management company, Stravinsky Brothers, which at the time included another soon-to-be platinum L.A. act, Great White on its books. Niven's involvement with Great White stemmed from his having worked for Enigma Records, then part of Greenworld Distribution, the independent import and distribution company which oversaw the release of the band's 1984 eponymous debut (Greenworld had also distributed Mötley Crüe's 1981, self-produced debut, *Too Fast For Love*).

Having grown up with a passion for all things rock 'n' roll, Niven learnt how to play guitar and began writing songs with a view to attracting like-minded musicians with whom to form a band. His strict disciplinarian father, however, had other ideas and believed a career in the military would march such frivolous notions out of his son's head. Rather than submit to his father's will or spend the rest of his life butting heads with the old man, Niven packed a bag and headed for America, arriving in Los Angeles in 1982.

Although Great White had a couple of accomplished songwriters in singer Jack Russell and guitarist Mark Kendall, Niven was anxious to be more than just their manager and contributed on several songs featured on the band's second album, *Shot In The Dark*, as well as the 1987 platinum-selling, *Once Bitten...*

The Gunners initially met with Niven at their new Hollywood Hills HQ, where, as Axl later recalled, their future manager arrived at the house bearing gifts, including several bottles of Jack Daniels No. 7, a couple of hardcore porno mags and a large pizza. Although it is fair to say there was no immediate rush of affection towards Niven, possibly due to his having delivered his brash sales pitch as though he was doing the band a favour – a fact which he subsequently admitted to Mick Wall – as well as to the Gunners' collective dislike for Great White.

Indeed, during the early days of their relationship, Niven made no bones about Great White remaining his first priority. Even *Appetite For Destruction* failed to shift his perspective. On his initial hearing of the Gunners' debut album Niven told anyone willing to listen that the band would be lucky to shift 200,000 units; and he positively scoffed at the idea of it containing a hit single.

The band did, however, sense a kindred spirit in Niven. They believed he would be sympathetic to their cause, and more importantly, would take no prisoners whilst protecting their best interests. The deal was supposedly sealed at a showcase gig at the Whisky A Go-Go on 23 August, 1986, where Axl allegedly tested Niven's patience by purposely turning up late, forcing the band to perform an impromptu jam. But according to G N' R legend, the deal was instead sealed at Barney's Beanery, the well-known West Hollywood watering hole, where Niven proceeded to impress his future charges by matching them drink for drink.

Although the introduction of the no-nonsense Niven was acceptable to both Geffen, and eventually the rest of the band, the ice never did quite thaw as far as Axl was concerned, which from the very outset, served to place an unnecessary strain on their working relationship. Niven, however, was content to put business before bad manners and believed if he could maintain some semblance of order and discipline within the G N' R camp then the band could go on to make a million dollars. Yet, despite being on hand to take care of the day-to-day chaos – which seemed to follow Guns N' Roses around like a star-crossed stalker – Axl, or the "red-headed dictator" as Niven subsequently referred to the Gunners' autocratic singer, was silently plotting a means of dispensing with the manager's services.

That opportunity came in May, 1991, shortly before the Gunners embarked on their mammoth *Use Your Illusion* world tour. Whilst Niven was fully occupied defending the band's decision to release two double-albums, the knives were being sharpened in his absence. Axl simply delivered an ultimatum to Geffen, whereby he refused to continue laying down his vocals for the new albums unless Niven was removed from office. When subsequently called upon by *Rolling Stone* magazine to explain his reasons for orchestrating Niven's removal in favour of Doug Goldstein, Axl gave the following perplexing response: "Everybody has a lot of good and bad. And with Alan, I just got sick of his fucking combo platter."

As Niven was forced to sign a confidentiality agreement as part of the rumoured $3 million kiss-off which prohibited him from discussing either Axl or Guns N' Roses in public, the matter was deemed to be concluded. This wasn't the end of Niven's association with all things Guns N' Roses, however, for when Izzy announced his own departure from the fold later that same year, he appointed Niven as his manager.

## NORTH GARDNER STREET

Before Guns N' Roses signed with Geffen, home was a ramshackle garage-cum-rehearsal space on North Gardner Street in West Hollywood.

Before Guns N' Roses attained stellar-stardom and were able to buy their own palatial houses, the five struggling musicians – as a means of cutting down on unnecessary expenditure – holed up together in a dilapidated storage unit on North Gardner Street, located just off Melrose Avenue. Slash, who along with Axl, was a full-time resident, would later describe their makeshift abode as a "very uncomfortable prison cell," which is pretty accurate given that it measured just 15 x 20 foot and lacked every modern convenience known to man. The place was one of three identical units, each with a corrugated aluminium roll-up serving as a front opening, and a communal bathroom located within a separate building. But having 'acquired' some wood to erect a makeshift loft space above Steven's drum kit, as well as installing a portable charcoal grill, the band renamed their abode the

'Sunset and Garden Hotel and Villas.

Despite their less-than-salubrious surroundings, Slash readily admits that their living together in such cramped confines was not totally bereft of positives as the sound was pretty good. Axl was equally charitable about his time on North Gardner, lamenting that, in some ways, he and the rest of the band missed it, or if not the place itself, then at least the camaraderie; "Every weekend, the biggest party in L.A. was down at our place." He later reminisced – albeit through rose-tinted spectacles. "We'd have five hundred people packed in an alley. And someone was selling beers for a buck out of his trunk. It was like a bar and everyone had their whisky."

And so, as was the Cavern to the Beatles, and Denmark Street to the Sex Pistols, North Gardner Street has become synonymous with the Gunners' early history.

# NOVEMBER RAIN

'November Rain', which appears on *Use Your Illusion I*, as well as reaching #3 on the Billboard 100 when it released as a single in 1992, became the most requested video on MTV.

Although the band has never confirmed as much, 'November Rain' is regarded by many fans as the second song in G N' R's unofficial '*Illusions*' power-ballad trilogy. Yet according to the English

writer, Chris Heath, in his 1993 Pet Shop Boys biography *Pet Shop Boys versus America*, Axl Rose supposedly paid the synth-pop duo a visit backstage during their 1991 North American tour and admitted to having taken his inspiration for 'November Rain' from their song, 'My October Symphony', which features on the duo's 1990 album, *Behaviour*. This is surely artistic license on Heath's part, for according to Slash, the ballad was already finished long before this time, and was initially intended for inclusion on *Appetite For Destruction*. The guitarist's claim is backed up – if any backing up were needed – by Tracii Guns, who says that he and Axl were working on 'November Rain' as early as 1983 whilst they were both in L.A. Guns.

Despite a running time of 8:57, which is regarded as anathema to the singles chart, 'November Rain' was the 'Bohemian Rhapsody' of its day. It was also a no-brainer for a single. And shame on those radio stations who, back in 1992, insisted on playing a truncated edit of the song, which omitted a solo

voted #6 in *Guitar World*'s '100 Greatest Guitar Solos. 'November Rain' is without doubt one of rock's most enduring ballads, and I can still remember being blown away upon hearing the song for the first time when the Gunners played Wembley Stadium in August, 1991.

Geffen, whose press release described the song as a melodic, mid-tempo ballad with a gorgeous lead vocal and an elegiac guitar lead, knew that 'November Rain' would appeal not just to the Gunners' burgeoning fan-base, but also to the mainstream record-buying public who wouldn't ordinarily rush out and buy a G N' R record. By 1992, sloppy rock ballads were two a penny, but although the rest of the band jokingly referred to it as "our Layla song", Axl, as with 'Sweet Child O' Mine', was savvy enough to avoid making the same mistake as (D)Eric Domino Clapton, or Barry Manilow (Mandy), Thin Lizzy (Sarah) etc and didn't put a girl's name in the song's title, thus ensuring it would strike a plaintive chord in the heart of every man. After all, there can't be many amongst us who haven't tried to banish the painful memories of a doomed relationship or attempt to resolve affairs of the heart whilst taking a solitary late-night stroll in the drizzling rain.

It is already well documented that Slash and Duff were both opposed to what they saw as a drift towards ballad-esque songs. But 'November Rain' was Axl's

grand opus. Indeed, the singer was so protective of the song that he'd warned those around him he would walk away from the music business if it wasn't recorded to his complete satisfaction. He'd also been desperate for the one-time ELO leader – and occasional Travelling Wilbury – Jeff Lynne to produce the track, but the proposal came to nought.

The accompanying video, which subsequently won an MTV Video Music Award for Best Cinematography, and reportedly cost an estimated $1.5 million to shoot, proved as captivating as the song itself. The viewer is taken on an emotional rollercoaster ride of 'life, love and loss', with the opening scene showing Axl downing pills to soften an, as yet unexplained pain, through to his marrying and burying his, then, real-life true love, Stephanie Seymour, all of which is interspersed with footage of the Gunners performing the song accompanied by a full orchestra. Stephanie looks ravishingly radiant as she walks down the aisle. But then again, she should in a wedding dress costing a reported $50,000.

Slash, who is the designated 'best man', has mislaid the ring. But Duff, who has either filched, or found the ring, hands it over to the relieved guitarist. Slash then passes the ring to the bemused priest before making his way outside the church, which has transformed from the ornate pillared basilica to a cute colonial structure akin to that from Laura Ingalls Wilder's *Little House On The Prairie*. The guitarist has also undergone a sartorial transformation and is now dressed in his more familiar leathers, and launches into his solo amid a swirling dust cloud kicked-up by the circling helicopter housing the film crew. The scene then switches back to the wedding, with Stephanie and Axl clambering into the back of a white Bentley convertible parked at the kerb, and the bride's ambiguous glance gives the viewer a first inkling that all is not well. And the storm clouds have quite literally gathered by the time of the lavish reception – complete with five-tier wedding cake – with the assembled guests (consisting of band members and friends) dashing for cover and sending the food and drink-laden tables flying as the heavens open. One of the guests accidentally knocks over a bottle of red wine, which cascades across a pristine white tablecloth – an image that serves as a subliminal precursor to the tragedy waiting to unfold.

Following a second 'tug-on-the-heartstrings' guitar solo from Slash – perched atop Axl's piano – the viewer is transported back to the church for Stephanie's funeral service. Axl sits gazing forlornly at his dead bride lying within an open casket. And with the service at an end, the casket is then carried out into the rain-soaked churchyard for burial. The final scene shows Axl lying on his bed. But instead of waking from the nightmare, he is instead transported back to the day of the wedding, where his dead bride, in the time-honoured tradition, throws her bouquet to the assembled guests. The bouquet sails in slow-motion through the air before pitching into her open grave and landing on the casket.

Incidentally, the guitar Slash uses in the video is a 1959 tobacco-sunburst Les Paul that once belonged to Aerosmith's Joe Perry. At the time, Joe was much more interested in snorting his fortune than he was in composing music, and his wife had sold the guitar in order to pay the bills. Slash willingly paid an L.A. collector $8,000 for the guitar, which had greater sentimental value to him than having once belonged to one of his heroes as he'd grown up with a poster on his bedroom wall of Joe playing that very same guitar.

# O'

## O'NEIL, SHAQUILLE

Shaquille Rashaun O'Neal, the renowned American basketball player who, in 2003, was ranked #9 in Slam Magazine's Top 75 NBC players of all time, is also a successful rap artist and has contributed to *Chinese Democracy*.

Aside from his prowess with the basketball, the 7ft 1 inch colossal, "Shaq" has released five rap albums, the first of which, *Shaq Diesel*, released in 1993, sold in excess of three million copies, and reached #25 on the Billboard 100. His involvement on *Chinese Democracy* came about totally

by accident as he happened to be recording in the same studio and headed over to say hello. As Axl was a fan of Shaq's talents both on and off the court, he invited him to 'freestyle' over one of the tracks intended for the album. "It was the first time I ever performed with a rock band, and it felt good." Shaq later admitted. Whether his vocal will survive to the finished mix, however, is anyone's guess.

## ONE IN A MILLION

'One In A Million', which is the final track on *GNR Lies*, landed Guns N' Roses – and Axl in particular – in hot water following the album's release in November, 1988.

When Guns N' Roses supported the Rolling Stones at the Los Angeles Coliseum in October, 1989, the opening act on the bill was Living Colour. And as all four band members were of Afro-American decent, it was inevitable they would be asked as to their opinion on the G N' R song which contained the words 'niggers' and 'faggots'. Indeed, it was they who fired the opening salvo when the band's frontman, Vernon Reid, participated in a radio phone-in at a local radio station the day before the opening Coliseum date. When one caller asked Reid – who was a prominent member of the Black Rock Coalition – for his verdict on 'One In A Million', the guitarist expressed a liking for Guns N'

Roses, but understandably took exception to the phrasing and sentiments contained within that particular song. The following night, Reid interrupted Living Colour's thirty-minute set to voice those same concerns from the Coliseum's stage. "If you don't have a problem with gay people," he informed the hushed audience, "then don't call them faggots. And if you don't have a problem with black people, then don't call them niggers." He finished off his sermon by adding that in his opinion, anyone who chose to call somebody a nigger – regardless of either the context, or the situation – was openly promoting racism and bigotry.

According to Reid, Keith Richards made a point of shaking his hand backstage after their set, whereas Axl seemed intent on shaking anyone connected with Living Colour by the throat, and challenged their bassist, Muzz Skillings, en route to the stage. After informing Skillings that he'd heard Reid's radio interview and didn't take kindly to his being perceived either racist or homophobic, Axl then astounded anyone within earshot by telling the bassist he'd never thought of them as 'niggers'. But before anyone could react, Alan Niven came rushing across and attempted to diffuse the situation by informing Living Colour's drummer, Will Calhoun, that Axl was from Indiana and therefore didn't know any better. The fact

Vernon Reid

that Niven remained both upright and in the band's employ was evidence enough that Axl failed to hear his cringe-worthy attempt to defend the singer's comments.

And when Mick Wall questioned Axl over the lyrical content of 'One In A Million' during an interview at·the singer's West Hollywood apartment in January, 1990, he told the journalist that the inspiration for the lyric came from his friend, West Arkeen, having been attacked and robbed by two black guys whilst out busking one Christmas. He then went on to defend his usage of such derogatory terms by arguing that the label 'racist' should only be applied to those individuals who chose to affix their personal feelings to the words; that the words themselves should not be considered racist. Although he readily admitted the word 'nigger' was offensive, he hadn't meant to denigrate the black race per se. A claim backed up by the fact that Slash is of mixed race himself and wouldn't have had anything to do with the song – let alone record it – if he'd thought Axl had maliciously intended to be insulting in that way.

It is interesting to note, however, that despite their attempts to justify 'One In A Million', Guns N' Roses haven't performed the song live since *GNR Lies* was released in November, 1988.

# P'

## PARADISE CITY

'Paradise City' is one of the stand-out tracks on Guns N' Roses' debut album, *Appetite For Destruction*, and reached #4 on the US Billboard 100 when it was released as a single in 1989.

According to legend, Slash first came up with the song's highly-infectious – and instantly recognisable – riff, played over the G, F and D chords, whilst he and Steven Adler were still ploughing a lone furrow in Road Crew. And little could the guitarist have imagined that he would one day be performing said riff as a climactic show-closer in front of hundreds of thousands of adoring fans in stadiums across the globe.

It has been suggested in some quarters that the lyrics to 'Paradise City' centre on the corruption of late '80s Los Angeles. But Axl, during a 1998 interview with *Hit Parader* magazine, shed some light on the matter by claiming the song's verses actually relate to "being in the jungle" that was – and is – downtown L.A., whilst the infectious chorus of 'Take me down to the paradise city/Where the grass is green and the girls are pretty' refers to "being back in the Midwest or somewhere." Knowing the band's penchant for drugs, however, the phrase 'where the grass is green' could well be a reference to weed, which is green the world over. And when Slash made a post G N' R appearance on the *BBC*'s satirical late-night music show, *Never Mind The Buzzcocks,* the guitarist jokingly stated the original chorus wasn't about the 'girls being pretty' but rather their being 'fat' and having 'big titties'.

The accompanying video is a colour/black 'n' white montage of live and off-stage footage filmed during two separate shows: the first being at the Giants Stadium in New Rutherford, New Jersey on 16 August, 1988 during G N' R's tenure opening for Aerosmith on the US leg of latter band's *Permanent Vacation* tour, while the second show is the ill-feted Monsters of Rock festival staged at Castle Donington two days later. The decision to use footage from Donington was the band's way of paying a proper and lasting mark of respect to the two fans that died during their set.

'Paradise City' has gone on to achieve near-legendary status amongst metal fans the world over, and deservedly ranks #3 in *Total Guitar* magazine's 100 greatest solos of all time, made

#21 on *VH1*'s 40 Greatest Metal Songs of All Time and came in at #453 in *Rolling Stone*'s 500 Greatest Songs of All Time. It also features on the soundtrack to the 1998 movie, *Can't Hardly Wait*, starring the delectable Jennifer Love Hewitt.

## PATIENCE

'Patience', which features on *GNR Lies*, became Guns N' Roses' fourth consecutive Top 10 US hit when it was released as a single in May, 1989. It also went Top 10 in the UK.

Although many G N' R fans initially believed that Izzy took his inspiration for 'Patience' from Axl's turbulent relationship with his then girlfriend, Erin Everly, it has since come to light the guitarist's heartfelt lyric was actually autobiographical and referred to his failed romance with model and aspiring actress, Angela Nicoletti (who subsequently went on to marry Hanoi Rocks' flamboyant guitarist Andy McCoy). The accompanying promo video – which again was directed by Alan Dick – features performance footage shot at L.A.'s Record Plant studios. Duff, clutching an acoustic guitar rather than his trusty bass, counts in the intro before he, Izzy, and Slash begin strumming the song's basic C, A, D chord pattern, while a sashaying Axl whistles along in accompaniment before kicking in with the vocals. It is interesting to note – given that the video was shot in February, 1989 – that he's reading the lyrics from a sheet of paper, yet the band first performed the song at the Cathouse on 21 January, 1988. As there is no call for percussion in Izzy's poignant ballad, Steven is left to twiddle his thumbs and idly toy with the props. The offstage footage was shot within the Ambassador Hotel where, twenty years earlier, Senator Robert Kennedy – the then Republican presidential nominee – was assassinated following a speech to the party faithful and had recently closed its doors for the last time.

Dick seems to have drawn his inspiration from Stephen King's fictional Overlook Hotel from the writer's 1977 horror novel, *The Shining*, as the band members are the only constants while ephemeral extras fade in and out of each scene. The shy and retiring Izzy is the only band member not to feature anywhere else in the video, whereas his axe partner, Slash is seen lying on a bed nonchalantly caressing his pet snakes – one of which is a six-foot red-tailed boa constrictor that was a gift from porn king, Larry Flint's daughter Lisa – while a procession of scantily-clad girls slip silently between the sheets. Duff, sporting a white tuxedo – like his hero Sid Vicious – is seen carrying a breakfast tray down to reception, where Steven is sat with a bevy of beauties who, like him, slowly fade away into the ether. Although no one could have known it at the time, 'Patience' would prove to be Steven's last cinematic appearance with the band before his dismissal several months later. Indeed, given that Izzy, Slash and Duff would subsequently follow the drummer out of G N' R's revolving door, the video has since taken on a whole new meaning owing to the final scene showing a despondent-looking Axl sat alone in a nondescript hotel room watching the Gunners' 'Welcome To the Jungle' promo video on TV.

'Patience' proved a favourite with fans, and remains in the Gunners' live set to this day. The ballad was obviously a firm favourite of Slash, Duff and Matt Sorum as Velvet Revolver covered it during their 2007 tour.

# PHOENIX

Arizona's state capital, Phoenix – the fifth largest city in the US – has proved something of an accursed place for Guns N' Roses as three of

their number have fallen foul of the local authorities there.

On 30 August, 1989, whilst en route from LAX to Indianapolis, Izzy was arrested at Phoenix's Sky Harbour airport for having verbally abused a female flight attendant, refusing to adhere to the flight's no-smoking policy and urinating in the aisle. Izzy was so out of it that he didn't actually wake up until the following morning – by which time he was in custody – with little or no recollection of what had occurred or why he was in jail. Although G N' R's management issued a press statement blithely dismissing the charges as "Izzy's way of expressing himself", the airline's authorities were understandably less accommodating. As Izzy had a prior conviction for possession, he was placed on probation and ordered to seek help for his spiralling drug dependency – including a 12-month period of random urine testing. This latest – and most shameful – altercation with the law served as Izzy's wake-up call. "That was the point where I said to myself this has got to stop," a detoxed Izzy later admitted. "I didn't wanna wind up dead, or worse, in prison,"

The Arizona state capital was also the setting for Slash's own heroin epiphany, which came several months after the Izzy debacle. The guitarist had followed Doug Goldstein to an exclusive luxury resort just outside Phoenix, where he was taking time

out for a little R 'n' R away from the G N' R maelstrom. As Slash remembers it, Goldstein was working on improving his golf handicap when a swarm of police officers came charging up the fairway to inform him they had one of his charges in custody for having assaulted a maid. Slash – who was stark naked at the time of his capture – had apparently gorged himself on a cornucopia of drugs and proceeded to 'trip out' whilst in the shower. Having escaped from his watery prison by smashing through the glass partition, lacerating his body in several places in the process, the guitarist then proceeded to run amok through the resort where, amongst other incongruities, he trampled over a petrified maid. Unlike Izzy, however, Slash somehow avoided being charged and immediately flew back to L.A., where he booked himself into a hotel under an alias and duly passed

out. Upon waking sometime the following day, and undergoing what he describes as an "intervention", the guitarist decided it was time to seek professional help. His one and only venture into rehab proved short-lived, however, as three days into his programme he decided he wasn't that fucked up, signed himself out, and flew to Hawaii to dry out at his leisure.

Axl also fell foul of Phoenix's finest whilst en route to Dr. Sharon Maynard's Arizona research institute in February, 1998. The singer's patience – already tested by interminable flight delays – was further aggravated when a member of Phoenix's Sky Harbor airport's security staff almost dropped a hand-blown glass sphere intended for Maynard's psychic perusal. Having both abused and threatened the bewildered staff member, Axl was arrested and spent several hours in the local jail. When the case came to court some twelve months later, he pleaded no contest to the misdemeanour charge and was duly fined $500.

# PITMAN, CHRIS

Chris Pitman, the Los Angeles-based multi-instrumentalist and songwriter, joined Guns N' Roses in 1998 as a second keyboardist. He also orchestrates and plays synthesisers during the band's live performances.

Chris was born on 25 February, 1976, in Independence, Missouri, and after finishing his schooling – which included studies at both the Art Institute of Kansas City, and the University of Missouri – began collaborating with several artists,

including the rapper, Dr. Dre. He was involved in forming electronic outfit ZAUM with Tool's Danny Carey, which subsequently led to his being invited to go out on tour with Tool and contributing to the track, 'Third Eye' on the band's 1996 album, *AEnima*. He also played a major part in forming The Replicants, who,like G N' R, released an album consisting entirely of covers, as well as psychedelic popsters Lusk, whose 1997 album, *Free Mars*, received a Grammy Award nomination in the 'Best Recording Package' category. In 1996 he contributed keyboards on Blinker The Star's album, *Bourgeois Kitten*, and co-wrote their 1998 single, 'Below The Sliding Doors'.

Although having been drafted into Guns N' Roses in 1998, Chris was still amenable to outside collaborations, and in 2004 he played synthesiser on the Electric Company album, *Creative Playthings*. In 2005, he again teamed up with Carey for the experimental project, 'Source of Uncertainty', which involved recording material using only pre-1960s musical devices.

Away from music, Chris is the co-founder of the Los Angeles-based conceptual art coalition, 'Priory of the North', which works primarily with Monotype Lithography using oils and metal. He is also actively involved with onsite land/environment projects on Midwest regional farmland sites in Lafayette and Johnson City,

Missouri. 2003 saw him set up a similar project in Rio de Janeiro titled 'Mind/Land', but the venture has been put on hold while the Brazilian authorities issue the pre-requisite visas and permits needed to import the necessary materials into the country.

# P.M.R.C.

The P.M.R.C., which stands for the Parents Music Resource Centre, was set up sometime in early 1985 by Tipper Gore, the wife of Al Gore, former senator for Tennessee, and the man who allegedly had the 2004 US election stolen from him by George Dubya Bush.

Tipper, having taken offence to the lyrical content on Prince's *Purple Rain* soundtrack album, which she'd purchased that day, decided to launch a crusade against what she saw as the slippery slope to moral turpitude. Firstly, she garnered support from her society friends, who also happened to be wives of highly prominent men in Washington, including Susan Baker (wife of James), and formed the P.M.R.C. to alert the general public to 'the growing trend in music towards lyrics that

are sexually explicit, excessively violent, or glorify the use of drugs and alcohol.' The P.M.R.C.'s first order of business was to call upon the R.I.A.A. (Recording Industry Association of America) to 'exercise voluntary self-restraint, perhaps by developing guidelines and/or a rating system, such as that of the movie industry'.

This was just one of six directives Gore and Baker were calling for. The other five, according to a 1985 issue of the *Washington Post*, were as follows: print lyrics on album covers; keep explicit covers under the counter; establish a ratings system for concerts; reassess the contracts of performers who engage in violence and explicit sexual behaviour on stage and establish a citizen and record-company media watch that would pressure broadcasters not to air 'questionable talent'. Guns N' Roses response was to place stickers on their subsequent albums which advised prospective buyers that said albums contained language which some listeners may find objectionable. And if so, they could always F?!* Off and buy something from the New Age section instead.

## POISON

Poison are an American glam-metal band who, during their 25 year-to-date career, have sold in excess of 25 million albums worldwide.

Much has been made of the enmity between Guns N' Roses and their mid-80s West Hollywood contemporaries. Indeed, the deep-seated animosity dates back to a time before Guns N' Roses even existed, when Slash, having passed an audition to join Poison, turned the gig down upon discovering that he'd be expected to dye his curls blond, wear satin chic, and daub his face with heavy make-up. Then, once G N' R were up and running, but prior to either band securing a record deal, they would occasionally appear together on the same bill at the Troubadour or one of the other clubs on Sunset Strip. As neither band had any real following at the time, they would take turns at headlining. But whereas the Gunners were happy with the arrangement, whenever it was Poison's turn to open, singer Bret Michaels would usually end the band's set by inviting the audience to a party. Since the crowd consisted largely of freeloaders who never needed a second invitation to a free bash, the Gunners usually ended up playing to a near-empty room.

The hostilities continued even after both bands had secured their coveted record deals and released their respective debut albums. Poison's new guitarist, C.C. DeVille (born Bruce Anthony Johannesson), who was only in the band owing to Slash's refusal, took to wearing a top hat on stage. Slash, although happy to admit to *Kerrang!* journalist Mick Wall that he

might not be the first rock 'n' roller to wear a top hat, he was certainly the only one to be doing so at that particular juncture. Having caught up with DeVille at the Rainbow one evening, he proceeded to get said point across by threatening to shoot the gullable guitarist.

Poison's unbridled hostility towards Guns N' Roses even extended beyond the band's members and their inner-circle. In 1987 a female Geffen publicist successfully sued Michaels and bassist Bobby Dall for assault for having dumped a bucket of ice water over her in what appeared to have been retaliation for various unsavoury comments made about their band by certain unnamed members of Guns N' Roses.

Poison's founding line-up of Bret Michaels, Bobby Dall, guitarist Matt Smith, and drummer, Rikki Rockett, all hailed from Mechanicsburg, Pennsylvania. The quixotic quartet formed in 1984 as Paris, but elected for the rather more confrontational-sounding Poison after seeing the name on a T-shirt worn by drummer Mick Shrimpton in the side-splitting *rock*umentary *This Is Spinal Tap*. They also decided on a change of location and moved to Los Angeles, where their penchant for make-up, garish stage costumes, and overblown hair-dos fitted in perfectly with the L.A. music scene of the mid-to-late 1980's. But the rockers had barely unpacked their hair bleach and curlers when Smith, who was about to become a father for the first time, quit the band and returned to Pennsylvania so he could be near his new-born child.

Having recruited C.C. Deville to replace Smith, the band signed to independent label, Enigma Records and headed into the studio to record their debut album, *Look What The Cat Dragged In*, which was released in May, 1986. And although their debut single, 'Cry Tough', failed to chart, the subsequent releases, 'Talk Dirty To Me', 'I Want Action' and 'I Won't Forget You' were all massive hits and contributed to the album accruing sales in excess of two million. This, however, was small potatoes next to the band's follow-up, *Open Up And Say...Ahh!*, which has sold over eight million copies worldwide and also spawned four US Top 10 hits: 'Nothin' But A Good Time'; 'Fallen Angel'; a cover-version of the Loggins and Messina hit, 'Your Mama Don't Dance' and the ballad which would prove the

band's biggest hit, 'Every Rose Has It's Thorn'.

By the time of their third album, *Flesh & Blood*, which was released in June, 1990 and also went multi-platinum, Poison had established themselves as the fourth best-selling hard rock act of the previous decade, behind Bon Jovi, Def Leopard, and their bitter rivals, Guns N' Roses. The record produced four gold-selling hit singles: 'Unskinny Bop'; 'Ride The Wind'; 'Something To Believe In' and the album's title track, 'Flesh & Blood (Sacrifice)', which, despite the accompanying video being banned from MTV due to its explicit nature, reached # 2 on the Billboard 100. This guaranteed the backcombed boys a headlining world tour, and saw them performing at the Donington Monsters of Rock festival in August of that same year. A number of shows were recorded on the *Flesh & Blood* tour with the best takes subsequently appearing on the band's fourth (double) album *Swallow This Live,* which also includes four new studio tracks – tracks which proved to be the last recordings the band would make with C.C. in the line-up.

Despite Poison's success, DeVille's cocaine and alcohol intake had become chronic and made him something of a liability, and the on-going conflict finally came to a head with Michaels and DeVille engaging in fisticuffs backstage at the 1991 MTV Video Music Awards. Michaels having finally lost patience when the erratic guitarist failed to remember which song he was supposed to be playing.

DeVille's replacement was 20 year-old Pennsylvanian-born, Ritchie Kotzen, who was installed in time to record Poison's fifth album, *Native Tongue*, released in February, 1993. C.C.'s departure also called time on the band's trademark anthemic party tunes and although the album generally received favourable reviews in the music press, it provided just one solitary single, 'Stand', and accrued just one million sales worldwide. Sometime during the resulting promotional tour, Kotzen was fired when it came to light that he had become romantically involved with Rockett's fiancée, Deanna Eve. Kotzen's replacement was Blues Saraceno.

In May, 1994, recording for what would be the band's sixth album, *Crack A Smile*, was brought to an abrupt halt when Michaels suffered multiple facial injuries and four broken fingers after losing control of his Ferrari. By the time the singer was able to resume recording, however, the industry had undergone a swift shift away from '80's 'hair-metal', which, coupled with the resulting loss of interest and support from their label, Capitol Records, saw the unfinished album shelved indefinitely. In November, 1996, Capitol did, however, release the *Greatest Hits 1986-1996* compilation, which achieved platinum status despite the lack of a promotional tour.

It wasn't until the summer of 1999, by which time Michaels and DeVille had ended their six-year spat and brought the cleaned-up guitarist back into the fold at the expense of Saraceno, that Poison finally went out on the road again, playing to ecstatic crowds – including a sell-out 18,000 at Detroit's Pine Knob Amphitheatre – and meriting an appearance on VH1's *Behind the Music*.

In March, 2000 *Crack a Smile... and More!* finally saw the light of day, and later that same year Poison released their eighth album, *Power to the People,* which is a combination of both brand-new studio songs and live tracks culled from recordings of the band's 1999 and 2000 tours. A ninth album, *Hollywierd*, which consists entirely of new material, was released in May, 2002 but failed to impress either the critics or the fans, who were equally scathing in their appraisal of its inferior production quality.

In the summer of 2006, Poison celebrated twenty years in the music business with their '*20 Years Of Rock*' tour, with fellow aging L.A. rockers, Cinderella in support. It proved so successful that the band released an anniversary, best-of album: *The Best Of Poison: 20 years Of Rock* the following April, which saw them grace the Billboard Top 20 for the first time since 1993.

# PRICE, BILL

The unassuming English-born engineer, who is best known for his studio work with both the Sex Pistols and The Clash, worked on both of the *Use Your Illusion* albums.

Having gained a qualification in electronics from working on missile guidance systems for Plessey, Price left the company in 1962 to embark on a recording career at Decca Records' West Hampstead studios, where he was called upon to apply his burgeoning talents to hits for the likes of Tom Jones and Engelbert Humperdinck. Although he was reasonably happy at Decca, Bill could not ignore the call from legendary Beatles producer, George Martin, who lured him away by offering him the position of chief engineer at his newly-formed AIR Studios in London's West End, where, amongst other things, he worked on the score for the James Bond movie, *Live And Let Die*, which was subsequently recorded by Guns N' Roses and appears on *Use Your Illusion 1*. It is, however, the now-defunct Wessex Studio in North London with which Price has become synonymous, for it was there that he worked on the Sex Pistols' seminal album, *Never Mind The Bollocks* as well as The Clash's double album masterpiece, *London Calling*. He was kept busy throughout the '80s working with the likes of Elton John, Pete Townsend, the Jesus & Mary Chain and Mick Jones' post-Clash outfit, Big Audio Dynamite, and the '90s saw him colluding with one-time Led Zeppelin frontman, Robert Plant, The Cult and, of course, Guns N' Roses.

Tom Zutaut had actually first approached Price back in 1986 with a view to his working on *Appetite For Destruction*. Negotiations were apparently well under way to bring the Gunners over to London to record the album at Wessex, when David Geffen had a change of heart and insisted that all the recording was to be done in Los Angeles. The last-minute change in location, however, meant an alternative producer would also have to be found as Price had long-standing commitments at Wessex and was also reluctant to leave his young family.

When the time came for Guns N Roses to begin work on what eventually became *Use Your Illusion I & II*, Geffen, realising that the colossal 30+ song project was running behind schedule – and over budget – again came a-knocking on Price's door, asking him to team up with Mike Clink. This time, however, although Price was willing to temporarily relocate to Los Angeles, Guns N' Roses was now not only the most dangerous band in the world, they were also the biggest, and the producer found himself having to audition for the job. As he was unfamiliar with all the new material, rather

than pick something compli- cated, Price chose the up-front, in-your-face rocker 'Right Next Door To Hell', which he set about by making a heavily compressed mix of the backing track before then adding Axl's vocal on top. Both Geffen and the band were delighted with the finished prod- uct, and Price returned to London to pack a larger suitcase.

With on-going support from both Clink and in-house engineer, Jim Mitchell, Price first worked his way through the twenty songs already down on tape before then working on each new track as and when it was ready. And as the albums weren't completed in time for the *Use Your Illusion* world tour, it was decided that Clink would get the band into whatever studio happened to be available on one of their days off between shows to record all the parts and then send the rough mixes back to L.A. Once Price had worked his magic, he would then jet out to whichever city the band happened to be playing in at the time and show them the finished results.

# R'

## RAINBOW BAR AND GRILL

The Rainbow Bar and Grill, which is located at 9015 Sunset, West Hollywood, is one of L.A.'s most renowned watering holes and features in several Guns N' Roses videos.

Although the Rainbow is a bar and restaurant in the traditional sense and is typical of the eating establishments dotted along Sunset Strip, the upstairs 'Over The Rainbow' room, which comprises of a full bar, dancefloor and DJ booth, has become the exclusive reserve of prominent musicians. During the 1970s, rock luminaries such as John Lennon, Ringo Starr, Keith Moon, Neil Diamond and Led Zeppelin could all be found at their favourite tables. And it was not unknown for the King, Elvis Presley, to drop by with his entourage at the end of a day's filming. By the late '80's, the L.A. music scene had drifted towards heavy metal and the Rainbow followed suit which saw Lemmy from Mötorhead, Mötley Crüe and, of course, Guns N' Roses taking up semi-permanent residence. Indeed, such was the Gunners' regard and affection for the Rainbow that it features in all three promo videos for the band's unofficial power-ballad trilogy: 'Don't Cry'; 'November Rain' and 'Estranged'.

The Rainbow was originally owned by movie director, Vincente Minnelli, father of Liza, who at the time, was married to Liza's mother, Judy Garland. This soon led to it becoming something of a favourite hangout for Hollywood's 'A-List' and it was the setting for Joe DiMaggio's first date with his future wife, Marilyn Monroe. It is also where John 'Jake Blue' Belushi ate his last meal (lentil Soup) before succumbing to a fatal drugs overdose in the nearby Chateau Marmont.

## RAPIDFIRE

Rapidfire was a Los Angeles-based quartet which featured Axl on vocals prior to his joining Hollywood Rose.

On 25 May, 1983, the quartet – which, apart from Axl, featured Kevin Lawrence on guitar, Mike Hammernik on bass, and drummer Chuck Gordon – recorded an 8-track, 5-song demo: 'Ready To Rumble'; 'All Night Long'; 'The Prowler'; 'On The Run' and 'Closure'. As this is the earliest known recording featuring Axl Rose's vocal talents, which according to Lawrence are reminiscent of those of Judas Priest's frontman, Rob Halford, there is much interest in the demo tape. Despite Axl's legal attempts to prevent him from doing so, Lawrence intends to release the songs commercially and the accompanying CD booklet is set to contain several photographs of the then non-tattooed future G N' R frontman.

# REUNION

The "will they, won't they?" question surrounding a possible reunion of the Guns N' Roses classic line-up of Axl, Slash, Izzy, Duff, and Steven, is still the subject of much debate amongst the band's fans.

I, like the majority of Guns N' Roses fans, have always believed that a reconstitution of the band's original line-up is highly unlikely to occur, largely owing to Izzy, Slash and Duff's respective grievances towards Axl. But, like many others, I allowed myself to be fooled into believing the impossible might well come to pass when snippets began circulating in the music press on both sides of the Atlantic – as well as appearing on various websites – that all five original members would come together to commemorate the 20th anniversary of the release of *Appetite For Destruction*. The proposed date and setting for this mouth-watering prospect was Saturday 28, July 2007, at West Hollywood's Key Club, where Steven Adler's new band, Adler's Appetite – with L.A. Guns in support – was booked to perform.

Needless to say, Axl failed to put in an appearance, but Adler's Appetite was joined on stage by Izzy and Duff for a thumping rendition of 'Mr. Brownstone' (Izzy also clambered back on stage for 'Mama Kin'), while Slash watched on from the wings before departing for a "prior commitment". Before leaving, the guitarist told reporters he'd been inundated with calls and e-mails ever since the reunion was first touted, and that although he was happy to come along and support Steven, who had finally put his well-documented drug problems behind him and was making music again, he'd purposely avoided getting up on stage in order to quash the mounting speculation that the Gunners would indeed be getting back together.

Steven, however, still remains hopeful that a full 'blow-out' Guns N' Roses reunion will take place sometime in the future. "I believe I made it this far for a reason," he told Billboard.com referring to his aforementioned drug problems. "I want to finish what we started.

And with the love and support I got from those guys (not to mention the $2.3 million in damages), I think we can reunite. I'm gonna leave it up to Axl. That's gonna be Axl's call. I love Axl, and I know he'll make the right call."

## REED, DIZZY

Dizzy Reed, born Darren Arthur Reed on 18, June, 1963 in Hinsdale, Illinois, joined Guns N' Roses as keyboardist in 1990, and aside from Axl Rose, is the band's longest-serving member.

Having been taught the rudiments of the organ at an early age by his grandmother, Dizzy played in a succession of local garage bands in Colorado, where the family had relocated. But, having decided to seek a professional career in music, he, like his future G N' R buddies Axl, Izzy and Duff, made the move to Los Angeles in order to realise his ambitions. Apart from knowing his way around a keyboard, Dizzy was also a budding guitarist, and shortly after arriving in L.A. he replaced August Worchell in a band called Johnny Crash. But that particular venture proved exceedingly short-lived as the band decided to split shortly after his inclusion.

His introduction to the wonderful world of Guns N' Roses came in 1985 when his group, The Wild, was rehearsing in a studio adjacent to the one the Gunners

were using. A shared passion for keyboards and pianos soon led to his striking up a friendship with Axl, and the two kept in touch even after G N' R's meteoric rise to stardom. Whether Dizzy was hoping anything would come of his friendship with Axl is a matter of conjecture, but in 1990 he was invited to join Axl and the rest of G N' R in the studio to add keyboards to several songs the band was currently recording for the *Use Your Illusion* albums. And as the Gunners would be going out on a massive world tour to promote the records, and would therefore require a full-time keyboardist, Dizzy was brought in as a permanent member. The induction did not go smoothly, however, and Slash and Izzy have both since gone on record to say that none of the band – with the exception of Axl, of course – spoke to Dizzy for at least two weeks after his joining.

They were not alone, as many of the band's ever-expanding legion of fans also held strong reservations about Dizzy's inclusion in the G N' R line-up. They felt the introduction of keyboards was taking the Gunners' sound ever further away from the rough and ready "street" sound so evident on *Appetite For Destruction* and that had attracted them to the band in the first place. But for every detractor still clinging on to the belief that keyboards had no place in rock music, there were scores of open-minded fans who appreciated Dizzy's skilful melodies on songs such as 'November Rain', 'Estranged' and 'Civil War'. And rather than risk enraging the diehards by drowning the band's back catalogue with keyboards during live shows, Dizzy chose to instead provide back-up percussion.

Of course, Slash's resentment of keyboards and keyboardists eventually mellowed and he subsequently invited Dizzy to play on the first Snakepit album. The keyboardist also guested on Duff's solo album, *Believe In Me*, as well as Gilby's post G N' R projects and current Gunners bassist, Tommy Stinson's solo album, *Village Gorilla Head*. It isn't only rock music which floats Dizzy's boat, however, for he is an aficionado of Christian Music pioneer, Larry Norman and appears on his 1998 *Copper Wires* album. He has also composed music for the score to director Joel Milner's movie, *The Still Life,* which was released in August, 2007, as well as appearing in Milner's latest movie, *Celebrity Art Show*, which is scheduled for release in 2008.

Today, beside performing with Guns N' Roses, Dizzy also plays keyboards and guitar in his own band, Hookers 'N' Blow, which belts out standard rock classics – as well as the occasional G N' R standard. His wife Lisa, although a teacher by profession, is an author by vocation, and her novel, *Ember's Flame*, was published in 2004 by Twenty First Century Publishing.

# RICHMAN, JOSH

Josh Richman is an actor, writer, producer and director who wrote the additional [spoken] verse for Guns N' Roses' cover of 'Knockin' On Heaven's Door' which appears on *Use Your Illusion II*.

Josh, who also goes by the name "8 Ball", was born on 21 November, 1962, in Los Angeles, California. His first acting job came in 1983 with an un-credited guest appearance in the American TV science fiction series, *V: Series 1*, alongside future Freddie Kruger star, Robert Englund. A second sci-fi role came in 1985 when he appeared as a teacher's aide in *The Twilight Zone*. His first significant role came the following year in *River's Edge*, starring Keanu Reeves and Dennis Hopper. Further roles followed in *Thrashin'*, *Modern Girls*, and *The Allnighter*, as well as the 1989 cult movie, *Heathers*, starring Winona Ryder and Christian Slater. Although these weren't exactly 'blink-and-you'll-

miss-'em' roles, they weren't going to see him strolling up the red carpet on Oscars night either. His latest role is in the 2007 movie, *The Education of Charlie Banks*, which was directed by Limp Bizkit frontman, Fred Durst.

At the time of writing, Richman is the club promoter at The Roxy on Sunset Strip, and he also manages a Los Angeles-based rock band, Deadsy, whose video for their single, 'The Key To Gramercy Park', was also directed by Fred Durst.

## RIGHT NEXT DOOR TO HELL

'Right Next Door To Hell', which opens the musical fare on G N' R's *Use Your Illusion I*, was written by Axl following an argument with his next-door neighbour, Gabriella Kantor.

In the early hours of Tuesday 30 October, 1990, a squad car from the nearby West Hollywood Sheriff's station responded to a late-night call from Axl's next-door neighbour, Gabriella Kantor.

The story goes that Kantor, having finally tired of Axl's now near-incessant arguing with Erin – which was usually accompanied by loud music blasting out from the G N' R singer's stereo – confronted Axl in the hallway. In a subsequent statement relating to her argument with Axl, Kantor claimed the singer had snatched her car keys away from her and thrown them from the twelfth-floor balcony of their apartment building into the bushes below, before then hitting her over the head with a wine bottle.

Axl's version of events is somewhat different. According to his statement, Kantor was a crazed, over-zealous fan, and that the fracas was just the latest episode in a long-standing feud between the two which had been going on ever since he'd moved into his apartment. He also claimed it was Kantor who had been making a nuisance of herself and that he had only gone out into the hallway to tell her to "shut the fuck up". He later told MTV's Kurt Loder that Erin had suffered a miscarriage the day prior to his fight with Kantor, which may have been the reason for his less-than-tactful response. Kantor, however, was not to know this and had retaliated by swinging the wine bottle she was carrying at him. Axl managed to prise the bottle away from her, but as he went to close the door Kantor flung her car keys over his head into his living area as a means of gaining access to his apartment.

Axl stood firm and slammed the door in Kantor's face, and it was while she was pounding away on the outside of his door that he despatched the keys over the balcony before calling the Sheriff's office.

But as Axl had previously filed a police harassment charge against that same Sheriff's office, it was hardly surprising that no one responded to his call. Less than an hour later, however, two deputies arrived in response to Kantor's own call, and rather than accept the singer's version of what had occurred – or his claim that any bruises Kantor might have on her person were self-inflicted owing to her having repeatedly thrown herself against his front door – the bemused deputies arrested the singer and bundled him off to jail. Axl was released sometime the following day, after posting $5,000 bail but the charges were subsequently dropped when he passed a lie-detector test which indicated that he had been telling the truth all along. Rather than risk further altercations with his irate neighbour, however, Axl moved out of the apartment building to take up residence in a newly-purchased house high up in the Hollywood Hills.

# ROCKET QUEEN

Rocket Queen, the rabble-rousing finale to *Appetite For Destruction*, is Axl's ode to a girl he knew – and possibly dated for a short period of time – shortly after moving to Los Angeles.

Axl later told *Hit Parader* magazine that at the time of their relationship, the girl in question was trying to put a band together which she intended to call Rocket Queen. He also revealed the song was in homage to her, and that the ultimate verse, which contains the lines 'Don't ever leave me/Say you'll always be there', was a personal message of hope and friendship.

'Rocket Queen' has to be unique in the pantheon of rock 'n' roll music in that it contains a recorded sex act within the mix. Legend has it that Axl, having come up with the idea to add pornographic sounds to the song, headed out into West Hollywood and came to some arrangement with a hooker – listed as Barbie (Rocket Queen) Von Grief on *Appetite*'s acknowledgements – brought her back to the studio and fucked her under the mixing consol. Ms Von Grief was apparently well known amongst West Hollywood's rock fraternity for she also received a credit on L.A. Guns' 1988 eponymous debut album. Another article, however, which subsequently appeared in *Classic Rock* magazine, wilfully named and shamed Adriana Smith – at the time the on-off squeeze of the soon-to-be-deposed Steven Adler, and also a close and intimate friend of Axl's – as the girl in question. Sources close to the Gunners, however, have since put the story of Smith's involvement down to nothing more than apocryphal journalism.

The somewhat bizarre scenario of Axl going hell for leather with the hooker – in keeping with the song's tempo – was backed up by Rumbo's in-house engineer, Steve Thompson. In an interview which can be found on www.heretoday-gonetomorrow.com, Thompson confirms that the singer did indeed bring a woman of questionable character into the studio, where up to thirty minutes of grunting and groaning was captured on tape and subsequently added to the song's final mix.

# ROCK IN RIO

Rock in Rio, and Rock in Rio Lisboa, is a series of rock festivals organised by Brazilian entrepreneur, Roberto Medina, three of which have featured appearances by Guns N' Roses.

Back in January, 1985, the year of the inaugural Rock in Rio festival, which featured a bill of both international and Brazilian artists alongside headline acts including Queen, Iron Maiden and AC/DC, Axl and Izzy were preoccupied honing their respective talents in Hollywood Rose, while Slash and Steven were likewise preoccupied in Road Crew and Duff was still in Seattle flitting from one dead-end punk band to another. But by the time of the second festival in January 1991, which was again staged in Rio de Janeiro, at the city's colossal 200,000 capacity Maracana Stadium, Guns N' Roses were the biggest band on the planet and were the obvious choice to co-headline the nine-day event alongside Prince and George Michael.

As with the first event, each headline act was required to give two performances, and the Gunners' first appearance, on 20 January, was their first live outing since Farm Aid IV the previous April. Not only was this Matt Sorum's first show since replacing Steven Adler, it also served as a means of introducing Dizzy Reed. Perhaps not surprisingly, given that the *Use Your Illusion* albums were currently being mixed back in Los Angeles, the set-list featured several of the songs scheduled to appear on the new records. This was by far the biggest audience the Gunners had yet faced, but instead of seizing the opportunity to justify the hype surrounding them, Axl brought the proceedings to an untimely conclusion some twenty minutes sooner than scheduled simply because he

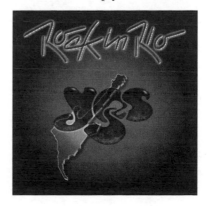

didn't feel the audience was being responsive enough.

Controversy also reared its ugly head on the night of the Gunners' second headline show three days later, on 23 January, when fellow rockers Judas Priest – who were second on the bill – were informed some three hours before they were due to go on that Axl was refusing to perform that evening unless their band was prepared to consent to his demands. Not only would the Brummie rockers have to agree to refrain from using any of their on-stage pyrotechnics, cut their set by twenty minutes and conduct one encore only, singer Rob Halford wouldn't be allowed to take to the stage – as he had done for the past decade – on the back of a motorcycle. And Judas Priest wasn't the only band to suffer. Michael Wilton and Scott Rockenfield, the guitarist and drummer from the American rock band Queensryche, who'd appeared on that same stage earlier in the evening, were forcibly ejected from the side-stage area by the Gunners' security – despite having earlier received permission from Axl to watch the show.

Despite Axl's prima-donna behaviour, Guns N' Roses were invited back to co-headline the third Rock in Rio festival in January, 2001. By this time of course, only the singer – unless one counts the long-serving Dizzy Reed – remained from the band's original line-up, but the 150,000 strong, largely Brazilian audience didn't seem to care and sang along to the old standards. Axl, however, still felt the need to explain the situation, and brought his Brazilian-born housekeeper, Beta Lebeis, out onto the stage to act as his translator while he took time out during the two-and-a-half-hour show to castigate his former bandmates for having supposedly worked very hard to do everything they could to prevent him from being there. And in what was surely meant as a slap in the face for Slash, Axl then lauded the guitarist's replacement, Paul Tobias, for having spent seven years working through the darkness to save Guns N' Roses.

Buckethead's untimely departure from Guns N' Roses in April, 2004, meant the band were unable to participate in the fourth Rock in Rio festival the following month, which had inexplicably relocated to Lisbon, Portugal. They did, however, appear at the second Lisbon RiR festival in May, 2006 where they headlined alongside Roger Waters, Red Hot Chili Peppers, The Darkness, and Kasabian.

# ROSE, W. AXL

W. Axl Rose, who was born William Brucc Rose Jr in the small college town of Lafayette, Indiana, on 6 February, 1962, is the long-serving singer in Guns Roses.

William Jr, or "Bill", as he was known, was just 2-years-old when his father, William Rose Snr, a renowned rabble-rouser and bar-room brawler, abandoned the family, never to be seen again. When his mother, Sharon, remarried two years later to local Pentecostal preacher, L. Stephen Bailey,

with whom she would have two more children – Amy and Stuart – her new husband kindly agreed to legally adopt young Bill and gave him his surname. And as Axl would have been too young to form any memories of that period, he grew up believing the stringent reverend was his biological father.

The Bailey household, however, was rarely a scene of domestic bliss, as the new patriarch was a deeply religious but often violent man, who Axl would later claim had sexually and physically abused both himself and his two siblings. His mother, despite herself suffering both extreme mental and physical abuse at the hands of her new husband, refused to leave Bailey, which, perhaps not surprisingly, led to the young and highly impressionable Bill accepting that domestic violence was normal behaviour in every American homestead. Indeed, in an interview with *Rolling Stone* in 1992, Axl even went so far as to blame his step-father's treatment

of his mother – and her failure to intervene on her children's behalf – for his own problems forming meaningful relationships with women. It wasn't until 1979, by which time the 17-year-old Bill had let his bronze-coloured hair grow out, and was singing in local rock bands – most notably 'Axl', which subsequently provided him with his lasting moniker – that

he discovered the truth about his biological father. In a fit of pique, he re-adopted his birth name but from that day on he would only refer to himself as W. Rose.

As with most victims of domestic violence, Axl developed a reckless attitude towards authority, and his delinquent tendencies, such as bunking school, public drunkenness and brawling in the street,

soon brought him to the attention of the Lafayette police. He would later claim to have been arrested and thrown in jail on more than twenty occasions, whilst admitting to having only been guilty of five of these incidents. Most of the offences were public disorder charges which warranted nothing more than a slap on the wrist, or at worst, a night in the slammer to sleep off a 'drunk'. But by becoming a 'repeat offender', he began to receive stiffer sentences, one of which resulted in his spending three months in jail following his failure to pay a fine for an undisclosed earlier offence. According to the Tippecanoe County Court records, from July, 1980 through to September, 1982, Axl spent a total of ten days in adult jail. As soon as Guns N' Roses hit the big time and the money began rolling in, he hired a lawyer to 'clean up' his dubious hometown past.

Axl's passion for singing first emerged when he was 5-years-old, singing gospel songs (the only music allowed in the Bailey household) in the choir at the local Pentecostal church, where he also performed at services with his siblings as the 'Bailey Trio'. In addition to singing in church, he also participated in his school chorus class and began studying classical piano, which would serve him well in later years. From 1980 onwards, having tired of living in Hicksville, USA, Axl began hitch-hiking out to L.A., where he often hooked up with his old high school friend, Jeff Isbelle, a.k.a Izzy Stradlin, who'd fled Lafayette immediately after graduation in search of rock 'n' roll stardom. (The scene was 'recreated' in the opening sequence to the 'Welcome To The Jungle' video). On 19 December, 1982, Axl, together with on-off girlfriend, Gina Siler, who claims to have paid for his now-famous W. Axl Rose tattoo, made the move permanent, and

the pair set up home at 1921 Whitley Avenue in Hollywood.

Somewhat surprisingly, given that Izzy himself was fresh out of Lafayette, his new friends looked upon Axl as a hapless hick and tended to keep him at arms length. But the aspiring singer was determined to succeed in the City of Angeles and began scouring the 'musicians wanted' section of the local music press. His first – short-lived – foray into West Hollywood's burgeoning music scene came with Rapidfire in early 1983, who, if it hadn't been for Axl's subsequent success with Guns N' Roses, would have long-since slipped into musical obscurity. That said, Rapidfire did at least provide Axl with the opportunity to flex his lungs in front of a discernable audience, and emboldened him to persevere with his dream. When Izzy first moved to L.A., he'd been befriended by budding musicians,

Chris Weber and Tracii Guns, and as he and Tracii were both occupied with their respective aspiring bands, he introduced Axl to Weber in the hope the two might get something going. This they did, and having assembled likeminded musicians, they formed the band Rose (Axl did initially toy with the idea of resurrecting his adopted moniker for the new venture before deciding on his surname instead). This in turn, was extended to the far glitziersounding Hollywood Rose, by which time Izzy had joined their number, and the band set about garnering attention by procuring any support slot available, as well as playing the occasional headline gig. Over the ensuing 12 months, musicians would come and go without much ado, but Axl and Izzy remained unfazed. And the two finally sensed a sea change in their fortunes when their new bass player, Duff McKagan, brought in Slash and Stephen Adler – and Guns N' Roses was born.

The Gunners' original five-piece line-up would remain together for the next five or so years, during which time they broke both chart and attendance records with consummate ease. But, as Axl himself subsequently sang in 'November Rain', nothing lasts forever, and the first indication of this sad yet perennial truth came with Steven's dismissal in 1990. This was largely due to Axl's escalating ego – coupled with a refusal to accept criticism from the ranks. Yet this was but the first schism, and one by one Izzy, Slash and lastly Duff, followed Adler out of the door. Instead of opting for a solo career – which in hindsight might have been the lesser of two evils – Axl believed he could prolong the life of Guns N' Roses' by bringing in a succession of musicians, who, despite their respective abilities, were never truly going to replace their more illustrious, and much lamented predecessors.

Although *Chinese Democracy* will eventually see the light of day – if not in February 2008 as currently being touted, then at some point in the near future – fifteen long years of relative obscurity have passed since Axl last released an album of any worth. And although he is an astute and talented musician who will have no doubt kept his fickle finger on rock's throbbing pulse – which will at least ensure a highly-polished, quality product – it is unlikely today's ipod generation will spare much thought to the ideals of a guy old enough to have been at school with their parents.

## ROSE TATTOO

Rose Tattoo is the Australian rock band whose song, 'Nice Boys (Don't Play Rock 'N' Roll)' was covered by Guns N' Roses and appears on the *GNR Lies* album.

Rose Tattoo was originally formed in Sydney in 1976. While the Aussie rockers recorded several impressive albums, one of which, 1982's *Scarred For Life*, would have a significant impact on Los Angeles' burgeoning metal scene, the band is largely remembered thanks to Guns N' Roses having covered one of their songs. Although it has to be said, their singer, Angry Anderson, is also remembered for the saccharine-soaked ballad 'Suddenly', which featured as the wedding theme for the fictional TV marriage of Scott and Charlene from the Aussie soap *Neighbours*. The popularity of the soap in the UK, where it had been screened five days a week since 1986, saw the song reach #3 in the UK charts.

In 1992, although he had carved out a successful solo career as well as being something of a TV celebrity in his homeland, Anderson received an offer he couldn't refuse when Guns N' Roses invited him to reform Rose Tattoo in order to support them on the

Australian leg of their *Use Your Illusion* tour. Although the reconstituted band was well received, instead of using the G N' R shows as a springboard to greater things, once the tour was over the band members went their separate ways.

1998, however, brought a collective rethink and Rose tattoo reformed and found their niche touring around Australia and Europe. In August, 2006, by which time four of Rose Tattoo's one-time members had succumbed to various forms of cancer, the band was inducted into the ARIA (Australian Recording Industry Association) Hall of Fame. Despite the tragedies, the band continued performing, and in 2007 they once again supported Guns N' Roses, this time on the Australian leg of their *Chinese Democracy* tour.

## ROXY THEATRE, THE

The Roxy Theatre, which is located at 9009 West Sunset Boulevard, West Hollywood, is one of L.A.'s most famous music venues, and in 1986 played host to the then up-and-coming Guns N' Roses.

The legendary venue first opened its doors back in September, 1973 when co-owners, Elmer Valentine and Lou Adler, along with sleeping business partners Elliot Roberts, Peter Asher, and David Geffen, took over the lease from the then occupier Chuck Landis who had run a strip club called The Largo on the premises. The inaugural show featured Neil 'Crazy Horse' Young.

The following year saw the Roxy play host to the debut American run of Richard O'Brien's side-splitting and decidedly risqué stage play, *The Rocky Horror Show*. Indeed, it had been Adler who was responsible for bringing the play to America. The show was such a runaway success that it was made into a movie the following year with Tim Curry in the starring role of Dr. Frank-N-Furter, the transsexual transvestite from Transylvania.

Thanks to the likes of Guns N' Roses, Mötley Crüe, Poison et al, by the mid-80s the Roxy had built up a reputation as "the placc to play in L.A.". But it wasn't only the local talent that plied their trade here, for established artists such as Bruce Springsteen, whose 1975 shows are still talked about to this day, David Bowie, Nirvana, Tori Amos, Miles Davis, Al Stewart and Jane's Addiction have all trodden the boards of the venue's small stage. And it was here during December, 1973 that the zany, and offbeat Frank Zappa and his Mothers of Invention recorded their celebrated album, *Roxy and Elsewhere*.

Somewhat surprisingly, Guns N' Roses only performed at the Roxy on three occasions. The first came on Saturday 18 January, 1986, when their 17-song set featured several covers, including early set perennials 'Jumpin' Jack Flash' and 'Mam Kin', as well as more rarely performcd versions of Elvis' 'Heartbreak Hotel' and Wings' 1979 hit 'Goodnight Tonight'. They returned to the venue two months later on Friday 28 March when they performed two sets, the second of which saw Axl gyrating on stage during 'Anything Goes' with a scantily-clad stripper. Their third and final Roxy tear-up came on Saturday 31 August, 1986, when they advertised themselves as "Diamonds In The Rough".

Today, however, as with the majority of the clubs dotted along Sunset Strip, the Roxy is a mere shadow of its former, glorious self, but fans can still get a feel for those halcyon days thanks to the extensive array of photographs that line the walls to serve as a constant reminder of its heady, decadent past. It wasn't only the stage that saw plenty of rock 'n' roll debauchery, for the club's small upstairs bar, On The Rox, overlooking Sunset Strip, has earned a lasting place in L.A. folklore as being where John Belushi partied the night away before shuffling off his cocaine-coated mortal coil. It was also a regular hangout for John Lennon, who spent a significant part of his legendary 'L.A. lost weekend' of 1975 here in the company of Alice Cooper, Harry Neilson and Keith Moon. In the 1980s the Roxy played host to sordid sex parties hosted by shamed Hollywood Madame, Heidi Fleiss.

# S'

## SALAS, STEVIE

Stevie Salas, the guitar prodigy and highly-successful solo artist, was brought in by Axl Rose to work on *Chinese Democracy*.

Stevie, who has since been rated one of the top fifty guitarists of all time, is of Native-American descent (Mescalero Apache) and grew up in San Diego, California with a love of the ocean and no musical aspirations whatsoever. But his life was set to change when aged 15, he was given a homemade guitar by his brother-in-law. Within a matter of weeks Stevie and his fledgling band were playing high school dances and local clubs, and having discovered he was a natural on guitar, he decided to embark upon a career in music. Shortly after graduation, he left the comforts of home, bound for Los Angeles.

At first, like Izzy and Axl before him – and countless other aspiring musos who'd relocated to L.A. dreaming of hitting the big time – Stevie had to deal with the harsh reality that the City of Angels owed no one any favours, regardless of their musical virtuosity. Living a hand-to-mouth existence and crashing on studio couches in search of a paying gig wasn't exactly how he'd imagined his life, and no one would have blamed him had he gone home to San Diego to fulfil his childhood aspirations of becoming a coast guard. Fortunately, Stevie persevered, and his break came when Funkadelic maestro George Clinton – who was in need of a guitarist – wandered into the studio where he was eking a living as a session musician. This in turn led to his being offered a sizeable recording contract with Island Records, and before the year was out he was touring with Stevie Vai and Joe Satriani, and jet-setting around the world with Rod Stewart and Mick Jagger.

Whether Stevie's licks will survive to the finished mix of *Chinese Democracy* is solely down to Axl, but many of you will already be familiar with the guitarist's fretboard dexterity from the 1989 movie, *Bill and Ted's Excellent Adventure*. Remember the blistering, demon riffs played by San Demus' 700-year-old resident, Rufus (Played by George Carlin)? Well, yes, that was Stevie Salas.

# SEYMOUR, STEPHANIE

Stephanie Seymour is the ex-supermodel who dated Axl Rose for two years during the early '90s and appears in the promo videos for 'Don't Cry' and 'November Rain'.

The stunning, blue-eyed, American supermodel, who in 2000 would be ranked #91 on lads mag *FHM*'s 100 Sexiest Women, was born in San Diego, California, on 23 July, 1968. Stephanie began her modelling career in 1982 working in a succession of hometown department stores, but her big break came the following year when, aged 15, she won the Elite Model Management 'Look of the Year' contest. Her shapely, 5'10" physique was ideally suited for modelling swimwear and lingerie which led to numerous appearances in *Sports Illustrated* – even making it onto the front cover. She is also credited with helping the then little-known *Victoria's Secrets* grow into one of the world's best known lingerie and

hosiery companies. Stephanie's curvy attributes hadn't gone unnoticed by Elite's CEO, John Casablancas, who, despite being married at the time, first wooed her into his bed, and then into his life. Their "scandalous" four-year relationship had been manna from heaven as far as America's gossip columnists were concerned. And their poison pens were soon dripping with scurrilous ink again when she embarked on a tumultuous two-year relationship with Axl Rose in 1991, shortly after walking away from a failed one-year-old marriage to another musician; the lesser-known Tommy Andrews, with whom she had a son, Dylan Thomas Andrews.

Some might view Stephanie's appearances in the G N' R videos 'Don't Cry' and 'November Rain', in which she and Axl pose as a bride and groom, as prenuptial nepotism. But such was the singer's infatuation with his new girl he went so far as to pretend he'd hired a genuine minister to appear in the video, which meant they were legally bound. The couple got engaged for real on 4 February, 1993, only to then break up three weeks later following Axl's claims of Stephanie's infidelity with movie star and legendary womaniser, Warren Beatty, whom she'd been seeing at the time of encountering Axl.

In October, 1993, Seymour filed a counter-sue lawsuit against her estranged lover claiming he had "kicked and grabbed" her at a party at their Mediterranean-style Malibu home the previous Christmas. It seems that Axl flew into a rage when she decided to press ahead with the party when he had wanted to cancel. She also claimed that as soon as their red-faced guests had fled the house, Axl set about smashing bottles and glasses, before dragging her barefoot through the broken shards leaving her feet and lower body covered in a myriad of cuts and bruises.

Axl, however, had already fired the first shot earlier in the year when he filed a suit against the model in August claiming she was refusing to return $100,000 worth of jewellery he'd given to her as gifts. The case – as with the one involving Erin Everly – was settled out of court, and it is rumoured that Stephanie received a payment of $400,000. Shortly after splitting from Axl, she became involved with *Interview* magazine publisher, Peter Brant, and nine months later gave birth to their first child, whom they named Peter. The couple married in 1994 and a second son, Harry, followed shortly thereafter, while daughter Lilly Margaret was born in 2004.

## SHAMROCK STUDIOS

Shamrock Studios is – or was – located at 5634 Santa Monica Boulevard, and it was here on 31 August, 1984, that Hollywood Rose performed a special 'after hours' show, taking to the stage at 2.am. The crudely-sketched flyer used to promote the show featured cartoon-esque images of Axl, Izzy and co, along with the band's logo.

## SILLY KILLERS

The Silly Killers was a Seattle-based punk band which briefly featured a pre G N' R Duff McKagan in its line-up.

The Silly Killers was formed in 1982, and along with The Fartz and Wad Squad, performed at the

very first punk gig in Tacoma, Washington that same summer. The show, which was staged in a dingy basement, was brought to an unscheduled and unsavoury conclusion, however, when a dozen or so of Tacoma's finest, dressed in full riot gear, stormed the basement under the mistaken assumption that an insurrection was taking place.

Later that same year – by which time Duff had departed the band, but was on hand to provide backing vocals on one of the tracks – the Silly Killers released their one and only vinyl offering, the 4-track 'Not That Time Again' EP, on Seattle's legendary punk label, No Three Records. Not surprisingly, the songs on offer – 'Not That Time Again', 'Social Bitch' (the song on which Duff provides backing vocals), 'Knife Manual' and 'Sissie Faggots' – were delivered in the typical 1-2-3-4 let's go punk style of the period, with perhaps just the faint whiff of a surf influence – especially on the opening riff to the title track. In 1992, Empty Records released

Gas Huffer's cover version of 'Knife Manual' as the b-side to a split single with Mudhoney, but as far as anyone can tell there don't appear to be any plans to reissue the Silly Killers' EP. That said, however, Duff McKagan's brief tenure with the band has ensured its name will live on, if only as a footnote in the Gunners' illustrious history.

## SIXX, NIKKI

Nikki Sixx is the bassist and main songwriter in American rock band, Mötley Crüe.

On the evening of 23 December, 1987, shortly after coming off the road opening for Alice Cooper, Slash, along with some of the guys from Megadeth, was standing within the ornate entrance of the Franklin Plaza Hotel – where he and the rest of the Gunners were now staying, having finally given up the rented apartment – awaiting the arrival of his favourite non-G N'R drug-buddy, Nikki

Sixx. Slash was intent on having a little festive fun chasing the Chinese dragon up, over and beyond the Hollywood hills before getting back into the groove with four shows over five nights at the Perkins Palace in Pasadena, commencing on Boxing Day.

Nikki, born Frank Carlton Serafino Feranna Jr. on 11 December, 1958 in San Jose, California, later reminisced in Mötley Crüe's collective autobiography, *The Dirt*, some fifteen years later, that by the time he and Ratt guitarist, Robbin Crosby arrived at Slash's hotel in a hired silver limousine, the pair had already gorged themselves on a gram of cocaine, causing the bassist to inadvertently throw-up over the beaver-haired top hat intended as a Christmas gift for Slash. Once Crosby had secured the narcotic necessaries from his dealer, the motley ensemble made a nuisance of themselves in the bars and clubs along Sunset Strip before returning to the Franklin to continue the party in Slash's room. They were somewhat surprised to find Crosby's dealer waiting for them with a stash of fine Persian heroin secreted about his person. Nikki, a latter-day Sid Vicious, in that he was well-known for using his body as a portable chemistry set and was happy to inject, smoke or swallow anything in search of the ultimate high, was too wasted to find a vein himself and had readily rolled up a sleeve and offered his outstretched arm to the dealer.

Although Slash hadn't partaken in the Persian, he'd knocked back enough Jack Daniels to fell a buffalo, and was therefore of little use when his girlfriend Sally tried to rouse him after finding a drooling Nikki lying comatose on the floor. Thankfully for Nikki, she'd had the wherewithal to call 911, otherwise the bassist might not be with us today.

Nikki, of course, has no recollection of the paramedics bundling him into an ambulance and ferrying him to the nearest hospital, but does remember having what he can only describe as an "out-of-body experience". He says he awoke to find himself floating around a brightly-lit emergency crash room, where two paramedics were frantically trying to save his sorry ass. Despite Nikki's heart having stopped for two full minutes, one of the paramedics – who Nikki says was a Crüe fan – saved him by injecting two vials of adrenaline into his failing heart. Several hours later, the hedonistic bassist – against medical advice – signed himself out of the hospital, returned to his apartment and administered a massive shot of heroin. This, the latest – and closest – in a line of near misses, was subsequently immortalised in the song, 'Kickstart My Heart', which appears on the band's *Dr. Feelgood* album.

This wasn't the first time Nikki's inability to 'just say no' had provided Mötley Crüe with a song. On Valentine's Day, 1986, follow-

ing a show at London's Hammersmith Odeon, the wayward bassist ended up OD-ing in a seedy West London opium den. In his eye-opening, best-selling book, *The Heroin Diaries: A Year In The Life Of A Shattered Rock Star*, he tells of how the fretful dealer – believing Nikki was dead – first attempted to revive the bassist with a baseball bat before giving up the ghost, carrying him outside and dumping his body in a skip. The experience was subsequently immortalised with the lyric 'Valentines in London found me in the trash', in the song 'Dancing On Glass' which features on *Girls, Girls, Girls*.

Another near-death incident occurred during the Mötley Crüe/ Guns N' Roses November '87 tour, when Nikki, Slash and Steven Adler sidled off to Slash and Steven's hotel room to shoot heroin. The West Hollywood alliance saw both bands drinking together on a regular basis, but it was the toxic trinity of Sixx, Slash, and Adler, who were responsible for the majority of the madcap mayhem. Mötley Crüe's irate manager, Doc McGee, went so far as to warn Slash that the Gunners would

be thrown off the tour unless he promised to stay away from both heroin and Nikki. The enforced abstinence, however, lasted just two days...

As the story goes, Slash became concerned for his friend when Nikki – who had told his compadres that he was going to his own room to fetch his bass for an impromptu jam – failed to return. When Slash and Steven entered Nikki's room they found the lanky bassist's blue-tinged body with the damning evidence still protruding from his tourniquet-clamped arm.

Slash, fearing that McGee would honour his earlier threat, dialled 911 while Steven dragged Nikki's unconscious form into the shower cubicle and attempted to revive him by dousing him with cold water. When that failed, and with no sound of an approaching siren, the drummer desperately began slapping Nikki about the face to bring him round.

Nikki sought professional help by entering rehab, but it wasn't until the band's reunion in 2004, that the father of five was finally able to declare himself sober. Following on from the short-lived Brides of Destruction, Nikki co-wrote songs for the bands Saliva, and Raven, as well as one song, 'The Monster Is Loose', for Meat Loaf's long-awaited *Bat Out Of Hell III*.

In September, 2007, Nikki's book, *The Heroin Diaries* was released in the US and soon shot into the *New York Times* best-sellers list. The book, which focuses on the bassist's journal entries in the 12-month period between Christmas 1986, and Christmas 1987 (when his drug intake was at its zenith), features present-day candid viewpoints from the bassist's fellow Mötleys, friends, family, business associates and ex-lovers. Together with his current side-project band, Sixx: A.M., Nikki also produced a soundtrack to accompany the book entitled *Life Is Beautiful* which was released on 21 August, 2007.

# SLASH

Slash, born Saul Hudson in Stoke-on-Trent, North Staffordshire on 23 July, 1965, was Guns N' Roses' lead guitarist from the band's incarnation in 1985, through to his untimely departure in 1996 following one too many fall-outs with Axl.

It was probably inevitable that Slash, given that both his parents made their living within the entertainment industry, would himself go on to find fame and

fortune in rock 'n' roll. His softly-spoken English father, Tony, was a graphic design artist and album sleeve designer during the 1970's. His most notable work came on Joni Mitchell's 1974, *Court And Spark* album, which reached #2 on the Billboard 100 and features the single, 'Free Man In Paris', which the Canadian-born singer/songwriter wrote about her then housemate – and Slash's future employer – David Geffen. His black, American-born mother, Ola, had been a moderately successful fashion designer for over a decade by the time she designed the costumes for David Bowie's 1976 cinematic debut in Nicholas Roeg's, *The Man Who Fell To Earth*. She had also designed the outfits the pop chameleon wore on the cover of his 1975, *Young Americans* album, and in addition had worked with Ringo Starr, John Lennon, Linda Ronstadt and James Taylor.

Ola returned to the US shortly after Slash was born in order to expand her business clientele, which forced Tony and his infant son to move in with his parents, where they would spend the next

four years before following Ola out to Los Angeles. They settled in Laurel Canyon, an elevated suburb of Los Angeles, and it was there that Slash's younger brother, Albion was born in 1972. By this time, however, the Hudson's marriage was in difficulty and the couple agreed to separate the following year. Shortly after the estrangement, Ola's relationship with David Bowie extended beyond the professional and surely made young Saul the envy of his classmates at Bancroft Junior High – one of whom was future G N' R collaborator, Steven Adler.

It was at his next school, Fairfax High, which also served as an alma mater to Red Hot Chili Peppers duo, Anthony Kiedis and Michael "Flea" Balzary, as well as future musical collaborators Dave Navarro, Dave Kushner and Lenny Kravitz, that Slash met life-long friend and confidant, Marc Cantor. Marc's family owned the famed L.A. institution Cantors Deli, located on North Fairfax, which in later years became something of a surrogate home to Slash, as well as a hangout for the pre-signed Guns N' Roses. It was also while he was at Fairfax that he received his monosyllabic nickname. As Slash later recalled, he, and just about every other Fairfax delinquent, tended to hang out and smoke pot at their buddy Matt Cassel's house. And it was Matt's father, Seymour – the character actor perhaps best known for his role as 'Dusty' in the 2001 movie *The Royal Tenanbaums* – who labelled the corkscrew-haired misfit "Slash", supposedly on account of his always seeming to be in a hurry to orchestrate his latest scam or hustle.

Although he had accrued an extensive knowledge of music, thanks to his parents' sizable record collection, the teenage Slash's interests lay in BMX biking. And such was his prowess that all around him believed he would have gone on to turn professional had it not been for his discovering the guitar. His first guitar – which came courtesy of his grandmother, with whom he was living at the time – was a battered flamenco one with only one string. One string, however, was

all it took to captivate the teenager's attention, and the old woman, perhaps sensing her grandson's embryonic talent for the instrument, went out and bought him an electric guitar. It mattered little that the Gibson Explorer copy was cheap and nasty and virtually impossible to keep in tune and Slash devoted much of his spare time to practicing, and developed his style playing along to his mother's record collection.

It soon became obvious to all who heard him play that young Slash was a natural, but he himself wasn't harbouring any thoughts of making it a career. He later told *Rolling Stone* that his epiphany came upon hearing Aerosmith's *Rocks* album for the first time, whilst he was trying to get to third base with an older girl. "It hit me like a fucking tonne of bricks," he told the reporter. "I sat there listening to it over and over, and totally blew off the girl. I remember riding my bike back to my grandma's house knowing that my life had changed forever. Now I identified with something."

As luck would have it, Steven had also been plotting a future in music and had been toying with the idea of taking up the guitar. He quickly abandoned that thought, however, upon realising that he was never going to hold a candle to his buddy, and instead opted to take up the drums. The pair formed the nucleus of what eventually became Road Crew, which introduced them to Duff McKagan, who in turn invited them to join an embryonic Guns N' Roses.

As with any band, it's the singer/lead guitar axis that tends to reap most of the plaudits and headlines, and Slash, with his trademark top hat (which he'd purloined from a second-hand clothing store called Retro Slut), and a bottle of Jack Daniels as a semi-constant companion, was the absolute embodiment of the rock god guitarist and was pivotal in G N' R's meteoric rise from aspiring glam-metal hopefuls to a global, multi-platinum selling phenomenon. Another reason for their success was undoubtedly the Gunners' collective belief in what they were trying to achieve, as well as an indomitable spirit, which saw them laugh in the face of early adversity. But 35 million album sales coupled with a 26-month, sell-out world tour will make a monster out of the most unassuming ego, and Slash found, to his dismay, that he and Axl were no longer on the same wavelength. So, on 30 October, 1996, the rock world was shocked to learn of the guitarist's departure from Guns N' Roses.

Instead of licking his wounds or avoiding the public's gaze by hiding away in his home high up in the Hollywood Hills, which had once belonged to movie moguls Cecil B DeMille and Roman Polanski, Slash hastily gathered his friends about him for the short-lived project, Slash's Blues Ball, as well as guesting on albums by the likes of Alice Cooper, Cheap Trick, Rod Stewart, Stevie Wonder and his old pal, Ronnie Wood. 2001, the same year he married girlfriend Perla Ferrar, (his five-year marriage to first wife, Renee Suran ended in divorce in 1997) saw the revival of his other side project, Snakepit, and the release of the platinum-selling album, *Ain't Life Grand*. The following year, Slash took to the stage with his old G N' R buddies, Duff and Matt, for a benefit/tribute show in honour of ex-Ozzy Osbourne drummer and mutual friend, Randy Castillo, who had recently succumbed to cancer. This in turn evolved into Velvet Revolver.

When he's not performing or recording with Velvet Revolver, Slash can be found relaxing at home with Perla, their two sons, London Emilio and Cash Anthony, and an ever-expanding menagerie

which includes fifty snakes, three cats and two iguanas.

## SLASH'S BLUES BALL

Slash's Blues Ball was the name given to Slash's two-year project which saw the guitarist's blues ensemble tour the US and Europe between 1996 and 1998, performing classic blues to appreciative audiences.

Although Slash announced his departure from Guns N' Roses in October, 1996, at the time of doing so even he couldn't have been sure whether his enforced exodus was going to be short-term or something rather more permanent. One option would have been to get on the phone and call up his old Snakepit buddies, but vocalist Eric Dover was no longer available and Gilby Clarke was busy putting a new solo album together. Although he had nothing to prove to anyone, Slash, like any other guitarist, needed to keep his fret fingers busy. And so rather than sit around waiting to see if Axl was gonna come to his senses, he set about re-assembling the coterie of blues freaks: G N' R hired-hand Teddy Andreadis; drummer Alvino Bennet; saxophonist Dave McClarem; rhythm guitarist Bobby Schneck and bassist and future Snakepit collaborator, Johnny Griparic, who'd accompanied him (as the makeshift Slash's Blues Ball) to headline that year's Sziget Festival in Budapest, Hungary, for what, at the time, the guitarist had intended as a one-off side project. The annual festival was in its third year and drew an audience of 206,000 and aside from Slash's blues combo, the line-up also included Iggy Pop, Sonic Youth, Stone Roses and Prodigy.

As the ad hoc combo's set-list comprised of the strongest songs from Slash's recently-released Snakepit album supplemented with traditional blues-rock classics such as Willie Dixon's 'Hootchie Cootchie Man', Albert King's 'Born Under A Bad Sign', Led Zeppelin's 'No Quarter', Jimi Hendrix's 'Stone Free' and Bob Dylan's timeless classic – and G N' R set perennial – 'Knockin' On Heaven's Door', they only needed to re-familiarise themselves with the Snakepit songs before heading out on a US tour which took in both seaboards and several states in-between. They also came over to the UK in late June, 1997, putting in two appearances over consecutive nights at London's Docklands Arena.

## SLASH'S SNAKEPIT

Slash's Snakepit was originally intended as a one album side-project, but the guitarist resurrected the band to record a second album following his departure from Guns N' Roses in 1996.

For the initial 1996 Snakepit – which he had been keen to stress was nothing more than a side-project whilst Guns N' Roses were in temporary hiatus – Slash brought in fellow Gunners Gilby

Clarke and Matt Sorum to play alongside Alice In Chains bassist, Mike Inez and ex-Jellyfish guitarist, Eric Dover, who provided the vocals. Legend has it the resultant album, *It's Five O'Clock Somewhere*, which was released in March, 1995, came about by accident rather than design. Slash, Matt, and Gilby, having set themselves up in Slash's home studio, known as 'The Snakepit' owing to its close – some would say too close – proximity to the guitarist's glass-partitioned reptile house, began working on ideas for potential new G N' R songs. When the demos were subsequently presented to Axl, the singer dismissed the fast-paced rockers as unsuitable for Guns N' Roses and rejected them out-of-hand. Slash, however, thought otherwise. Although he accepted Axl's decision, he wasn't prepared to let the songs to go to waste and brought in Inez and Dover with a view to releasing a solo album. He had initially wanted to call the makeshift group simply 'Snakepit', but as Geffen would be funding the project, he reluctantly consented to having his name added in order to boost sales.

Axl may have deemed the songs inferior, but G N' R's fans were rather more open-minded and the album, with its title taken from a passing comment made by a flight attendant and artwork provided by the guitarist's younger brother, Ash (who was following in his

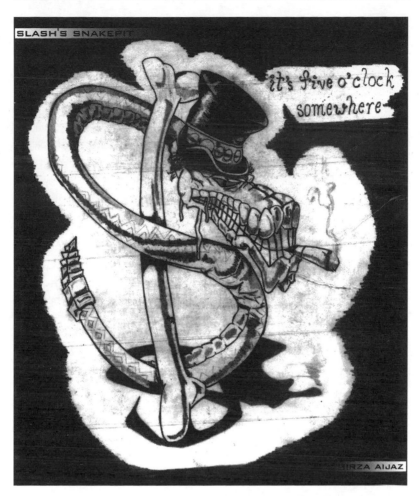

father's creative footsteps), went on to achieve platinum status.

Frustrated by the ever-expanding period of inactivity within the G N' R camp – and some gentle persuasion from the powers-that-be at Geffen – Slash agreed to take his makeshift band out on the road for a six-month promotional tour. Of the five musicians that had recorded the album, however, only Slash, Gilby – who was a free agent again, having recently been unceremoniously sacked from G N' R by Axl – and Eric Dover were able to sign up for the tour. Mike Inez was committed to Alice In Chains, while Matt had been forced to step aside in order to placate an irate Axl, who, despite having dismissed Slash's offerings, was angered at the press and record company attention being shown to his lead guitarist. Their replacements were future Megadeth bassist, James 'JLo' Lomenzo and drummer, Brian Tichy.

In early 2000, by which time Slash had long-since departed

from Guns N' Roses, the guitarist resurrected Snakepit, albeit with a completely different line-up consisting of vocalist Rod Jackson, bassist Johnny Griparic, guitarist Ryan Roxie and drummer Matt Laug. The resulting album, *Ain't Life Grand*, released in October that same year, was somewhat less well received than its predecessor, which led to Slash calling time on the project.

# SORUM, MATT

Matt Sorum was Steven Adler's replacement as drummer in Guns N' Roses. He joined the band during the summer of 1990.

Matt, who is of English and Norwegian descent, was born in Long Beach, California, on 19 November, 1962. His mother, Joanne being an opera-loving music teacher – as well as a fan of the Beatles – meant Matt was introduced to music at an early age. Having two older brothers who were both rock aficionados also provided him with a good grounding on the likes of Jimi Hendrix, Cream and The Doors. Having decided on becoming a drummer, Matt formed his first band, Prophecy, while he was still in high school and by the time he was 14 he was playing in clubs such as The Starwood, Gazzarras and the legendary Whisky a Go-Go. After graduating from school, however, Matt called time on the band, packed his belongings into

the back of his beat-up '64 Rambler station wagon, and headed for the bright lights of Los Angeles with just $40 in his pocket.

It was while he was jamming at the Central Club on Sunset Strip (now the Viper Room), that he hooked up with a guitarist called Greg White and agreed to accompany him on a tour of the southern states – including shows at legendary New Orleans clubs such as Jimmy's, and Ol' Man Rivers.

Upon his return to Los Angeles, Matt began plying his trade in earnest and his seemingly-effortless ability to juggle ten bands at any one time whilst also working as a session drummer for the likes of Shawn Cassidy, King Solomon Burke and Belinda Carlisle, meant he soon built up a solid reputation. It was whilst he was drumming for a now long-forgotten band at an airport hotel that he encountered Tori Amos, who was playing in the hotel's piano bar. The two struck up a conversation which led to a two-year collaboration on a project they called Y Kant Tori Amos. The duo also secured a recording deal with Atlantic Records. But when Tori announced she wanted to strike out alone in 1987, Matt wished her well and teamed up with the Jeff Paris Band and recorded an album for PolyGram Records.

Matt's big break came in 1988, when, through a chance conversation, he learnt British goth-rockers, The Cult were on the lookout for a new drummer. He went along to the auditions and having sufficiently impressed Messrs. Astbury and Duffy, spent two thrill-filled years on the road with the band, including lengthy US tours with both Metallica and Aerosmith. It was after a Cult show in Los Angeles during the summer of 1990 that Matt was approached by Slash and Duff and offered the now-vacant drum stool in Guns N' Roses. Needless to say, Matt leapt at the chance, and after a month of

solid rehearsals he accompanied his new band into the recording studio to begin work on the *Use Your Illusion* albums.

The first song Matt recorded with Guns N' Roses was a cover of the Bob Dylan classic, 'Knockin' On Heaven's Door, which had already been earmarked for the soundtrack to Tom Cruise's latest movie, *Days Of Thunder*. His live debut – as a fully-fledged Gunner – came on 20 January, 1991, at the

Rock in Rio II festival staged at the Maracana Stadium in Rio de Janeiro in front of 140,000 screaming Brazilians. Over the next three years Matt toured the world twice over with Guns N' Roses on the band's massive *Use Your Illusion* world tour. Although the tour saw him perform alongside Elton John, Brian May, Jeff Beck and Ronnie Wood, the highlight, as far as he was concerned, came with a four-night stint at The Forum in his hometown of Inglewood, California. He also recorded *The Spaghetti Incident?* and received two Grammy nominations, as well as two MTV awards during his seven-year tenure with the band.

In 1997, Matt either left or was dismissed – depending on one's point of view – from Guns N' Roses following a heated debate with Axl which saw him make several unsavoury comments about the singer's buddy, Paul Huge, who'd recently replaced Slash in the band. Although Axl took Matt's derogatory comments about Huge (who was present at the time) in his stride, it was the drummer's stinging remark that 'he had to be smoking crack if he thought Guns N' Roses could continue without Slash' that triggered his departure.

Aside from providing the beat for the Neurotic Outsiders, Matt also helped out on the first Slash's Snakepit album, as well as contributing to Duff and Gilby's solo albums. He also recorded with the Buddy Rich Orchestra on the drumming legend's Atlantic releases, *Burnin'*, and *For Buddy*, which were both produced by Rush drummer, Neil Peart. In May, 1996, he was invited to perform at the grand opening of the Hard Rock Hotel and occupied the drum stool in an ad hoc houseband which included guitaring greats B.B King and Bo Diddley.

Following his departure from Guns N' Roses, Matt briefly worked with Sammy Hagar before forming Orange Curtain Productions with his friend Larry Cordola to work on movie scores. The duo has also notched up several production credits for the likes of blues-legend, Little Milton, Cypress Hill's Sen-Dog and Ronnie Spectre. In 1999, Matt rejoined The Cult for a sell-out, summer US tour. He remained with the band through to 2001, during which time they recorded *Beyond Good and Evil* with legendary producer Bob Rock and also undertook an extensive world tour to promote the album.

In 2003, by which time he was already involved in Dave Navarro's side-project, Camp Freddy, Matt teamed up with his ex-G N' R buddies Slash and Duff and ex-Wasted Youth guitarist, Dave Kushner, to form Velvet Revolver. On 1 June, 2004, his debut solo album, *Hollywood Zen* – on which he sings, as well playing drums and guitar – was released on Brash Records. He describes the album, which chronicles his own experiences of life on the road, addictions, relationships, and his adopted home town of Los Angeles, as a very personal reflection of his two decades in rock 'n' roll.

## STINSON, TOMMY

Tommy Stinson, who was born Thomas Eugene Stinson on 6 October, 1966, in Minneapolis, Minnesota, is Guns N' Roses' incumbent bass player. He joined the band in 1998.

Stinson first made a name for himself in 1979, when, at just 12-years-old, he helped form the legendary 1980s alternative rock outfit, The Replacements, and he would remain in the line-up until the band's eventual demise in 1991. In 1993, when Guns N' Roses were probably the most famous band on the planet, Stinson formed the short-lived Bash & Pop, but the resulting album, *Friday Night Is Killing Me*, failed to cause much of a stir. His next – equally short-lived – musical venture, Perfect, released the EP: 'When Squirrels Play Chicken' in 1996, but by the following year the bassist's career appeared to have flatlined when the outfit's debut album, *Seven Days A Week*, was unexpectedly shelved owing to problems with their record label.

In 1998, however, Stinson's career was resuscitated when he – along with one-time Nirvana drummer and Foo Fighters

frontman, Dave Grohl – guested on a rock remix of Puff Daddy's 'It's All About The Benjamins'. That same year he was invited to join Guns N' Roses. At the time of writing, Stinson is still an active member of G N' R – a tenure which has lasted some eight years – and it is fair to say he will continue to do so for as long as his heart desires, for he has stood within the eye of Axl's wrath and lived to tell the tale. On 24 November, 2006, during a Guns N' Roses show in Cleveland, Ohio, the bassist took exception to Axl having referred to the support band, Eagles of Death Metal – the band that he had personally recommended – as the "Pigeons of Shit Metal". He hurled his bass to the floor and insulted Axl, before storming off stage. While he sheepishly returned after missing four songs, those present that night would surely have kept an eagle eye on G N' R's official website in expectation of the official posting notifying them of Stinson's departure from the band. Somewhat surprisingly, no such notice appeared. And when radio silence was finally broken a week or so later, it was Stinson who was doing the talking. In a message posted on his MySpace website, the bassist admitted to an error of judgement over his choice of opening act, before then attempting to rationalise his bass-throwing antics of eight days earlier with the following statement: "In the past I have thrown my bass, but I have never thrown it at Axl or anyone else in the band, nor have they thrown my bass back at me… yet. Axl has been a dear friend to me for nine years. We have no problem communicating, and wish that people would stay the fuck out of shit they know nothing about."

Away from Guns N' Roses, Stinson has released a solo album, *Village Gorilla Head* (2004), which was well received by both fans and music press alike. And his return to the 'main stage' with G N' R paved the way, so to speak, for the release of the shelved Perfect album which was re-titled *Once, Twice, Three Times & Maybe*. In 2005, Stinson took time away from Guns N' Roses to team up with his old high school buddy and Soul Asylum frontman, Dave Pirner for a series of shows to pay tribute to the band's bassist Karl Mueller, who'd recently succumbed to throat cancer. He also toured with the band in 2006.

In the autumn of 2005, Stinson teamed up with fellow ex-Replacements, Paul Westerberg and Chris Mars, to record two new songs for a proposed Replacements compilation album, and in 2006, he and Westerberg also collaborated on the soundtrack to the computer-animated movie, *Open Season* featuring the voices of Martin Lawrence, Ashton Kutcher and Billy Connelly.

# STRADLIN, IZZY

Izzy Stradlin, born Jeffrey Dean Isbell on 8 April, 1962 in Lafayette, Indiana, was Guns N' Roses' rhythm guitarist from the band's inception in June, 1985, through to November, 1991.

The young Jeff Isbell spent his formative years smoking pot with friends and listening to the likes of Alice Cooper, the Rolling Stones and Led Zeppelin. Having decided to try his hand at music, he pestered his blue-collar parents into buying him a drum kit – an instrument he would stay with for several years before finally switching to guitar. The transition, which came in early 1983, was due to it being much easier to write songs with an acoustic guitar than it was with a high-hat and snare drum. It was whilst he was recruiting like-minded souls at Jefferson High School that Jeff first encountered the then shy and retiring William "Bill" Bailey, who was going by the name of Axl. "In high school you were either a 'jock', or a 'stoner'," Izzy later recalled. "We weren't jocks; we had long hair so we ended up hanging out together. We'd play covers in a friend's garage. And as there were no clubs in Lafayette, we never actually made it out of the garage. Axl was really shy about singing back then, but I always knew he was a singer."

Having acquired the happy-go-lucky nickname Izzy Stradlin, the budding guitarist decided that if he was going to fulfil his musical aspirations then his future lay elsewhere than Indiana. So, immediately after graduating (the only original member of Guns N' Roses to do so), Izzy packed his guitar and drum kit into the back of his car and hit the I65 heading for Los Angeles. Upon arrival in the West Coast's music capital during the summer of 1983, he tried his luck as a drummer with a couple of bands, one of which was called The Atoms. But this venture quickly came to nought, and after briefly trying his hand at bass, he made the permanent switch to guitar. He, like many of L.A's young Turks, began hanging out on Sunset Strip – particularly the Rainbow Bar & Grill. At the time, Izzy was playing in another no-hope outfit called Little Women, but having struck up a friendship with fellow Rainbow residents and aspiring musos, Tracy Ulrich (Tracii Guns) and Christopher Weber, the three decided to pool their talents.

It was around this time that Izzy was joined in L.A. by Axl, and as Izzy was hoping to get something going with Ulrich, he introduced Axl to Weber in the hope that his Lafayette friend might do the same. Within a matter of weeks, however, Izzy had thrown his lot in with Axl and Weber and the trio began recruiting like-minded musicians for their band, Rose, which in turn became Hollywood Rose. 1984 proved to be a period of upheaval for Izzy as Hollywood Rose developed something of a revolving membership; even Axl temporarily abdicated to team up with Tracii Guns in his new band, L.A. Guns. Having become disillusioned with the whole scene, Izzy also jumped ship for a brief stint in the Sunset Strip staple band, London, only to then follow Axl's lead by returning to Hollywood Rose.

The transition from Hollywood Rose to Guns N' Roses was not without its pitfalls, but suffice to say, neither Izzy nor anyone else connected with the band could have expected G N' R to become so big so quickly. Indeed, Axl was once quoted as saying Izzy would have been happy for Guns N' Roses to reach a level of success similar to that of the Ramones, and play 2,000 capacity venues. The overwhelming and unprecedented success of *Appetite For Destruction*, however, saw the band propelled into super-stardom, and Izzy's aversion to being in so large a spotlight led to his seeking solitude and solace in drugs and alcohol.

In 1988, *Kerrang!* Journalist, Mick Wall jokingly informed Slash that the five members of Guns N' Roses were all odds-on favourites on the music magazine's in-house list of rock fatalities. But whereas Slash and Steven continued with their respective habits, Izzy decided there had to be more to life than getting obliterated every day. He later cited that year's US summer tour with the rehabilitated Aerosmith as a major source of inspiration to weaning himself off smack, but his epiphany didn't come until the following August, when he was arrested at Phoenix's Sky Harbor airport, whilst enroute to Indianapolis, for abusing a stewardess and urinating in the

aeroplane's galley. And the final straw came with his being subjected to random urine tests.

Izzy's decision to clean up meant he was forced to travel separately from his fellow Gunners – with only his Swedish girlfriend, Annica and his dog, Treader for company – during the *Use Your Illusion* world tour if he was to have any hope of resisting the omnipresent toxic temptations. But the rest of the band, instead of supporting Izzy's attempt at abstinence, thought him unsociable and aloof. The endless hours on the road gave Izzy plenty of time to consider his position, and these petty and unwarranted grumblings only served to enforce the guitarist's belief that life in Guns N' Roses was no longer fun. While he'd contributed more songs to the *Use Your Illusion* albums than any of the others, he didn't care for the band's new over-elaborated

direction; and nor did he care for playing in front of 50,000+ stadia crowds. His last live performance as a member of Guns N' Roses – although he didn't officially quit the band until 7 November – came on Saturday 31 August, 1991 at London's Wembley Stadium. There would be no fanfare, no press release, and no interviews with the press to explain his reasons. He simply packed up his guitars and walked away.

Despite Izzy's well-publicised contempt for his home state – he was once quoted as saying Indiana had no place being on his resume – it was here he retreated to following his departure from Guns N' Roses. The prodigal son returned to Lafayette, not on a mule, or donkey – nor even a car – but on a gleaming Harley Davidson. It was during his recuperation that he set about penning the songs which would subsequently appear on his debut solo album, *Izzy Stradlin and the Ju-Ju Hounds*. The record garnered favourable reviews upon its release in 1992 and, despite his aversion to touring, Izzy took his new band out on a promotional world tour. But in May, 1993, he briefly resumed his G N' R duties as a temporary stand-in for Gilby Clark following the latter's involvement in a motorcycle accident.

Following on from the Ju-Ju Hounds tour, Izzy took a five-year sightseeing sabbatical which saw him travel the world on his Harley, but in 1998 – having recharged his batteries – he announced his return to the scene with his second solo offering, *117 Degrees*. The album contains some of Izzy's best work to date, but his reluctance to promote the album meant it failed to trouble the Billboard 100; and the knock-on effect from this saw him fall foul of Geffen's latest bout of corporate restructuring and he was dropped from the label. His third solo release, 1999's *Ride*

*On*, on the Universal Victor label, was only made available in Japan, which did at least see him undertake a mini promotional tour of the country.

In 2002, by which time he had released two more solo albums, *River,* and *On Down The Road*, Izzy was invited to link up with Slash, Duff and Matt for what evolved into Velvet Revolver. But

although the guitarist had long-since renewed his friendships with both Slash and Duff, his aversion to lead singers and touring saw him decline the invitation. Instead, he chose to persevere with his solo career and went into the studio to record *Like A Dog,* but the album, his sixth solo effort, didn't appear until 2005, and even then it was another internet only release. May 2006 saw Izzy renew his friendship with Axl when he made a guest appearance at Guns N' Roses' fourth and final warm-up show at New York's Hammerstein Ballroom – the first time he and Axl had shared the same stage in thirteen years. Since then he has gone on to make regular appearances with the band on their on-going *Chinese Democracy* world tour, and in May, 2007, he released his seventh solo album, *Miami,* which was yet another exclusive iTunes only release.

## SUNSHINE, GARY

Gary Sunshine is an American playwright and television screen-writer. He also teaches guitar, and it was his teaching Axl Rose that led to him being invited to appear on the G N' R song, 'Oh My God'.

The Brooklyn-born playwright has neither interest in nor intention of becoming a permanent member of Guns N' Roses – and if truth be told, it was only through his showing his new best buddy, Axl

where to place his fingertips on the fretboard that he was invited to play on the song at all. Gary's published literary works include *Reasons To wake Up,* *A History of Plastic Slipcovers* (his father apparently made his living from cutting said slipcovers), *Al Takes A Bride* and *Five Ways In.* And his best-known work, *What I Want My Words To Do To You* – which he co-wrote, co-created and co-produced – won several awards, including the Sundance Film Festival's Freedom of Expression Award and the Heartland Film Festival's Audience Award.

Gary embarked on his writing career soon after graduating from Princeton University, where he majored in English and also received an MFA (Master of Fine Arts) from New York University's Dramatic Writing Program. In December, 2004, he took up residence at the Royal National Theatre Studio in London and the following year received the Helen Merrill Award for Emerging Playwrights.

# SWEET CHILD O' MINE

'Sweet Child O' Mine' – the third single to be culled from *Appetite For Destruction* – was released on 21 August, 1987 and is, to date, Guns N' Roses' only US number one.

The song topped the American Billboard Hot 100 Chart for two weeks in September, 1988, but, if Slash is to be believed, then the instantly-recognisable E-flat-based intro to the song – recently voted the #1 riff of all-time by the readers of *Total Guitar* magazine – started out as nothing more than a string skipping exercise he would occasionally use to limber up his fingers before getting down to some serious fretwork. Indeed, his so-called 'circus riff' only came to light when the top-hatted guitarist decided to lighten the mood during an ad hoc G N' R jam session. And he couldn't believe his ears when the others insisted that he keep on playing the infectious riff while they found the requisite chords and knocked it into shape. Axl was particularly enthusiastic because the new melody fitted in perfectly with the gushing poem he'd recently written in homage to his then girlfriend – and supposed soul mate – Erin Everly. Indeed, much has been made of the heartfelt emotion Axl placed within the lyric, which aside from being an ode to the then love of his life and future bride, contains autobiographical references to the childhood abuse he suffered at the hands of his step-father.

The accompanying video, which was designed to capture the Gunners in a relaxed rehearsal mode, surrounded by their girlfriends and various hangers-on, was filmed at Los Angeles' Huntingdon Park Ballroom on 11 April, 1988. The subsequent heavy rotation the video received on MTV, as well as every other music video channel, guaranteed its mainstream success. The outcome would surely have been different, however, if Axl had had his way. In 2006, the singer confided to New York DJ, Eddie Trunk that his concept for the promo video had not only centred on drug-trafficking, but also featured a dead infant whose

lifeless body is found packed with heroin. Given that the idea of a promo video is to maximise a single's sales potential, and that a video featuring dead babies stuffed with highly-illegal substances was sure to receive a media blanket-ban, it's little wonder Geffen rejected the singer's proposal.

In order to make 'Sweet Child O' Mine' more radio-friendly, manager Alan Niven took it upon himself to edit the song down from its original 5:56 to 4:20 – with much of Slash's intro being wiped. Although Niven had the band's best interests at heart, his actions drew indignation not only from Slash, but also from Axl and no doubt played a part in his being expunged from the band's inner-circle. During a subsequent 1989 *Rolling Stone* interview, the singer admitted to having "hated" the edit as the intro had been his favourite part of the song. "There was no reason for it [the intro] to be missing." he ranted, "Except to create more space for commercials so the radio station owners can get more advertising dollars. When you get the chopped-down version of 'Paradise City', or half of 'Sweet Child O' Mine' or 'Patience' cut, you're getting screwed!" Axl had every right to be bitter about what he saw as both a flagrant act of betrayal on Niven's part and Geffen's willingness to pander to corporate interests instead of adhering to their initial promise of allowing Guns

N' Roses full artistic license over their material.

'Sweet Child O' Mine' has gone on to be voted #196 on *Rolling Stone*'s 500 Greatest Songs of All Time as well as featuring in the same magazine's 40 Greatest Songs that Changed the World; #6 on *Q Magazine*'s 100 Greatest Guitar Tracks; #37 on *Guitar World's* list of 100 Greatest Guitar Solos and #3 on *Blender*'s 500 Greatest Songs Since You Were Born. Yet even now, some twenty years later, Slash still insists he only played the riff as a joke. But if that's the case, there's many an aspiring axe-man who would gladly give their left nut to share his sense of humour.

## SYMPATHY FOR THE DEVIL

'Sympathy For The Devil' is a Rolling Stones song which was covered by Guns N' Roses in 1994 for the Neil Jordon movie, *Interview With The Vampire* starring Brad Pit and Tom Cruise.

'Sympathy For The Devil', which appears as the opening track on the Rolling Stones' classic 1968 album, *Beggars Banquet*, was written by Mick Jagger and Keith Richards. In a 1995 *Rolling Stone* interview Jagger believed the inspiration for the lyrics came from the writings of French poet, Charles Baudelaire (1821-1867), but the song's opening line, 'Please allow me to introduce myself/I'm a man of wealth and

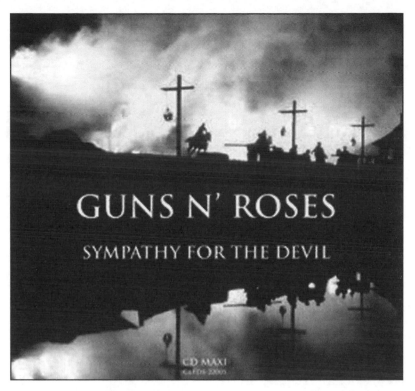

taste' is strikingly similar to the opening phrase in Mikhail Bulgakov's 1967 novel, *The Master and Margarita*: 'Please excuse me,' he said, speaking correctly, but with a foreign accent, 'for presuming to speak to you without an introduction.'

As the Stones' previous long-player was titled *Their Satanic Majesties Request,* certain sections of the media instantly picked up on the title of the new album's opening track and – aided and abetted by overzealous religious groups – began spreading ridiculous rumours that the band's members were devil-worshippers intent on corrupting Britain's youth. Yet a closer inspection of the lyrics would have revealed it to be a monologue of atrocities carried out by man in God's name, such as the Russian Revolution of 1917, World War II and the assassinations of John and Robert Kennedy. Indeed, Bobby Kennedy's assassination occurred while the Stones were in the studio recording the song, which brought about a revision of the lyric from 'who killed John Kennedy?' to 'who killed the Kennedys?' 'Sympathy For The Devil' is also the title of a 1968 film by French director Jean-Luc Godard. The film, which is more of a documentary loosely based on the late-60s counter-culture movement, also features the Stones recording the song in London's Olympic Sound Studios over 5/6 June. Jagger and

Richards (whose idea it was to add samba-style backing percussion) can be seen performing backing vocals, but the scene was staged for the director's benefit.

By the time G N' R went into L.A.'s Complex Studios to record the song for the *Interview With The Vampire* movie in August '94, Axl's relationship with Slash was already in freefall. But the singer's decision to bring in his old Lafayette buddy, Paul Tobias, a.k.a Paul Huge, as Gilby's replacement proved the final nail in the G N' R coffin as far as the guitarist was concerned. Indeed, in his autobiography, Slash cites 'Sympathy For The Devil' as the one Guns N' Roses song he never again wishes to hear again as it's the sound of Guns N' Roses breaking up. The guitarist, despite hating Jordan's adaptation of Anne Rice's novel, had arrived at the studio hoping that recording the song might at least serve as a catalyst to bringing everyone back into the fold. But his illusion was shattered the moment he entered the studio to find the obnoxious Huge unpacking his guitar. Although he could understand Axl wanting to bring in someone known to the band rather than an outsider, he couldn't believe the decision had seemingly been made without any consultation with himself and Duff. In fact, his anguish was so overwhelming he later admitted to contemplating killing himself; and might have done so if he'd been able to lay his hands on a gun or a half-ounce of heroin.

Speaking about the incident in 2002 – by which time Huge had also departed – Axl defended his actions by saying he'd merely brought Huge in as a means of complementing Slash's style, but the sorry situation was best summed up by a friend of the band: "Huge was a nice enough guy," the friend recalled. "But they're Guns N' Roses for God's sake. Huge simply didn't have the chops."

'Symphony For The Devil' was co-produced between the band and Mike Clink and engineered by Clink's long-standing sidekick, Jim Mitchell, with Bill Price once again called in to do the mixing. Yet despite this array of engineering expertise, the song lacked the G N' R bite we'd come to expect. Even Slash, although begrudgingly admitting that their version "sorta sounded like Guns N' Roses", thought it lacked spark and admitted that if he'd had any say in the matter then it wouldn't have been released. 'Sympathy For The Devil' is indeed a great song, but perhaps not one best suited to Guns N' Roses. And one can only assume their involvement was solely down to the movie being a Geffen Pictures production.

'Sympathy For The Devil' isn't the only Rolling Stones song associated with Guns N' Roses. The Gunners also performed the English rockers' 1971 hit, 'Wild Horses' during the *Use Your Illusion* world tour, when Axl would use the song as a means of introducing Gilby Clarke to audiences.

# T'

## TEGELMAN, JUSSI

Jussi Tagelman, the Finnish-born, Havana Black drummer, was a temporary stand-in following Steven Adler's dismissal from Guns N' Roses in 1989 and receives an acknowledgement on both the *Use Your Illusion* albums.

## TEN MINUTE WARNING

Ten Minute Warning was a Seattle-based hardcore punk band which featured Duff McKagan in its original line-up.

It was actually Duff, along with ex-Fartz guitarist Paul Solger, who formed Ten Minute Warning, perhaps the best-known of the bassist's hometown bands before he abandoned the Pacific Northwest in search of fame and fortune. Having recruited vocalist, Steve Verwolf and drummer Greg Gilmore – who would accompany Duff to California before returning to Seattle and eventually finding a modicum of fame with Mother Love Bone – Ten Minute Warning adopted a style which was not only of a much slower tempo than that of the Fartz, but also dared to introduce a psychedelic element to their sound. Although such heretical leanings were anathema to Seattle's punk rock purists, the band stuck to their guns and received critical acclaim from fellow artists such as Black Flag's Henry Rollins, who dubbed them "A punk rock Hawkwind", while Pearl Jam guitarist, Stone Gossard has since credited Ten Minute Warning as the band that inspired him to pick up a guitar.

In early 1984, Ten Minute Warning headed into the studio and recorded an album's worth of songs – including a cover of Pink Floyd's 'The Nile Song' – but this was before Nirvana or the ensuing Grunge movement placed Seattle

on the musical map, and the lack of an accommodating independent record label such as Sub Pop, meant the album never saw the light of day. With little prospect of their being picked up by one of the majors, the band gave one final farewell performance at Seattle's Lincoln Arts Centre before going their separate ways.

In 1997, by which time Duff had left Guns N' Roses and returned to his native Seattle, Ten Minute Warning announced they were reforming – albeit without Duff or singer Verwolf, who was currently unavailable owing to his incarceration in Washington's State Penitentiary. Legend has it the band's decision to dust off their guitars was due to Duff's celebrity Grunge buddies having gushingly heaped praise on the bassist's former outfit. The band's nine-track, self-titled album was released the following year on the Sub Pop label. The reformation, however, proved short-lived, and on 22 August, 1998 – Paul Solger already having quit – the band played their last ever show at the Roseland Theatre in Portland, Oregon.

## THE SPAGHETTI INCIDENT?

*The Spaghetti Incident?*, released in 1993, was Guns N' Roses' fifth studio album, and while consisting entirely of cover-versions, at the time of writing it is the latest record released by the band. The tracks featured are:

*Since I Don't Have You* (4:19) (**The Skyliners**); *New Rose* (2:38) (**The Damned**); *Down On The Farm* (3:28) (**UK Subs**); *Human Being* (6:48) (**New York Dolls**); *Raw Power* (3:11) (**Iggy & The Stooges**); *Ain't It Fun* (5:02) (**Dead Boys**); *Buick*

*Makane* (2:39) (**T-Rex**); *Hair Of The Dog* (3:54) (**Nazareth**); *Attitude* (1:27) (**The Misfits**); *Black Leather* (4:08) (**Sex Pistols**); *You Can't Put Your Arms Around A Memory* (3:35) (**Johnny Thunders**); *I Don't Care About You* (2:17) (**Fear**); *Look At Your Game Girl* (2:34) (**Charles Manson**). LP, CD, Cassette, Geffen Records 1993

If the *Use Your Illusions* albums can be said to have captured Guns N' Roses at the height of their creativity, then *The Spaghetti Incident?* surely serves as the band's nadir. Having sat down and chosen their respective favourite punk tracks, the band then recorded these songs – along with The Skyliners' 'Since I Don't Have You', T-Rex's 'Buick Makane' and Nazareth's 'Hair Of The Dog' – during the *Use Your Illusion* sessions, with a view to releasing an EP at a later date. The later date came and went, and by the time the band came off the *Use Your Illusion* tour in July, 1993, their ever-expanding legion of fans were again clamouring for new product. Geffen, although doing very nicely from the recent release of Nirvana's follow-up album, *In Utero*, were also keen to get Guns N' Roses back onto the Billboard chart. But the idea

of releasing a punk rock karaoke album at a time when Grunge was ruling the airwaves was commercial suicide. Indeed, the album's obscure title and unimaginative artwork – a staid photograph of tinned spaghetti – seemed to show a total lack of interest from both label and band alike. And although there were enough G N' R 'completists' around to ensure healthy sales, it proved a monumental failure compared to the sales generated by any of its predecessors.

Several stories – all of which involve Steven Adler – have since emerged in regard to the album's bizarre title. The first tale relates to an incident which occurred whilst the Gunners were out on the road, when one of the band surreptitiously ate the drummer's pasta-based evening meal. Another – equally lame – offering, tells of how the band had come to a collective decision never to partake of spaghetti in Adler's company on account of his having repeatedly agitated his parents by smearing his face with the tomato sauce whilst eating it as a child. There is also the tale which tells of a sordid sex act involving one or more band members, a female of dubious character, and a can of spaghetti. The most likely explanation, however, comes from Duff, who subsequently admitted in an interview that the spaghetti incident occurred in 1987 whilst the band was in Chicago. They'd been staying in a guesthouse located above an Italian restaurant, where Adler, as a means of keeping himself and the rest of the band out of trouble, had elected to use 'spaghetti' as the codeword for his heroin stash. The only problem was, he failed to let anyone other than Axl know of his cunning subterfuge. So when Duff woke the following morning to find the highly-agitated drummer tearing the room apart searching for his 'spaghetti', the bassist fell about in hysterics.

As to the album itself – which once again saw Mike Clink at the consol – the track selection is as follows: 'Since I Don't Have You', the song which Axl was forever whistling at rehearsals, had originally been recorded back in 1959 by Pittsburgh doo-woppers, The Skyliners. The Gunners released the song as a single in 1994, but it failed to trouble the charts, stalling at #69. Next up is the Damned's seminal punk offering, 'New Rose', which is sung in true '76 punk spirit by Duff. Another of Duff's selections was 'Down On The Farm', which had originally been recorded by second-generation punk outfit, UK Subs, and sees Axl inexplicably adopt a risible Dick Van Dyke 'Mockney Poppins' accent. It is difficult enough trying to figure out why the bassist selected the UK Subs, let alone one of their more obscure songs. A safer bet would have been to cover a track by The Adverts, Buzzcocks, or even Stiff Little Fingers' Alternative Hollywood/Alter Your Disneyland.

As all five band members were huge fans of the New York Dolls, it was perhaps inevitable that one of their songs would appear on the album. And although the version of 'Human Being', which appears as the ultimate track on the Dolls' second, and final, album, *Too Much Too Soon*, was a passable attempt, it doesn't hold a candle to the original version. Duff also both selected and sang Johnny Thunders' lament to lost love, 'You Can't Put Your Arms Around A Memory' as a tribute to the Dolls backcombed guitarist and one-time Heartbreakers frontman, who was found dead in a New Orleans hotel room on 23 April, 1991.

One of the few highlights on the album is the Gunners' version of the Stooges' 'Raw Power', which was the title track of the Motor City, Michigan band's third album and has since been hailed as one of the progenitors of punk rock. Another punk fatality, Stiv Bators, who tragically died in his sleep in Paris in 1990 after being struck by a car earlier that same day, is also commemorated with the Dead Boys track, 'Ain't It Fun', which sees Axl sharing vocal duties with Michael Monroe. The next two selections, T Rex's 'Buick Makane' (the actual spelling was Buick Mackane), from the glam band's 1972 *Slider* album, and Nazareth's 'Hair Of The Dog', the title track from the Scottish rockers' 1975 album, both came from Slash. Duff's punk heritage

was again called to the fore for The Misfits' 'Attitude', and as no punk tribute album could be considered complete without a Sex Pistols song, the band blast their way through 'Black Leather'. While the song is credited to the Sex Pistols, it is really more of a Professionals track – The Professionals being Steve Jones and Paul Cook's first post-Pistols project. Shortly after the release of the album, Slash encountered Jones at a mutual friend's wedding. Steve was naturally curious as to whether G N' R's version was better than The Runaways 1978 offering, and was no doubt surprised to be told it was also better than the original.

According to the track-listing, Fear's 'I Don't Care About You' – which appeared on the L.A. punksters' 1982 debut album, *The Record*, and was another personal favourite of Slash's – is the final song on the record. But if one refrains from hitting the eject button, then the lilting sound of psychotic killer Charles Milles Manson's 'Look At Your Game Girl' fills the air. The song appears as the opening track on Manson's 1968 album, *Lie, The Love & Terror Cult*. Despite vociferous protests from both his bandmates – who refused to record the track – and his Geffen paymasters, Axl was insistent that it should appear, albeit unaccredited, on the album. And many believe he did so as a dig at his ex-lover, Stephanie Seymour. Taking to the stage sporting a T-shirt bearing the image of the man behind the infamous LaBianca/Tate murders of August, 1969 was one thing, but recording one of the convicted killer's songs was going beyond the pale. The Gunners subsequently – and shamefacedly – pledged to donate royalties to the relatives of Manson's victims. In 2000, Axl, still seething over what he saw as the media's misinterpretation of his interest in Manson, announced that the track was to be removed from the album's reissued version. This, however, wasn't an admission to his earlier foolishness, but rather because, in his view, the 'misunderstanding public no longer deserved to hear it'. At the time of writing, however, the track-listing remains unchanged.

# TOBIAS, PAUL

Paul Tobias, a.k.a. Paul Huge, is a childhood friend of Axl Rose. The Los Angeles-based guitarist was also an official member of Guns N' Roses from 1997 – 2002.

It was during Guns N' Roses 1 January, 2001 show at Las Vegas' House of Blues – their first live performance for eight years – that Axl lauded Tobias as the man who'd helped him keep Guns N' Roses together. Little could the Axl exalted guitarist have known, however, that the band's next live show, on 31 December, 2001 – again in America's gambling cap-

ital – would prove to be his last with G N' R. The reason given for Tobias' departure was his aversion to touring, and he was replaced by Richard Fortus.

Tobias, aside from being a childhood friend of Axl's, has a long-standing connection with Guns N' Roses which stretches back to the time of Hollywood Rose, when he co-wrote 'Shadow Of Your Love' (which earned him a thanks in the credits for *Appetite For Destruction*), and 'Back Off Bitch' which appears on *Use Your Illusion 1*. In 1994, Axl invited him to play on the Gunners cover of the Rolling Stones' 'Symphony For The Devil', intended for the *Interview With The Vampire* movie soundtrack. Slash, although still smarting from Axl's high-handed show of nepotism in replacing Gilby Clarke with his old buddy Tobias, was initially open to the idea of their working together. It didn't take long for Slash to realise things weren't going to work out though, as aside from taking an immediate and intense dislike to the obnoxious and arrogant Tobias, he didn't even rate the newcomer's style or technique as worthy of Guns N' Roses. Duff and Matt had also taken a strong dislike to Tobias, but Axl refused to waiver. Indeed, it was Matt's derisive comments about Tobias's shortcomings which led to his dismissal from the band in 1997. By this time, of course, Slash had long-since departed and Tobias had officially been unveiled as his replacement. Aside from 'Symphony For The Devil', Tobias also played on the Gunners' follow-up single, 'Oh My God', which appears on the soundtrack to Arnold Schwarzenegger's 1999 movie, *End Of Days*, as well as 'IRS', which is set to feature on *Chinese Democracy*.

In September, 2002, by which time Tobias had left Guns N' Roses, his former band, Mank Rage sought to release an album consisting of material recorded prior to the guitarist's involvement with G N' R. The proposal was shelved owing to record company indifference, but in 2006, three of the songs eventually surfaced on the band's MySpace site.

## TROUBADOUR, THE

The Troubadour, located at 9081 Santa Monica Boulevard, is one of the best known clubs on Sunset Strip, and the place where Guns N' Roses cut their teeth and honed their sound.

Although Hollywood Rose played the Troubadour several times during 1984 and early '85, the night which has gone down in L.A. folklore came on 6 June, 1985, when the newly-constituted Guns N' Roses made their inaugural appearance. And seeing new boys Slash and Steven up on the stage might have caused some confusion amongst those in attendance that night because the crudely-drawn flyer – which cited the event as a "rock 'n' roll bash where everyones (sic) smashed" – still bore images of the now-departed Tracii Guns and Rob Gardener.

By the summer of 1985, the Troubadour was the epicentre of L.A.'s rock scene, but when it first opened its doors back in

1957, the venue had served as a safe haven for flowery folk acts owing to owner, Doug Weston's predilection for the genre. The original venue was located on La Cienega in West Hollywood, but moved to its present location in 1961, where it soon found a niche hosting Monday night hootenannies which provided budding folk singer-songwriters with an open stage where they could try out their material on an appreciative and like-mined audience. The "Troub", as it became known to locals, also served as a springboard for the likes of Tom Waits, Emmylou Harris, Jackson Browne and The Eagles. Even Elton John, who completed a residency here in 1970, now cites the Troubadour as being pivotal in helping him achieve mainstream American success.

Six years on from Elton's now famous tenure, however, the Troubadour's halcyon days were a distant memory. And in 1976 the club closed its doors, seemingly for the last time. Twelve months later, however, the venue reopened for business, but rather than try to breathe life into the now-decaying folk corpse, Weston began booking local rock acts. He was even willing to embrace punk, but a mini-riot during a performance by local ragtag outfit, The Bags, brought about an urgent rethink, which saw both punk bands and their disorderly audiences receiving a lifetime ban.

By the mid 1980s, the club's modest stage had been taken over by the glut of glam-metal bands currently plying their trade along Sunset Strip. And the fact that these bands were all vying with each other for gigs, in conjunction with the local authorities' recent decision to outlaw fly-postering, meant the club could rewrite the rules. The days of bringing along thirty-to-forty friends to supply the necessary ambience were over. Now the bands were obliged to sell their full quota of tickets before being allowed to play.

As Friday night was the dream gig all the hopefuls aspired to, the Troubadour initiated a pecking order system whereby each new band would be given a Monday or Tuesday night 'graveyard slot' – these being traditionally quiet nights on the Strip – and those who proved themselves capable of shifting tickets were then promoted to a Wednesday or Thursday night slot before then finally being given a shot at the title. Of all the bands that were in vogue on the Strip during the mid-'80s, Guns N' Roses were selling the most tickets – and doing so most often. Before long they were regarded as the Troubadour houseband.

The Gunners' final appearance at the venue – which they cheekily advertised as their "Farewell to Hollywood" show – came on 11 July, 1986, and during the performance Axl took time out to personally thank the audience for having – albeit inadvertently – helped in getting the band signed to Geffen.

# USE YOUR ILLUSION 1 & 2

## Use Your Illusion 2
*Civil War* (7:42); *14 Years* (4:23); *Yesterdays* (3:14); *Knockin' On Heaven's Door* (5:36); *Get In The Ring* (5:29); *Shotgun Blues* (3:23); *Breakdown* (7:03); *Pretty Tied Up* (4:48); *Locomotive* (8:42); *So Fine* (4:07); *Estranged* (9:23); *You Could Be Mine* (5:42); *Don't Cry* (alternative lyrics) (4:45); *My World* (1:23).
2xLP, CD, Cassette
Geffen Records, 1991

The *Use Your Illusion* double albums, which were released simultaneously in the US on 17 September, 1991 and on 16 September in the UK and Europe, are Guns N' Roses' third and fourth studio albums. Although *Use Your Illusion 2* proved the more popular of the two by pipping its sibling to #1 on the Billboard Hot 100, both albums went on to sell over seven million copies.

## Use Your Illusion 1
*Right Next Door To Hell* (2:58); *Dust 'N' Bones* (4:55); *Live And Let Die* (2:59); *Don't Cry* (Original) (4:42); *Perfect Crime* (2:22); *You Ain't The First* (2:32); *Bad Obsession* (5:26); *Back Off Bitch* (5:01); *Double Talkin' Jive* (3:19); *November Rain* (8:53); *The Garden* (5:17); *Garden Of Eden* (2:36); *Don't Damn Me* (5:15); *Bad Apples* (4:25); *Dead Horse* (4:17); *Coma* (10:13).
2xLP, CD, Cassette
Geffen Records, 1991

*Appetite For Destruction* and *GNR Lies* had collectively sold some 15 million copies and propelled Guns N' Roses into rock's elite pantheon, but by the summer of 1989, the band's voracious fans were clamouring for new product. And needless to say, David Geffen and the rest of the label's execs were equally keen to get the band into the studio. Indeed, they would probably have been content just to get the five musicians in the same room together as the Gunners appeared to be drifting apart. Although no one was pressing the panic button, there were a few furrowed brows pacing up and down Geffen's corridors of power. Between December, 1988 and January, 1991, Guns N' Roses, a band which prided itself on its live shows and had spent the previous two years constantly out on the road – aside from the odd awards ceremony, guest appearance, or warm-up show – put in just four live appearances, and these all came supporting the Rolling Stones in October, 1989.

It wasn't – as reported in some quarters – a case of collective writers block that was holding things up regarding new material. In fact, the band already had the bare bones of several songs, including 'Civil War', 'You Could Be Mine', 'Estranged', 'Pretty Tied Up' and 'Dust 'N' Bones' in the can. To get these songs knocked into shape – as well as get the creative juices flowing again – the decision was made to reconvene in Chicago, where a three-month block-booking had been arranged at the Cabaret Metro, the famous

rock venue located on the outskirts of town. Slash, Duff and Steven duly arrived for rehearsals the first week of July, 1989, but Axl, who'd decided to make the 2000 mile journey from L.A. by car, didn't put in an appearance until the last week of the scheduled rehearsals, while Izzy failed to show at all. The trio had formulated several ideas for new songs, but when Axl did finally show up, he was only willing to work on 'Estranged'. These non-rehearsals proved Steven's last involvement as a member of Guns N' Roses, for by the time the band relocated to West Hollywood's A&M Studios

at the end of September to begin writing in earnest, the drummer had been replaced by Matt Sorum.

With one druggie having been shown the door and Slash and Izzy having kicked their own heroin habits, the Gunners were soon back to firing on all cylinders and laid down the backing tracks to over forty songs in less than a month, before then moving on to Record Plant Studios to continue with the recording. The initial itinerary had called for work to begin at noon, but as musicians are like vampires in that they seem to do their best work at night, the band quickly settled into a regime where they began recording at six or seven in the evening and worked straight through to the following morning. Once again Mike Clink was at the production helm, with award-winning engineer Bob Clearmountain brought in to assist. Halfway through the mixing process, however, the band decided they were unhappy with Clearmountain's efforts, and started again from scratch with English engineer Bill Price. Although the studio was supposedly off limits to anyone outside the band's inner-circle, this rule didn't appear to apply to Axl's new celebrity friends Naomi Campbell, Johnny Depp, Sean

Penn, and Bruce Springsteen, which led Matt to jokingly liken the late-night, candlelit sessions to being in a Fellini movie.

The recording sessions proved something of a mixed blessing as far as the Geffen execs were concerned. For although they were doubtless delighted at the band's prolific output, they were rather less enthralled with Axl's insistence that all the recorded material should be released simultaneously. The singer's proposal to put out a quadruple box set was rejected out of hand, but Tom Zutaut came up with a suitable compromise by suggesting the initial release of one double-album, which could then be followed up in twelve months time with a single album – possibly together with one of the covers EPs the band were keen to record – and then finish off with a live album once the Gunners had finished the accompanying world tour. Axl, however, having already won one battle in getting rid of Alan Niven, refused to waiver and argued the thirty-odd songs in the can represented a particular period of time in the band's history and could well lose all relevance and meaning in the intervening twelve months. Indeed, several of the new compositions, including 'Ain't Goin' Down', which subsequently appeared on a Guns N' Roses pinball machine, 'Too Much Too Soon', 'Sentimental Movie', 'Just Another Sunday' and 'Bring It Back Home', had already been discarded, and the ensuing tour would surely provide the band with fur-

ther inspiration. Geffen, realising Axl was holding all the aces, capitulated and agreed to releasing two double-albums simultaneously. Axl even had a title for the body of work: Use Your Illusion. The singer had come across American artist Mark Kostabi's painting of the same name in a Los Angeles gallery and was so taken with its thought-provoking imagery – which Kostabi had lifted from Raphael's fresco, *The School Of Athens* – he had one of his people contact Kostabi to ask the artist's permission to use it on the cover.

Although each album features an epic ballad ('November Rain' on *Use Your Illusion I*, and 'Estranged' on *Use Your Illusion II* - as well as alternate versions of 'Don't Cry'), *Use Your Illusion I*, with titles such as 'Right Next Door To Hell', 'Live And Let Die', 'Double Talkin' Jive' and 'Don't Damn Me', is generally regarded as being the angry 'ying' to accompany the sister album's bluesier 'yang'. Aside from the songs which feature elsewhere in this book, the highlights of *UYI I* include 'Dust 'N' Bones', Izzy's Stones-esque lament to man's 'threescore and ten', the highly underrated 'Perfect Crime', which served as an occasional show-opening rocker and wouldn't have sounded out of place on *Appetite For Destruction*. 'Bad Obsession' is Izzy's ode to the darker side of drug addiction, while 'Back Off Bitch' serves as Axl's misogynistic rant at women in general – and ex-wife Erin Everly in particular. The self-explanatory 'Double Talkin' Jive', which is driven along by a masterful solo from Slash, is another of Izzy's underrated *UYI I* gems, while 'Garden Of Eden' lambastes organised religions for making a mockery of humanity. 'Dead Horse', which sees Axl provide an autobiographical insight into his troubled childhood, begins with an acoustic intro played by the singer himself, and although the track was never released as a single, it does have an accompanying video.

Stand-out tracks on *Use Your Illusion II* include '14 Years', which provides Izzy with another opportunity to show off his vocal prowess and the sentimentally-sweet 'Yesterdays', which was subsequently released as a single and is the only song within G N' R's considerable canon that gives a writing credit to three non-band members: West Arkeen, Del James, and Billy McCloud. 'Get In The Ring', with its opening salvo: 'Why do you look at me when you hate me' was aimed at the band's critics and detractors, while the slow-tempo ballad 'So Fine' is Duff's mournful lament to the passing of his punk hero Johnny Thunders, who'd died whilst the Gunners were in the studio. 'Pretty Tied Up', another Izzy number – which the guitarist introduces with some subtle sitar playing – tells the tale of a dominatrix he knew operating from her home on Melrose Avenue. 'Shotgun Blues', the only other UYI track to feature Axl on guitar, is supposedly a tirade aimed at his Mötley Crüe nemesis

Vince Neil, while the melancholic mini-epic 'Breakdown', featuring dialogue from Cleavon Little's character 'Super Soul' in the 1971 movie *Vanishing Point*, is the singer's bitter-sweet introspection on the inequities of this thing we call life ('Just because you're winning, don't mean you're the lucky ones').

Despite the wealth of great material on the double albums, the general consensus amongst G N' R fans has always been that a truncated, single *Use Your Illusion* would have been a serious contender for 'greatest rock album of all time'. In 1998, it seemed Geffen had also come around to this way of thinking. But instead of selecting killer tracks, the label released a US only sanitised and expletive-free 12-track album to satisfy the morality-mongers at the country's leading chain-store outlets, Wal-Mart and Kmart, which both refused to stock any albums carrying a parental advisory sticker.

As previously stated, the albums came out in the UK on 16 September, which being a Monday, meant I could only realistically afford to purchase one or the other without skinting myself and going hungry until payday. I'd made my way into town that particular morning believing *Use Your Illusion I* was the CD for me as it featured 'November Rain', which had blown me away at the Gunners' Wembley show two weeks earlier. But my mind was in turmoil upon perusing the track-listing on *Use Your Illusion II*. And suffice to say, I went hungry.

# USE YOUR ILLUSION WORLD TOUR, 1991 – 1993

The colossal, eight-leg *Use Your Illusion* world tour which Guns N' Roses undertook between May, 1991 and July, 1993, with 192 dates played to some seven million people in 27 countries across the globe and grossing an estimated $58 million, is the largest rock tour in history.

In May, 1991, with the thirty songs which would make up the two *Use Your Illusion* double albums currently being mastered by George Marino at Sterling Sound in New York, Guns N' Roses announced three 'warm-up' shows in preparation for the mammoth world tour they were about to undertake. The first two shows, played at San Francisco's compact Warfield Theatre and Los Angeles' Pantages Theatre on 9 and 12 May, 1991 respectively, were rapturously received. But it was the band's third and final "live rehearsal" – as Axl jokingly referred to the warm up shows – at New York's Ritz Theatre on 16 May that really caught the Gunners at their blistering best. Billed as 'An Evening With The Doors', the ecstatic audience was treated to *Appetite*'s standards as well as several new songs from the long-awaited album(s), including the forthcoming single, 'You Could Be Mine', which had already been

earmarked as the theme tune for Arnie's latest blockbuster, *Terminator 2: Judgement Day*. The only downside to the evening came when Axl tumbled from one of the onstage monitors injuring his left ankle. The tour's opening date was only a week away, and the band – not to mention the Geffen hierarchy – was anxious the tour should go ahead as scheduled. With this aim in mind, experts from sports-shoe giants *New Balance* were hurriedly brought in to design a specially-crafted 'space-age' boot, which, although limiting Axl's mobility, would at least allow him to get about the stage.

## First Leg
## 24 May, 1991 – 9 April, 1992.
## USA and Europe

On 24 May, 1991, the tour got underway with the first of two sell-out shows at the Alpine Valley Music Theatre in East Troy, Wisconsin, with Sebastian Bach's Skid Row as support. Gone were the days of borrowed cars and cramped tour vans, the Gunners, their management team and select members of the band's inner circle flew to Wisconsin in a luxurious 747 jet owned and leased by the MGM Grand Hotel in Las Vegas. Their starting the tour in what was – at least in musical terms – a mid-western backwater, was due to Axl having recently purchased a sizeable plot of land in the area, where he not only intended to build his dream home, but also be buried – he would subsequently

change his mind on both counts and sell the land.

The next show, at the 17,000 capacity Deer Creek Music Centre in Noblesville, Indiana, where the band again performed two sell-out shows over consecutive nights, was even more personal to Axl as it was a return to he and Izzy's home state. It had been three years since Guns N' Roses last performed in Indiana and Axl wasn't about to let the occasion pass without venting his pent-up angst at those nameless, faceless bureaucrats who'd imposed a state-wide curfew requiring all outdoor public gatherings to be concluded by 10.30pm. Though

Axl was himself partly to blame for having kept the audience waiting for two hours before going on stage – an occurrence that became something of a regularity as the tour progressed – he laid into the local authorities by comparing them to Hitler's Nazis. He also likened his 'subjugated' audience to inmates of the notorious Nazi death camp, Auschwitz, which brought unwanted and unnecessary publicity, making headlines across America. "I just wanted to tell them that they could break away too," the despondent singer told reporters.

On 17 June, at a show at the Nassau Coliseum in Uniondale,

New York, Axl took his tardiness to new extremes by keeping the audience waiting until midnight. Mick Wall, in his unofficial Axl Rose biography, suggests this was done in petty retribution for Slash having had the audacity to decline the singer's invitation to an impromptu party at a Manhattan restaurant the previous evening. Instead of challenging Axl's adopted 'higher-than-thou' attitude, Slash and Duff preferred to seek solace in their respective drug de jour, while Izzy, although equally disillusioned with Axl, had never been one for confrontation and retreated deeper into his shell. His decision to clean up his act following the fracas over Phoenix – which had earned him the sobriquet "Whizzy" amongst band and crew members alike – meant it was virtually impossible for him to spend time with his fellow Gunners who, with the possible exception of Axl, were drinking copious amounts of alcohol as well as dabbling in one or more illegal substances. His decision to travel separately from the rest of the band wasn't meant as a slight to the others, it was simply a means of resisting the everyday temptations and staying on the wagon.

On 2 July, the chickens well and truly came home to roost during a performance at the recently-opened Riverport Performing Arts Centre, some fifteen miles west of St. Louis in Maryland Heights, Missouri. The band were ninety minutes into the set when Axl brought the proceedings to a premature halt to draw the ven-ue's in-house security team's attention to an audience member who was harassing other fans and preventing them from enjoying the show. The guy in question happened to be Stump, the leader of a local biker gang known as the Saddle Tramps, and as the security staff were either friends of Stump's or were afraid of whatever retribution he and his biker crew might inflict on them once Guns N' Roses had left town, they were reluctant to intervene. And to show he was untouchable, the biker goaded Axl further by waving a video camera in his face. The band's contract specifically prohibited the use of cameras and video recording equipment, so when the security staff continued to ignore Axl's pleas, the singer took matters into his own hands and dived into the audience to confront the biker. The security team now felt compelled to act, and during the ensuing scuffle Axl punched one of their number – and received several blows in return – before the band's roadies succeeded in pulling him back up onto the stage. Axl was beside himself and informed the bemused crowd that thanks to the lame-ass security he was going home. The rest of the group continued playing for several minutes before sidling from the stage once it became clear their singer wouldn't be returning.

Axl later claimed he'd fully intended to continue with the show, and had only left the stage in order to replace a contact lens he'd lost during the scuffle. The audience, however, knew nothing of what was going on backstage and began expressing their displeasure by barracking the band. Instead of going back out to at least placate the audience, Axl and co remained ensconced within their dressing room while the road crew went out to dismantle the equipment. This was the spark to ignite the powder keg, and certain sections of the crowd began tearing out seats and hurling them at the hapless roadies, at which point the venue's manager, realising he had a potential full-scale riot on his hands, called in the police. In the ensuing carnage, which saw every available police officer in the St. Louis county area arrive in full body armour and armed with batons, fire hoses and cans of Cap-Stun (a cayenne pepper aerosol similar to Mace), sixty fans were injured and another sixteen were arrested. The venue suffered damages totalling some $200,000, and the band lost all their equipment.

Slash, who watched the destruction from the backstage area, later bemoaned: "I lost all my amps, and my guitar tech Adam [Day] got a bottle in the head. Someone got knifed, and all our stage and video equipment and Axl's piano were trashed. I don't know. It was a fluke. It shouldn't have happened... but it did." The loss of so much equipment forced the band to cancel forthcoming shows in Kansas, and Chicago.

The following day saw the show's promoters, Contemporary Productions, in conjunction with the venue's owners, file lawsuits against Guns N' Roses. Worse was to follow three days later when the St. Louis authorities issued a warrant for Axl's arrest on no less than five misdemeanour charges – four of 'assault' and one of 'property damage'. The St Louis riot and the ensuing adverse headlines, which followed the band around like a bad smell, may have put a dampener on subsequent shows in Texas, Colorado, Utah and Washington, but the five saddle-sore Gunners found a renewed spring in their cowboy-booted heels upon their return to Los Angeles for four sell-out shows at the Great Western Forum. Indeed, such was the demand for tickets for the local-boys-done-good that the promoter had offered the band eight shows.

Eight days later, on 12 August, the band arrived in Helsinki, Finland, where they were scheduled to perform two shows over consecutive nights at the Finnish capital's Jäahalli ice arena. Duff, Slash, Matt and Dizzy – as well as the guys from Skid Row – fought off the jet lag and went to watch the Black Crows performing at the nearby Tavastia Club. This was the Gunners first European jaunt since the UK tour of four years earlier and everyone was in good spirits. Yet it seemed Axl hadn't learned anything from the St Louis debacle, for the irascible singer stomped off stage midway through 'Welcome To The Jungle' leaving the rest of the band to continue the song as an instrumental.

With the song ended and with Axl showing no sign of returning, Izzy was summoned from the shadowy periphery to sing '14 Years', which was followed by a drawn out, improvised drum solo from Matt and an equally-protracted guitar solo from Slash, before Axl nonchalantly reappeared on stage behaving as though it was all part of the act. If any doubt remained as to Axl's scant regard for anyone other than himself, it came in Stockholm four days later, when he purposely chose to spend three hours playing roulette at the Sheraton Hotel's casino before summoning the limo to the Globen arena where the rest of the band were waiting. He didn't even arrive at the venue til gone midnight, and the rumour – albeit an unsubstantiated one – was that the singer had stopped off en route to watch the Vallenfestivalen firework display. Worse was to follow in the Danish capital, Copenhagen on 19 August, when Axl again called a halt to the proceedings and challenged the idiotic fan who'd thrown a firework up onto the stage to come forward. When the culprit failed to comply, he led the group from the stage and didn't return for some twenty minutes. The singer was so incensed by the firework incident that he took his ire out on the band's Norwegian fans by refusing to catch the flight to Oslo, where they were scheduled to play on the 21st. Slash and Duff again chose to avoid confrontation and sank deeper into their respective oblivions, leaving a red-faced Izzy to explain to the manager of

Oslo's Spektrum arena that the show would probably have to be cancelled – as indeed it was – since no one was quite sure of Axl's whereabouts. Later that evening, Axl's personal assistant phoned Doug Goldstein to inform him the singer was in Paris taking a "much-needed break" and would join up with the band in Mannheim, Germany, where they were scheduled to play in five days time.

One week on from the Mannheim show, the band flew into London's Heathrow airport for the final European date – a 72,000 sell-out show at Wembley Stadium on 31 August. All five members – especially Slash, being English-born – had been looking forward to playing London's illustrious, twin-towered dame which was steeped in history, having staged the 1948 Olympics and the 1966 World Cup Final, as well as the Live Aid extravaganza of six years earlier. The tickets had sold out in a matter of hours. But not everyone was enthralled with Guns N' Roses' return to the UK. Wembley's borough council, in an attempt to keep the band on as tight a leash as possible, were insistent that Axl and co. should refrain from any unnecessary on-stage obscenities during their performance. Needless to say, Axl didn't take kindly to being given such high-handed orders and retaliated in kind by ordering the Geffen representatives to buy up every available inch of billboard space within a five-mile radius of the stadium and plaster them with a poster which read: Guns N' F-----g Roses, Wembley F-----g Stadium, Sold F-----g Out!!!.

This was the Gunners first UK appearance since the ill-feted Donington Festival of three years earlier, and although no one knew it at the time – with the possible exception of girlfriend Anneka – the Wembley show would also result in a casualty, as it proved to be Izzy's last as a member of the band. The disillusioned guitarist had initially tended his resignation shortly after the group returned to L.A., only to then undergo a change of heart. But a month or so later, haunted by the prospect of having to go back out on the road, he gave notice a second time. Izzy's departure from Guns N' Roses was officially announced on 17 November.

By the time they hit the road again in December, with Izzy's replacement, ex-Kill For Thrills guitarist Gilby Clarke primed and ready for action, the band had been augmented by keyboard and harmonica player, Teddy Andreadis, an all-girl trio of backing singers and an all-girl, three-piece horn section dubbed the 976-Horns. The *Use Your Illusion* albums were both sitting pretty at the top of the Billboard 200, as well as in every other music-loving country in the world, and it seemed that nothing – not even the emergence of scuff-punk trio Nirvana, and the Seattle-based Grunge movement – could derail the G N' R juggernaut. And three sell out shows at New York's Madison Square Garden on 9, 10 and 13 December merely served to confirm their status as the biggest band on the planet. The group kick-stared 1992 with a sell-out show on 3 January at the LSU Assembly Centre in Baton

Rouge, Louisiana, and followed this with several more US dates before flying out to the far east for three gigs in Japan, the last of which was recorded and subsequently released as the *Use Your Illusion* double video set. Following two shows at the Palacio De Los Deportes in the Mexican capital, Mexico City on 1 and 2 April, they returned to the US to complete the first leg of the tour with shows in Oklahoma City, and Rosemont, Illinois.

## Second Leg
## 16 May – 2 July, 1992.
## Europe

The second leg got underway at the picturesque setting of Dublin's Slane Castle in front of 40,000 ecstatic Irish fans. The Irish have long been renowned for their warm-hearted nature, and Slane village's 1,200 inhabitants, instead of bemoaning their village being invaded by an army of tattooed, leather and denim-clad rockers, welcomed the G N' R army with open arms. To add to the Irish flavour, the Gunners invited local up-and-coming band, Little Funhouse (a recent Geffen acquisition) to open the show. The band arrived at the venue to find a crate of forty-year-old Blackbush Irish whiskey and a barrel of Guinness waiting for them backstage, courtesy of Ireland's greatest musical export, U2. The Gunners would get to thank the Irish rockers in person when their paths crossed in Vienna later in the month. The Gaelic bonhomie even extended to the local press, and the previous day's *Irish Independent* carried a photo of a beaming Axl upon its front page. The local clergy, however, were concerned that the Emerald Isle's respectable Colleens might emulate their American and English cousins by baring their breasts on the giant video screens. Some 800 Garda officers – one tenth of Ireland's entire force – were on duty that day, but apart from the expected drunkenness and minor drug offences, the show passed trouble free. And Slash, who thoroughly enjoyed his time in the Irish capital, later commented: "I can always tell a drinking town when the locals get drunk before I do."

Following shows in Czechoslovakia, where Vanessa Warwick, the hostess of MTV's late-night rock show 'Headbangers Ball', caught up with the band, and Austria, where U2 – who were due to play there the following night – were Axl's honoured guests, the Gunners arrived in Berlin for a 40,000 sellout show at the German capital's Olympic Stadium on 26 May. The following night saw the band perform in front of the largest crowd of the tour so far – 75,000 people at Stuttgart's Cannstatter Wasen – which was staging a rock concert for the first time. The final German date – at Cologne's Müngersdorfer Stadion on 30 May – was marred by torrential downpours, but the band remained upbeat and Axl jokingly described the sodden crowd as "the biggest wet T-shirt contest in the world".

On 6 June, the band arrived in Paris for a pay-per-view show at the French capital's Hippodrome De Vincennes. During the set they were joined on stage by Slash's pal, Lenny Kravitz for a version of Kravitz's hit, 'Always On the Run', as well as Aerosmith's Steven Tyler and Joe Perry for an extended encore of the Yardbirds' classic, 'Train Kept A-Rollin'' and their own 'Mama Kin'. As the show was to be broadcast in both the US and across Europe via satellite uplinks, the various TV and radio networks created a 'media city' larger than the Gunners own sizeable compound. The initial idea had been for ex-Yardbird, Jeff Beck to join the band on stage for 'Train Kept A-Rollin'', but the plan was scuppered when the guitar legend suffered a recurrence of the tinnitus (an infection of the middle or inner ear brought on by over-exposure to excessively loud noise) which had blighted his career. Although Slash, who had idolised Beck since first taking up the guitar, was downhearted at the news, he was the first to acknowledge the show wasn't worth his risking permanent damage to his hearing. "Just playing together during rehearsals and bullshitting together off-stage was fucking great. It was an honour just to be on the same stage as him," he later gushed.

Before flying to Manchester for the scheduled show at Manchester City's Maine Road football ground on 9 June, the band took 48 hours out for a little downtime in the French capital. Paris being

the 'city of love', Axl had hoped his latest squeeze, Stephanie Seymour, would be able to join him. But when the model cried off owing to previously unmentioned work commitments, the singer flew into a rage believing she was seeing her former lover, the actor Warren Beatty.

The strain of performing and travelling – not to mention the mental anguish over what Stephanie might be up to – was beginning to take its toll on Axl, and the following evening a doctor was summoned to the sumptuous five-star Hotel De Crillon where he and the rest of the band were staying and diagnosed the singer as suffering from 'complete physical exhaustion'. He recommended that Axl take an immediate forty-eight hours rest. This would, of course, mean cancel-

ling the Manchester show, yet the official announcement confirming said cancellation wasn't made until the day of the show, which meant thousands of fans – including yours truly – had already taken time off work. In order to placate all concerned, the show was rescheduled for that coming Sunday so as not to inconvenience the fans any further, while the now superfluous backstage catering was donated to a local hospice. Before the rescheduled Manchester show, however, the Gunners returned to Wembley on the Saturday for another 72,000 sell-out gig which left both fans and critics breathless. For the first encore, the band was joined on stage by Brian May for blistering versions of the Queen anthems 'Tie Your Mother Down' and 'We Will Rock You'.

Following the third and final UK date at the 25,000 capacity Gateshead International Stadium, the band returned to London for a couple of days rest before flying out to Germany for a show at the Talavera-Mainweise airfield in Würzburg. As luck would have it, the area suffered one of the worst electrical storms in recent years. But despite the torrential thunderstorms – which were even more spectacular than the onstage pyrotechnics – the band completed their two-and-a-half-hour set. Another sell-out show followed in Basle, Switzerland, but by this time Duff was feeling the effects of having played out in the elements, and doctors were called in when his condition deteriorated. The tour was thrown into even greater jeopardy when Axl was found to be suffering from a sore throat, and the flight to Rotterdam – the next date on the itinerary – was delayed so that both Axl and Duff could receive medical treatment to get them through the show. The subsequent delay in getting to Rotterdam, however, resulted in the band arriving at the venue two hours late and they didn't take to the stage until gone 10pm. The Dutch authorities, although sympathetic to the Gunners' plight, were only willing to extend the 11pm curfew by thirty minutes. Axl informed the audience they'd paid their money and were entitled to a full show, and had his blessing to express their discontent any way they saw fit. Perhaps he wasn't exactly inciting a riot, but his words left little to the imagination. Thankfully, however, common sense prevailed and the powers-that-be agreed the band could play unencumbered by time restrictions. Duff managed to get through the show, but the medication had worn off by the time the band arrived back at their hotel and a local doctor ordered the bassist to rest for 48 hours, which unfortunately resulted in the following night's show in Belgium being cancelled.

With an unexpected break before the next show, in Turin on 27 June, the band flew to the Italian fashion capital, Milan, but the entourage was so large they were forced to book into two adjoining hotels as no single one was big enough to hold them. While Duff recuperated, Slash, Gilby and Teddy Andreadis flew to Munich to appear in the video to Michael Jackson's 'Give In To Me'. Axl, meanwhile, was in seventh heaven now that Stephanie had finally joined him (she would remain with her lover for the remainder of the tour), and the couple – probably at Stephanie's behest – visited the showrooms of top Italian designers such as Gianni Versace and Armani. Later that same evening, he and Stephanie dined with Donatella Versace, her model husband Paul Beck, and supermodel Naomi Campbell. Duff had fully recovered by the time of the Turin gig and the band treated the ecstatic 65,000 Italians inside the Della Alpi stadium to one of the best shows of the entire tour. As the next appearance was in Seville in southern Spain, the band travelled by coach to the Italian port of San Remo, where they celebrated Duff's engagement to girlfriend and future wife Linda by renting a 180-foot luxury motor cruiser for a two-day sightseeing and water-sports cruise along the Italian coastline. The Seville show, staged at the city's Estadio Benito Villamarin on 30 June, was delayed until midnight so the crowd could enjoy the full benefits of the spectacular lightshow.

History was in danger of repeating itself, when on 2 July – exactly one year on from the St. Louis riot – Guns N' Roses performed at Lisbon's Alvalade Stadium. One might have expected the painful memories of twelve months earlier to have ensured everything went according to plan, but the Portuguese crowd was left standing for five interminable hours before the band finally appeared. The fans were far from happy and expressed their displeasure by pelting the stage with a hail of plastic water bottles – not all of them empty. Axl, however, was in no mood to play dodge ball and threatened to leave the stage unless the barrage stopped. It didn't, and he and the rest of the band sloped off. They

returned some fifteen minutes later, but the disgruntled audience was in an unforgiving mood and began hurling firecrackers and lighters around the stadium, which resulted in the band downing instruments a second time. When a Portuguese official's plea for calm failed to restore order it seemed as though a repeat of 12 months earlier was unavoidable, but thankfully the band succeeded in pacifying the audience by playing the aptly-named 'Patience'.

The 4 July 'Independence Day' show – the last of the European leg – at Madrid's Vicente Calderon Stadium had to be cancelled when it was discovered the venue's concrete construction was badly affected by aluminosis. The crew had already begun work at the stadium and were placed on permanent standby should an alternative venue be found. When

none emerged, the show was rescheduled and Slash and most of the others took advantage of the situation by flying back to the US the following morning. Axl, however, knowing a fugitive warrant awaited his return, headed back to San Remo with Stephanie and spent the next few days getting reacquainted. The couple eventually returned to the US on 12 July, and sure enough Axl, had barely cleared customs at New York's JFK airport when he was arrested over the outstanding charges relating to the St. Louis riot. Two days later, the singer appeared before a judge in Clayton, Missouri, where he pleaded innocent to all five counts. The judge, however, thought otherwise and a court date was set for 13 October. This would have meant interrupting the next leg of the tour, but the judge was happy to allow the band to proceed on condition they placed a $100,000 bond, which Axl put up himself. Axl was subsequently found guilty on all counts, but instead of the four-and-a-half year jail term the St Louis prosecutor Robert McCulloch had been pressing for, the singer got off with two years' probation, and was ordered to donate $50,000 to local community groups.

## Third Leg
## 17 July – 6 October, 1992.
## 25-date US Stadium tour with Metallica

When the tour reconvened at the RFK Stadium in Washington DC on 17 July, instead of taking stock of his life now that he had avoided serious jail time and reconnecting with Slash and Duff, Axl distanced himself even further by surrounding himself with an even larger coterie of helpers and professional hangers-on. Now, aside from the usual retinue of bodyguards, personal assistants and his brother Stuart and sister Amy, who'd both come along for the ride, the singer brought in his psychiatrist Suzzy London, a stunning brunette who also appears in the 'Don't Cry' video, and a rather less attractive professional psychic by the name of Sharon Maynard.

When the G N' R/Metallica double-header (with Faith No More opening the proceedings at the majority of the shows) was first announced back in May, the prospect of seeing America's two biggest and best rock acts on the same stage had left fans drooling, and each of the 25 dates sold out in no time. Indeed, several did so within hours of the tickets going on sale, and the gigs at the Giants Stadium in New Jersey (18 July), and Pasadena's Rose Bowl (3 October) both sold-out in less than an hour. The tour was not without incident, however, for during the encore at the second of two sets at the aforementioned Giants Stadium on 29 July, Axl was struck in the genitals by a low-flying cigarette lighter and had to vacate the stage in agony, leaving Duff to take over vocal duties. Although the singer would subsequently make light of the matter by saying he'd been "hit in the dick by a bic", the tour was forced into temporary hiatus with the next three shows (Boston, South Carolina, and Minneapolis) being rescheduled for September when he was diagnosed as having sustained 'severe damage to his vocal chords' – a condition even professional vocal coach Ron Anderson couldn't alleviate. Axl's sore throat and swollen nads paled into significance compared to the injury which befell Metallica's frontman, James Hetfield at Montreal's Stade Du Parc Olympique on 8 August. A misunderstanding over the on-stage pyrotechnics led to Hetfield suffering severe burns to his left arm, bringing Metallica's set to an immediate halt. Seven dates would have to be rescheduled while Hetfield recovered from his injuries, and even when he did return, Metal Church's John Marshall filled in on guitar while he sang. Instead of going on earlier than scheduled to compensate the Canadian fans as arranged, Axl brought another evening to a premature close claiming he couldn't hear himself through the on-stage monitors. And although he informed the disgruntled crowd their money would be refunded, more than 2000 of their number ran amok in the surrounding streets and clashed with local police.

The final G N' R/Metallica show – which, according to Slash should have been the final date of the *Use Your Illusion* tour – came on 6 October in Duff's hometown of Seattle. The Gunners had been on the road for 14 gruelling months, but whereas Metallica – who were earning the same fees – kept expenses to a minimum, the union dues incurred owing to Axl's terrible timekeeping and the singer's insistence on throwing lavish after show themed parties – which saw band and crew gorge themselves on lobster and champagne suppers whilst scantily-clad girls gyrated to a musical backdrop of Motörhead, Aerosmith and Sex Pistols – had significantly eaten into the band's profit margin.

## Fourth Leg
### 25 November – 13 December, 1992.
### A nine-date tour of South America

The extended itinerary kicked off with a show in front of 45,000 ecstatic fans at the Poliedro de Caracas in Venezuela – Guns N' Roses first headline tour of South America. The absence of a suitably-sized venue, however, meant the show – which was the largest ever held in the country – was actually staged in the parking lot outside the arena. The performance passed without incident, but unbeknownst to anyone – especially the band – the Venezuelan air force was plotting a military coup to seize control of the country. The coup failed, but although the band managed to escape the following day, the majority of their equipment – along with several anxious crew members – was left stranded at the airport. The next

stop on the tour was the Columbian capital, Bogotá, where the Gunners were scheduled to perform two shows over consecutive nights at the city's 60,000 capacity El Campin Stadium. But with the vast majority of their equipment still stranded in Venezuela, coupled with the logistical nightmare of attempting to ferry in new gear from the US, it was decided the two shows should be rolled into one. The band did offer to re-jig their itinerary and make Sunday's tickets valid for the Monday, but the promoters decided against this as the majority of those with tickets for the Sunday show would have travelled long distances and couldn't afford the added cost of remaining in the capital for an extra night.

The stranded equipment didn't arrive at the venue until around 7pm on the Saturday evening, so while an ever-increasing number of fans occupied themselves in erecting makeshift encampments outside the stadium, the 80-strong crew worked through the night to erect the 200 x 80 foot stage in time for the following night's show. This was just one of three separate stages which piggy-backed from venue to venue so each one was utilised every third gig. The crew's already Herculean task was not made any easier by the torrential rain, and disaster struck when the stage's six-tonne roof, complete with lighting rig, came crashing to the ground. (A subsequent inspection revealed that the locally-supplied base structure had been unable to cope with the additional weight of the accumulating rainwater). The sound of buckling metal gave the stagehands ample warning to flee the scene, but with no time to rebuild the roof, the set was hastily redesigned with the lights repositioned on the set's side walls. This was but one example of the crew's dedication and determination to get the job done, which saw the US trade magazine *Performance,* name them 1991's 'Crew of the Year'.

The band's 55,000 sell-out show in Santiago, Chile on 2 December was marred by the Chilean media's scurrilous – and unfounded – reports that Axl had been drunk for the performance; and that a quantity of drugs had been found in the band's rooms at the Sheraton San Cristobel hotel. Although both Doug Goldstein and the hotel manager vehemently denied the allegations, Goldstein did admit representatives of the CDI (Chilean Department of Investigation) had paid an unannounced late-night visit to the hotel to conduct a fruitless search of several of the band's rooms – including Axl's. Following two capacity shows at Buenos Aires' Estadio River Plate in Argentina over the weekend of 5/6 December, the band arrived

in Sao Paulo, Brazil. The first performance at the city's Estacionamento Do Anhembi stadium went ahead despite incessant torrential rain. But when the deluge continued into the next morning – flooding both the venue and surrounding area – the local officials insisted on cancelling the second night's show. The final appearance of the South American tour was staged at Rio de Janeiro's enormous Autodromo stadium on 13 December before band and crew returned to the US for a month-long festive break.

## Fifth Leg
### 12 January – 6 February, 1993.
### Japan and Australasia

The final six of the 30-month world tour got underway on 12 January, 1993 with the first of three sell-out shows at the futuristic Tokyo Dome. Although Axl still insisted on being accompanied by his support team and assorted 'suck-ups', cost-cutting forced the band to dispense with Teddy Andreadis, the backing singers and horn section. The first Tokyo

set went without a hitch, with even Axl making it onto the stage at the appointed hour. But by the second show the singer had reverted to type and kept the audience waiting for ninety minutes. For the third and final Tokyo gig Ronnie Wood joined the band for an extended version of 'Knockin' On Heaven's Door'. The Stones guitarist had performed a solo show in the Japanese capital the previous evening and had invited the Gunners to his aftershow party at the Lexington Queen nightclub.

The band flew out to Australia the following morning but took a two-week sightseeing break before performing at Sydney's Eastern Creek Raceway, which was the largest musical event staged in Australia. Next up was Melbourne's vast Calder Park Raceway stadium on 1 February, which, despite torrential rain, broke national attendance records. The tour then moved on to New Zealand where band and crew spent the evening before the show in a plush restaurant overlooking Auckland harbour helping Axl and Duff – along with tour inveterate Del James – celebrate their respective birthdays. And as the show – at the city's Mount Smart Stadium – fell on Axl's 31st birthday, the crew brought proceedings to an unscheduled stop midway through the set to present the singer with an enormous candle-lit birthday cake while Slash led the audience in a heart-warming rendition of Happy Birthday. Following a day spent sightseeing, the band

returned to the US, where, owing to the difference in time zones, they arrived at LAX three hours before they left New Zealand.

### Sixth Leg
### 23 February – 13 July, 1993.
### USA

The sixth leg of the world tour – dubbed the 'Skin and Bones' tour – kicked-off at the 17,000 seater Frank Erwin Centre in Austin, Texas on 23 February. Although the set predominantly remained the same, the audience was treated to a mid-show 'acoustic easy hour', which saw the relaxed Gunners gather around a sofa and coffee table placed in the centre of the stage to perform several acoustic numbers – including three of the four acoustic tracks from *GNR Lies*: 'Used To Love Her'; 'Patience' and 'You're Crazy'. Not surprisingly, 'One In A Million' remained hidden away in the G N' R locker. The next show, in Birmingham, Alabama went according to schedule, but the following four, in Ohio, North Carolina, New York and Rhode Island had to be rescheduled owing to adverse weather conditions. Water also effected the 3 April show at Sacramento's Arco Arena when Duff was rendered unconscious by a flying plastic water bottle, while the show at Atlanta's 17,000 Omni Arena was cancelled when Axl discovered it was the same venue where he'd been arrested six years earlier, following a scuffle with an overzealous security guard during the Mötley Crüe tour of 1987. The singer was still technically on parole over the St. Louis incident and was also all-too-familiar with the heavy-handed tactics of Georgia's State Police.

The tour – which had already seen cancellations (enforced or otherwise), injuries, riots and drug-raids – took another bizarre twist at the end of April when Izzy returned to the fold – albeit on a temporary basis – as stand-in for his replacement, Gilby Clarke. Gilby had broken his left wrist whilst practicing for a celebrity charity motorcycle race which saw the four remaining US dates cancelled. But rather than cancel the forthcoming European festival shows, and with no time to break in a new guitarist, Axl asked a favour, which made perfect sense given Izzy's familiarity with the songs.

## Seventh Leg
## 22 May – 13 July, 1993.
## Europe

With Izzy (now sporting dreadlocks) once again prowling the shadowy no-man's land at the rear of the stage, the Gunners opened the penultimate leg of the tour – dubbed the 'Get In the Ring Motherfucker Round II' – at Hayarkon Park in Tel Aviv, which saw more than 40,000 fans turn up for what was later declared the largest music concert ever staged in Israel. Axl was in fine form and took to the stage sporting a custom-made 'Guns N'

Moses' T-shirt. Following shows in Greece and Turkey, the band arrived in the UK for two gigs at the Milton Keynes National Bowl over the weekend of 29/30 May, where Axl's friend, Shannon Hoon's band Blind Melon was one of the support acts. Unfortunately for all concerned, the English weather was true to form and the near-incessant downpour turned the open-air amphitheatre into a quagmire. The second show proved to be Izzy's last, as by this time Gilby's wrist had healed well enough for the guitarist to grasp a fret board. During the now-familiar mid-set acoustic session, the band was joined on stage by Gilby, ex-Hanoi Rocks frontman and Axl acolyte Michael Monroe and Ronnie Wood. Izzy, although having enjoyed the opportunity to absorb the culture of ancient cities such as Athens and Istanbul, hadn't enjoyed any other aspect of the G N' R travelling circus and was happy to be on his way. He later admitted he didn't bother to say farewell to any of the guys as – with the possible exception of Axl who was now a devoted exerciser and had replaced alcohol and drugs with bottled mineral water and high-protein vitamin shakes – they'd been too fucked up to notice his return.

Gilby's first full show came on 2 June at Vienna's Praterstadion and the guitarist took no chances by having a specialist flown in from the US to oversee his on-going recovery; and to help reduce the swelling, he packed his left arm in ice before, during and after the show. Following dates in Holland and Denmark, the band played another sell-out gig at Oslo's Valle Hovin stadium. Before the show each member of the band was presented with a platinum disc for having sold more than 300,000 records in Norway, which was something of an achievement given Norway's entire population is little more than four million. The next concert, at Stockholm's Olympic Stadium on 12 June, was marred by incessant rain, and as the band was leaving the stage Slash jokingly invited the sodden Swedish audience to an aftershow party at Dizzy's room back at the Sheraton Hotel. Fortunately for the keyboardist, only a fraction of those in attendance understood English.

The highlights of the June 16 show at the St. Jakub Fussballstadion in Basle, Switzerland was the inclusion of the Rolling Stones song 'Dead Flowers', which subsequently appeared on Gilby's debut solo album, *Pawnshop Guitars*, and a naked Shannon Hoon arriving on stage to deliver a pizza during the acoustic set. The Gunners then headed across the border into Germany for five shows, the first of which, at Bremen's Weserstadion on 18 June, coincided with Dizzy's 30th birthday. The second, at the 50,000 capacity Wildparkstadion in Karlsruhe, descended into chaos when it came to light that opening act, Suicidal Tendencies, had been double-booked and

the band was in Italy touring with Metallica. To add to the confusion, Brian May, who was also on the bill, arrived late owing to traffic congestion in the city, but the guitarist did at least agree to play a longer set to compensate. And to cap the evening off Guns N' Roses also arrived at the venue some 40 minutes late owing to their helicopter pilot somehow deviating off course on what should have been a routine 20 minute flight.

Following on from two storming sets in Modena, Italy on 29 and 30 June, the band took time out to recharge their batteries before flying on to Spain. The first Spanish show was staged at Barcelona's spectacular 60,000 Estadi Olympic, where Del James donned the Domino's Pizza uniform to deliver the mid-set pizza before then grabbing up the congas and joining in on 'Used To Love Her'. After a relatively incident-free show at Madrid's Vicente Calderon Stadium on 6 July, the Gunners flew to Nancy in north-eastern France for the first of three French performances at the city's Zenith de Nancy arena. The final show of the European leg came in Paris at the French capital's Omnisports de Bercy stadium. And as the band were due to fly straight to Buenos Aires early the following morning, immediately after the two-hour show they returned to their hotel, the Royal Monceau, and took up residence in the bar until it was time to leave for the airport.

## Eighth Leg
## 16 – 17 July, 1993.
## Argentina

The final two dates of Guns N' Roses' mammoth 30-month tour were staged in Argentina, at the city's 70,000 capacity Estadio River Plate on 16 and 17 July. Friday night's show was delayed some 75 minutes, however, owing to a visit to the band's hotel by 50 officers belonging to the city's narcotics division. The officers had apparently been tipped off that the band was carrying a large amount of cocaine. But the allegations proved unfounded and their two-hour search failed to yield anything untoward. A simultaneous – and equally fruitless – search of the band's equipment was also carried out at the stadium.

As Saturday night's show was being broadcast live on TV in Argentina and neighbouring Uruguay, proceedings got underway at the appointed hour. The Gunners ended their twenty-song set – and the 30-month tour – with 'Paradise City', and although the ecstatic Argentineans clamoured for more, the proverbial fat lady was the only one left singing. The band headed straight back to their hotel and took up residence in the bar, where they remained until dawn, doubtlessly reminiscing on the highs and lows of the tour. And little could Slash, Duff or Matt have known at the time, that the second Buenos Aires show would be the last time they would share a stage with Axl.

# VELVET REVOLVER

Velvet Revolver is the name of the Grammy Award-winning group featuring ex G N' R stalwarts Slash, Duff McKagan and Matt Sorum.

In 2002 Velvet Revolver emerged like a phoenix from the rock 'n' roll wreckage that was Guns N' Roses following a reunion, of sorts, when Slash, Duff, and Matt – along with rappers B Real and Sen Dog from Cypress Hill – appeared on stage together for the first time in six years at a benefit concert for their friend and fellow musician Randy Castillo, who'd tragically succumbed to cancer in March of that year. Although Slash had recently contributed to albums by Michael Jackson, Iggy Pop and Carole King, the guitarist was at something of a loose end; as were Duff and Matt following the demise of the Neurotic Outsiders. While the Key Club benefit show was only intended as a one-off, it reignited Slash's passion for rock 'n' roll, and upon learning Duff and Matt had been equally invigorated, the three decided to take things a stage further by inviting Izzy to join their, as yet, unnamed project. But although Izzy had rebuilt many bridges in the intervening decade since he'd pulled the emergency break on the G N' R juggernaut, his aversion to being part of a band – any band – remained as strong as ever. He was happy to jam with his old buddies and share war stories, but

he was unwilling to commit to the cause. Disappointed, but far from disheartened, the trio turned to ex-Wasted Youth guitarist, Dave Kushner, who'd recently collaborated with Duff on the bassist's Loaded project.

The news that three ex-members of Guns N' Roses were putting a new band together hit 6.8 on the Richter scale and had every music channel and magazine clamouring for more information – with VH1 even going so far as to send a camera crew to West Hollywood to film their search for a singer. Amongst those invited to audition were an English vocalist called Steve, one-time Faith No More frontman Mike Patton, the Cult's Ian Astbury and Buckcherry's Josh Todd. But perhaps not surprisingly – given his past history with Guns N' Roses – it was ex-Skid Row singer Sebastian Bach who ended up hogging the limelight on the VH1 special. Bach had just signed up to appear as Jesus in Andrew Lloyd Webber's *Jesus Christ Superstar*, and although he was willing to shed his false beard and halo, the three ex-Gunners felt his similarity in style to a certain W. Axl Rose would prove too heavy a cross to bear. One name that had constantly come up in conversation during the fruitless auditions was Stone Temple Pilots frontman, Scott Weiland. Scott was flattered and had also been suitably impressed with the demos Slash had dropped off at his apartment, but although the Stone Temple Pilots were having their problems, they were still an on-going band and Scott felt obliged to stick with them. Slash, Duff and Matt went back to trawling through the mountain of demo tapes gathering dust at the rehearsal studio, but several months later news filtered through that the Stone Temple Pilots had broken up and Scott was in. And having decided on the name Velvet Revolver, the five-piece played its first gig at L.A.'s El Rey club in June, 2003.

By the time the band headed into the studio to record their debut album, *Contraband* in December, one of their songs, 'Set Me Free' had already appeared on the soundtrack for Ang Lee's movie *The Hulk*, while their version of Pink Floyd's 'Money' had featured in that year's remake of *The Italian Job* starring Scarlett Johansson and Mark Wahlberg. The finished album was released on 8 June, 2004, and such was the enthusiasm amongst G N' R fans who were desperate to hear new product from their heroes – regardless of the fact they were no longer active members of Guns N' Roses – it entered at #1 on the US Billboard chart and at a respectable #11 on its UK counterpart. *Contraband* would go on to sell close to three million copies in the US alone, making it the best-ever debut by a rock act, while the accompanying single, 'Slither' won the 2005 Grammy for 'Best Hard Rock Performance'. The album spawned another two singles: the hard-rocking 'Dirty

Little Thing' and the hauntingly exquisite ballad 'Fall To Pieces', which Axl would surely have been proud to call his own. The band's fourth single, 'Come On, Come In' features on the soundtrack to the 2005 movie *Fantastic Four* starring Jessica Alba.

Of course Slash, Duff and Matt couldn't hope to shake their G N' R past, but all three were keen to stress Velvet Revolver was a new band looking forward to entering a new era. A new beginning it may have been, but certain hatchets remained unburied and the band declined an invitation to tour with KISS when it came to light their old adversaries Poison would also be on the bill. In August, 2005, the group participated in Live 8, but, while they performed a three-song set, only 'Fall To Pieces' made it to the commemorative DVD. Despite the resounding success of *Contraband*, Velvet Revolver was not a band content to rest on its laurels, and in late 2005 they announced that their follow-up album, *Libertad*, was under production with renowned rock producer Rick Rubin. This collabo-ration proved short-lived, however, with Rubin being replaced by former Stone Temple Pilots producer, Brendan O'Brien. The switch brought untimely delays, but the band placated their fans by releasing the 5-track EP 'Melody and Tyranny' – which features a cover of the Talking Heads classic, 'Psycho Killer' – on 6 June, 2007. The 12-track album also features a 10-minute video documentary called "Re-Evolution: The Making of Libertad" directed by Rocco Guarino, and came out four weeks later, on 3 July. Although *Libertad* debuted at #5 on the Billboard 100, selling 92,000 copies in its first week of release, a surprising lack of promotion saw the album slip quickly from the charts. To date two singles have been lifted from the album: 'She Builds Quick Machines' and 'The Last Fight', which were released in May and August 2007 respectively. But of the two, only the former found its way onto the Billboard chart, and even then it failed to make the 100, stalling at #104.

# VRENNA, CHRIS

Chris Vrenna is a Grammy-winning producer, sound engineer and one time Nine Inch Nails drummer who briefly worked on *Chinese Democracy* in 1997.

Vrenna was born on 23 February, 1967 in Erie, Pennsylvania, but as Erie was devoid of a music scene, the multi-talented musician moved to Cleveland, Ohio in the early '80's, where he played in a band called the Exotic Birds with future Nine Inch Nails frontman, Trent Reznor. Having decided the Exotic Birds weren't going to realise his musical aspirations, he relocated again, this time to Chicago, where his production, mixing and engineering talents saw him become an active figure on the windy city's industrial music scene. While he was in Chicago, Vrenna again hooked up with Reznor, which in turn led to his being invited to take up the drum stool with Reznor's new

band, Nine Inch Nails. Vrenna would remain with the industrial rock progenitors through to 1997, but during that same period he also went out on tour with industrial outfit KMFDM.

Following his departure from Nine Inch Nails, Vrenna teamed up with the Smashing Pumpkins, and it was while he was out on the road with Billy Corgan's outfit in May, 1997 that he received the call from Axl Rose inviting him to participate on *Chinese Democracy*. Vrenna was a man very much in demand, having collaborated with the likes of Green Day, David Bowie, U2, Rob Zombie and Marilyn Manson – with whom he is still involved as a live keyboardist. So sitting around the studio from 10pm to 6am each and every night, twiddling nothing other than his thumbs with whoever else happened to be in the G N' R line-up at the time, whilst waiting for Axl to grace them with an appearance was never going to sit well, and he left after two weeks. "It was going to be a long commitment," he said following his departure to work on his own projects. "There was no firm line-up. Axl had a definite direction he ultimately wanted to head toward, but at the time there wasn't even a song."

To date Vrenna has released two solo albums: *The Attraction To All Things Uncertain* (2001) and *2am Wake Up Call* (2004), both of which were released under the pseudonym 'Tweaker'.

# W'

## WALL, MICK

Mick Wall is a renowned writer who first cut his teeth reporting on the nascent UK punk scene for *Sounds* back in 1977, before going on to help establish heavy metal magazine, *Kerrang!*

Mick first entered G N' R's orbit backstage at the Manchester Apollo on 6 October, 1987 whilst covering their five-date return to the UK for *Kerrang!*, which at the time was the only magazine giving any column inches to the group he would later dub 'the most dangerous band in the world' in his 1991 book of the same name. Kerrang!'s championing of Guns N' Roses saw Mick warmly received into the Gunners' camp, and his willingness to pen only favourable articles and reviews subsequently provided him with access to the group's inner sanctum which might otherwise have been denied. The band rewarded his efforts by presenting him with a gold disc bearing his name for *GNR Lies*.

As Mick's relocation to Los Angeles happened to coincide with the Gunners' meteoric rise to stardom, it was inevitable their paths would cross on both a professional and social basis. Indeed, Mick eventually began to view the five members as friends – particularly Slash and Duff, with whom he counted down the chimes ushering in the 1990s – but little could he have known at the time that his expulsion from the court of King Axl would come just a few months into the new decade. In January 1991, having received a late-night call from a highly-agitated Axl, Mick clambered into his car and headed across town to the singer's West Hollywood apartment. He'd struggled to keep awake during the drive but became instantly fully alert upon witnessing the singer's feral rage over Mötley Crüe frontman, Vince Neil's disparaging remarks about Izzy in a recent *Kerrang!* article.

Mick could hardly contain himself as he activated his tape recorder and sat back while the wild-eyed Axl not only set the record straight about what really happened during Vince's supposed confrontation with Izzy at last year's MTV awards, but also openly challenged Vince to a showdown involving "knives or guns". These are the situations journalists live for. And since He'd taken the precautionary measure of validating the inflammatory quotes with the G N' R frontman before going to press with the article (which hit the newsstands that April), Mick was left flabbergasted – not to mention deeply hurt – when Axl not only denied having made the comments, but even went so far as to accuse him of having fabricated the entire article. Axl's newfound contempt for Mick did not end there, however, for he was one of several scribes – or "punks in the press" as the singer forever immortalised them – caustically castigated on 'Get In The Ring' which appears on *Use Your Illusion 2*.

## WALLACE, ANDY

Andy Wallace is a Grammy Award-winning studio engineer who, in 2006, was invited to work alongside Axl Rose on *Chinese Democracy*.

Although Wallace first came to prominence in 1986, thanks to his innovative production skills on the Run DMC/Aerosmith collaboration 'Walk This Way', it was his engineering on Nirvana's seminal 1991 debut, *Nevermind* which had the likes of Rage Against The Machine, Bad Religion, Faith No More, System Of A Down and Slipknot all clamouring for his services. His Grammy Award for Best Engineered Album, Non-Classical, which he shared with Tchad Blake and Trina Shoemaker, came in 1999 for his work on Sheryl Crow's album, *The Globe Sessions*.

News of Wallace's involvement on *Chinese Democracy* came in October, 2006, as part of a *Rolling Stone* feature on the long-awaited and highly anticipated forthcoming Guns N' Roses album. The article not only mentioned Wallace was serving as both co-producer and mixing engineer, but that the G N' R management team were said to be "delighted" with the results.

This wasn't Wallace's first collaboration with the G N' R fraternity, however, as in 2004 he was called upon to mix Velvet Revolver's debut long-player, *Contraband*.

## WAYNE NEUTRON

Wayne Neutron was the name used by Duff McKagan and Matt Sorum for a one-off show staged at The Joint in Las Vegas on 10 March, 1995.

For the Vegas show, Duff and Matt, along with guitarists Eric Mesmerize and Steve Stevens, who'd provided the licks to many of Billy Idol's mid-'80s hits, were joined on stage by Billy himself for a lip-quivering cover of Johnny Kidd and The Pirates' 'Shakin' All Over' and his own 1986 hit 'Rebel Yell'. Iggy Pop was also on hand to treat the celebrity-studded audience, which included blues guitar legends BB King and Bo Diddley as well as singers Sheryl Crow and Seal, to raucous versions of 'Raw Power' and 'I Wanna Be Your Dog', on which he was suitably aided and abetted by Steve Jones who also ran through the Sex Pistols ditty, 'Black Leather'. It was this informal gathering which led to Duff, Matt and Steve joining forces to form the Neurotic Outsiders.

# WELCOME TO THE JUNGLE

'Welcome To The Jungle', which ranks #2 on *VH1*'s 40 Greatest Metal Songs, is the opening track on *Appetite For Destruction*, and was also Guns N' Roses' first US single release in 1987.

'Do you know where you are? You're in the jungle, baby, you're gonna die…'

Today, the opening lyric to 'Welcome To The Jungle' is instantly recognisable wherever music is played and is also used as a chilling portent to psyche out opponents at sports stadia throughout America. As with the Sex Pistols and their 1976 debut offering, 'Anarchy In the UK', 'Welcome To The Jungle' served as G N' R's call to arms, and it was little wonder Geffen selected it as the band's debut US single. The Gunners themselves were also hip to the impact the song had on their audiences, and subsequently began using it to open their set. During a 1988 interview with *Hit Parader* magazine, Axl said he wrote the song's lyric whilst the band was in Seattle during the so-called 'Hell Tour' of three years earlier, and had done so as a means of differentiating between a big city such as Seattle, and the sheer sprawling, vast metropolis that is modern-day Los Angeles. "It's a big city", he said of the Evergreen State's capital. "But at the same time it's still a small city compared to L.A., and the things that you're gonna learn. It seemed a lot more rural up there [Seattle]. I just wrote how it looked to me." And speaking of his adopted city he added, "I just wrote how L.A. looked to me. If someone comes to town and they want to find something, they can find whatever they want. Plus, I had just been to New York... and it's like, I love L.A., I just know a lot of people there and I know where everything's at."

The inspiration behind the song's opening line, however, supposedly comes from an earlier incident when Axl – along with an unnamed companion – ran away to New York, where they were confronted by a homeless black guy who'd stumbled upon them whilst they were sleeping rough in a fenced-in schoolyard in Johnny Thunders' old stomping ground of Queens. Some writers have stated that Axl and Slash wrote the song whilst both were in the band London, but this isn't possible if, as Axl says, he wrote it about Seattle, since he didn't set foot in Duff's home town until August 1985, by which time both he and Slash were in Guns N' Roses.

Although the lyrical content of 'Welcome To The Jungle' was unlikely to win many supporters on mainstream TV, Geffen decided to go with an accompanying promo video. And so on Saturday 1 August, 1987, the day after the worldwide release of *Appetite For Destruction,* the band – together with British-born director Nigel Dick – headed down to La Brea in West Holly-wood to set up the cameras, with the on-stage footage shot at the nearby Whisky A Go-Go.

In keeping with the song's autobiographical theme, the video opens with Axl – looking every inch the wide-eyed, Midwest country hick, complete with dilapidated string-wrapped suit-case and a blade of straw jutting from his mouth – stepping off the Greyhound bus where Izzy, portraying the stereotypical L.A. drug dealer, is waiting ready to pounce. Slash also features in the opening scene, playing a hapless wino swigging from a concealed bottle whilst Axl stands staring at the bank of TV screens in a store window showing a demented, straitjacketed figure – played by himself – writhing about in an electric chair. The TV screens flick through a montage of war imagery and other scenes of man's destructive force, which serve to brainwash Axl and transform him into the streetwise rocker he ultimately becomes.

As predicted, MTV refused to play the video and only relented as a result of David Geffen personally calling in a favour from the music channel's chief executive, Tom Freston. And even then, the channel was only willing to air the video once at 3:00 am EST (Standard Eastern Time), and midnight in Los Angeles. One airing, however, was all it took for the MTV switchboard to light up like Times Square as rock fans on both seaboards called in demanding repeat plays. It seemed no

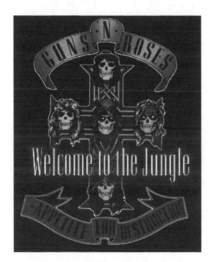

one could get enough of this new, exciting band that was breathing life back into rock's decaying corpse, and within days 'Welcome To The Jungle' was the channel's most requested video. Today, MTV is happy to bask in the glory of having been the first music channel to champion Guns N' Roses, but Tom Zutaut's former A&R (Artist and Repertoire) partner, Teresa Ensenat, remembers things somewhat differently. "It took about six months of consistent lobbying to get anybody at MTV to play that video," she told Danny Sugarman for his 1992 tome, *Appetite For Destruction: The Days Of Guns N' Roses*. "Now they show ads saying 'You saw 'em here first'. They resisted to the very last inch. It was ridiculous what that channel put us through to get them to play this band."

Another vehicle which helped push the song into the wider public arena was its featuring on the soundtrack to Clint Eastwood's 1988 'Dirty Harry' movie, *The Dead Pool*, starring Clint, Liam Neeson and Jim Carrey. It seemed that Clint's son, Kyle, who was already a huge fan of the band, was the one who put their name forward. The five band members were also invited to appear in the movie, whose storyline has a film crew forming a betting circle whereby each crew member chooses ten (fictional) celebrities they believe will go to meet their maker much sooner than their allotted 'threescore and ten'. Although it was obvious Clint knew nothing about Guns N' Roses, or the song itself, their cameo survived to the final edit; and they also got to meet an all-American hero.

In December, 1989, 'Welcome To The Jungle', made the news when it – along with Van Halen's 'Panama' and The Clash's 'Rock The Casbah' – was used as part of 'Operation Just Cause', which was the codename for the US invasion of Panama to oust the Central American country's military dictator, General Manuel Antonio Noriega. Although the recently-deposed dictator had escaped capture by seeking sanctuary in the Apostolic Nunciature (the Holy See's embassy in Panama), the building was quickly surrounded by US troops who subjected Noriega – as well as anyone else within earshot – to an endless barrage of non-stop, loud rock music. The psychological warfare only ceased following an intervention from the Vatican to the then US President George H.W. Bush.

## WHISKY A GO-GO

The Whisky A Go-Go is another legendary L.A. hotspot which played host to the then emerging Guns N' Roses in 1987.

By the time of G N' R's emergence during the mid-to-late-80s, the Whisky A Go-Go, the three-storey former bank located at 8901 Sunset and Clark, had already achieved a lasting place in rock folklore for having staged shows by Janis Joplin, Smokey Robinson and the Miracles, the Beach Boys, Buffalo Springfield and The Doors, who served their apprenticeship as the club's resident house band. An up-and-coming guitarist by the name of

Jimi Hendrix was also a regular attendee who needed no encouragement to get up on stage and jam with whoever happened to be playing at the time.

The Whisky first opened its doors on 11 January, 1964. Its owners, Elmer Valentine and his tough, no-nonsense, ex-Chicago cop partner Mario Maglieri, whose former occupation saw him offering counsel to Joplin and Morrison on the perils of drink and drugs, had taken their inspiration for their new venture from the racy Parisian discothèques they'd frequented on a recent trip to Europe. The seductive interior – complete with beautiful, scantily-clad young ladies gyrating to the beat from within cages suspended above the dance floor – soon established the Whisky as the number one club on Sunset Strip. The first act to tread its famous boards was

a young Southern rocker called Johnny Rivers, whose performance was subsequently released on the live album: *Johnny Rivers Live at the Whisky-A-Go-Go*. Legend has it that the 150 or so punters in attendance that night dutifully made their way to the recording studio a fortnight later to redub and enhance the 'live' ambience. The album was produced by Lou Adler (no relation to Steven), who subsequently became an equal partner in the Whisky alongside Valentine and Maglieri, and the three-man coalition has since taken ownership of The Rainbow Bar & Grill and The Roxy. In 1971, by which time the Whisky's itinerant triumvirate of Joplin, Morrison and Hendrix had each shuffled off their respective mortal coil, the club was forced to close following a $100,000 fire supposedly caused by a careless smoker. The revamped Whisky, now featuring a large portrait of Lizard King, Jim Morrison hanging behind the bar, and a bathroom door reportedly from the Doors old recording studio, re-opened its doors several months later. And while it may have lost its original décor, the flames hadn't robbed the club of its stature as the Strip's premiere venue, and it soon regained its prominence by staging shows by Anglo rock luminaries such as Led Zeppelin, Cream and Traffic.

Guns N' Roses made their live debut at the Whisky on Saturday 5 April, 1986, and the promo flyer, which provocatively asked: 'When Was The Last Time You Saw A Real Rock 'N' Roll Band... At The Whisky A Go-Go?', served as a statement of intent. And it was here, on 8 January, 1987, that the Gunners shot the live footage for the promo video to 'Welcome To The Jungle'.

The venue also embraced Grunge, and played host to Nirvana and other Seattle bands such as Soundgarden and Mudhoney. But by this time, the Whisky's glory days were little more than sepia-toned memories, despite its owners' attempts to recapture the magic, first by turning the club into a 'records only' disco, and then again as a live venue. The days of big, named acts treading the Whisky's boards are now long gone as the venue has since adopted a policy whereby it leases out to local promoters, who then charge up-and-coming bands for the chance to play and gain some exposure.

## WHITE TRASH WINS LOTTO

White Trash Wins Lotto is a Broadway-style, satirical musical with a central character loosely-based on Axl Rose.

White Trash Wins Lotto, written by one-time mortuary attendant and ex-Wall Of Voodoo frontman Andy Prieboy, has been cited as the West Coast equivalent of 'Hedwig and the Angry Inch'. It was first performed at Los Angeles' trendy dinner-theatre venue,

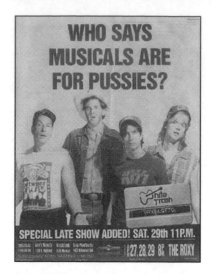

**WHO SAYS MUSICALS ARE FOR PUSSIES?**

SPECIAL LATE SHOW ADDED! SAT. 29th 11P.M.

Largo in 1997 and was also staged at Guns N' Roses' old stomping ground, The Roxy for three sold-out weekend-long engagements. At the time, Prieboy had recently been dropped by MCA – who released his debut solo offering, *Upon My Wicked Son* – and he retreated to his studio to lick his wounds. It was whilst he was trying to pen a hit song to resuscitate his ailing career that he hit upon the idea for a stage play lampooning America's clichéd rock scene. As Prieboy tells it, the (unseen) musicians in the adjoining studio spent every hour of the day hammering away at the piano trying to come up with suitable show tunes for whatever project they were working on. It was whilst listening to the budding Rogers and Hammerstein duo that the idea flashed through his mind of what might happen if someone were to accidentally stumble upon the Guns N' Roses story without actually knowing anything about

the band; and how they might make Axl Rose acceptable to the Broadway stage. With the opening lines 'I wanna be in a metal band/please let me sing for you' dancing around inside his head, Prieboy put pen to paper.

Although the show's central character – played brilliantly by Brian Beacock – is Axl Rose in that he's a Midwest hick who rises to rock superstardom before retreating into a hermit-like existence, Prieboy is quick to point out that it isn't a show about Guns N' Roses per se. Against a backdrop of guitar-free music, which almost gives it a Gilbert and Sullivan feel, Prieboy masterfully narrates the story which follows the backward baseball cap wearing hero from Nebraska to Los Angeles, and then through various locales, such as Jumbo's Clown Room where would-be rock stars mingle with aspiring starlets, backstage with the Rolling Stones and then on to Jim Morrison's grave in Pere La Chaise celebrity cemetery in Paris (a pilgrimage which Axl himself made in January 1990).

Prieboy, who was born and raised in East Chicago, Indiana, and a mere 100 miles from Axl's hometown of Lafayette, was keen to stress that, as a fellow musician, he appreciated just how difficult it would have been for someone like Axl Rose to rise from obscurity to the top of the rock pile. He even invited the reclusive G N' R singer to attend performances on several occasions, but Axl reportedly refused to even acknowledge the show's existence and is said to have taken it as an insult to his hard-earned achievements.

# WHOLE LOTTA ROSIE

'Whole Lotta Rosie' is a well-known AC/DC song which was covered by Guns N' Roses in their pre-*Appetite For Destruction* days.

'Whole Lotta Rosie' first appeared as the last track on Aussie rockers AC/DC's fourth studio album, *Let There Be Rock*, which came out in 1977, before subsequently being released as a single the following year. Indeed, the song has become so synonymous with AC/DC that it has featured on all six of the band's official live albums to date. The song is said to be about an obese woman – a "Tasmanian, 19-stone she-devil named Rosie" with whom the band's original singer, Bon Scott, supposedly had a relationship. Scott subsequently died due to acute alcohol poisoning in London on 19 February, 1980 whilst the band was on a UK tour, and it was 'Whole Lotta Rosie' (along with Ike & Tina Turner's 'Nutbush City Limits') that his successor, ex-Geordie frontman Brian Johnson sang at his audition.

The song's now instantly-recognisable riff – which saw it placed at #16 on *Q Magazine*'s Top 100 Greatest Guitar Tracks in March, 2005 – originally featured on an earlier recording entitled 'Dirty Eyes', which was slower in tempo than 'Rosie' and featured alternate lyrics as well as a different chord progression on the chorus. Guns N' Roses, whose raucous sound was similar to that of the Bon Scott era AC/DC, adopted the song as a staple encore to their early repertoire, and the blistering version lifted from the band's third and final Marquee show on Saturday 28 June, 1987 subsequently appeared on the now long-deleted Japanese-only EP, 'Live From The Jungle'.

# WILLIAMS, ROBERT

Robert Williams is the renowned and controversial painter and founder of *Juxtapoz Art & Culture Magazine,* who achieved lasting recognition within the rock world when his painting, *Appetite For*

*Destruction* was chosen as the artwork – and title – of Guns N' Roses' debut album.

Fantasy artist Williams created *Juxtapoz Art & Culture Magazine* in 1994, at the age of 43, to celebrate the genius of 'lowbrow art', and was already no stranger to controversy, as he – along with fellow underground contemporaries Robert Crumb and Gilbert Shelton – had cut his teeth as part of the *Zap Comix Collective* during the late '60s. But, as he put the finishing touches to Appetite For Destruction, little could he have imagined the hullabaloo that lay in store for him. The painting depicts a rape scene where a human-sized robotic creature leers over a semi-conscious young saleswoman whilst destroying a quantity of her quirky 'Mr Mini-Mite' robotic gadgets. The girl is slumped on the ground with her uniform salaciously ripped open to reveal one of her breasts, while her white panties are provocatively poised below her knees. The despicable robot's end appears nigh, however, for a monstrous, mechanical, blood-red nightmare is set to pounce whilst shedding skull and cross-boned minions like so much confetti. Had William's design been placed on display within the confines of a stuffy museum, it would no doubt have been considered 'art' by the cognoscenti. But its application to a rock 'n' roll album sleeve – where it would be in the public realm – somehow rendered it obscene and caused uproar in the US and the UK, as well as many other countries around the globe. Needless to say – and despite Geffen's claim to the contrary – the furore surrounding the sleeve was a publicist's dream, for it only served to draw more attention to the album, which in turn accrued more sales. But mounting pressure from the PRMC eventually forced Geffen into withdrawing the albums still bearing the offending sleeve, which was moved to the inside cover and replaced with the death's-head crucifix tattoo design inked upon Axl's right forearm.

## WOOD, RONNIE

Ronnie Wood, the legendary Rolling Stones guitarist and successful artist, has featured one way or another in Slash's life since the latter was 15 years-old.

Ronald "Ronnie" David Wood was born on 1 June, 1947 in Hillingdon, London, and was the first member of his gypsy family to be

born on land. He began his four decade-and-counting musical career as the bassist in The Birds (not to be confused with L.A. band, The Byrds). Following a brief spell with The Creation he – along with the then unknown Rod Stewart – joined The Jeff Beck Group, but the ex-Yardbird called time on his eponymous outfit in 1969 after recording just one album. Ronnie then accompanied his new best mate Rod into the Small Faces, who, having truncated their name to simply 'The Faces', went on to rival the Rolling Stones in popularity before splitting in 1975. By this time of course, Ronnie had already left the Faces to replace Mick Taylor in the Rolling Stones.

His expertise on both slide and pedal steel guitar has led to collaborations with the likes of Prince, David Bowie, Eric Clapton, Bo Diddley and Bob Dylan. Ronnie's most-memorable non-Stones performance surely came at the stateside Live Aid show in Philadelphia on 6 July, 1985, whilst he and fellow Stone, Keith Richards, were accompanying Dylan on 'Blowin' In The Wind'. The trio were halfway into the song when Dylan broke a string, but rather than bring a halt to the performance, Ronnie handed the bemused Dylan his own instrument and switched to air guitar until a roadie brought him a solid-bodied replacement. Aside from his guitar prowess, Ronnie is also an accomplished painter, having trained at the Ealing College of Art before opting for a career in music. His paintings, prints and drawings, which feature his fellow Stones and musical contemporaries as well as other icons of popular culture, have been displayed all across the globe, and sales of his work have earned him an estimated $10 million.

Slash was first introduced to Ronnie back in 1980 at his friend Matt Cassel's house. The then 15 year-old had accompanied Matt to a Stones gig at the L.A. Coliseum, and little could he have known as the pair walked back to Matt's place, each humming a Stones classic, that there was still one more encore to be played out. Matt's father, the actor Seymour Cassel – and the man who'd given Slash his one-syllable moniker – was renowned for throwing the best parties in town, and Ronnie and the other Stones turned up for an 'after after' show. Although Slash was still only in his teens, there was something about the corkscrew-haired, coloured kid which appealed to the eternally free-spirited Ronnie, and the pair developed a friendship that survives to this day.

# WONG, ESTHER

Esther Wong was a music promoter and owner of Madame Wong's East, where Hollywood

Rose made their live debut on Friday 16 March, 1984.

Esther Wong was born in Shanghai, China on 13 August, 1917, and after many years travelling around the world helping her father with his import business, in 1949 she emigrated to the US in order to escape China's harsh Communist regime. She settled in Los Angeles and spent the next twenty years working as a clerk for a shipping company before she and her husband, George, opened Madame Wong's East at 949 Sun Man Way in the city's Chinatown district in 1970. The restaurant initially featured Polynesian bands, but when her clientele began to dwindle, she reluctantly agreed to put on rock acts in an attempt to resuscitate her ailing business. With groups such as the Ramones, The Knack, The Motels and UK reggae punksters, The Police regularly treading the boards, the restaurant began drawing crowds in excess of 300, which saw the colourful and oft-controversial Esther being given the nickname

"Godmother of Punk". Although willing to accept the new form of music, Esther was a strictly no-nonsense business woman and once brought a Ramones show to an unscheduled halt so that two of its red-faced members could slope off to the bathroom to erase the graffiti they'd written on the walls.

Although the flyers for Hollywood Rose's debut appearance at Madame Wong's East – which show Axl and Izzy striking suitable rock poses – state Hollywood Rose, at this particular juncture in the band's career, they were in fact still trading as 'Rose'. What these flyers do, however, is serve as a clear indication that Axl was intent on augmenting – as well as glamorising – the band's name. Although when they returned to the venue the following month, on 20 April, said augmentation had yet to take place.

The mercurial Esther stunned her clientele by announcing the closure of Madame Wong's East in the summer of 1985, just as the L.A. metal scene was growing in stature. Her alternative venue, Madame Wong's West – located in Santa Monica, and where Hollywood Rose put in a solitary appearance on 16 June, 1984 – remained in operation for thirteen years from 1978 – 1991. Esther died at home on 14 August, 2005 following a long battle against lung cancer and emphysema.

# WYLDE, ZAKK

Zakk Wylde, the singer/song-writer best known for his role as founding member of Black Label Society, was drafted in as a hired gun by Axl to work on *Chinese Democracy*.

Zakk was born Jeffrey Phillip Wiedlandt in Bayonne, New

Jersey, on 14 January, 1967. He grew up in nearby Jackson, where he reportedly spent every waking hour practicing on his guitar. His first musical ventures with local bands didn't look like amounting to anything, but Zakk persevered and was rewarded for his toil in 1987, when the then unknown 20-year-old landed the coveted role of lead guitarist with Ozzy Osbourne – a collaboration which lasts to this day. The story goes that Wylde's then girlfriend – and now wife – Barbaranne, was listening to Howard Stern on the radio when the shock-jock announced on air that Ozzy was on the lookout for a new guitarist to replace the outgoing Jake E. Lee. Zakk, who'd been working as a gas attendant at the time, was encouraged to send an audition tape to Ozzy by a local photographer. Though he surely never expected anything to come of it, he was stunned when Ozzy's

wife Sharon called to inform him she was sending him a plane ticket to fly out to Los Angeles for an audition.

Today, Slash believes Axl brought in Zakk as a means of placating him over Paul Huge's largely unwanted presence at rehearsals during the summer of 1996. Slash and Zakk had been friends for nigh on a decade by this time, and although Slash respected Zakk's guitar skills, he was used to working with and playing off low-key rhythm players such as Izzy and Gilby, and couldn't really see what his friend – an equally consummate lead guitarist – could possibly bring to the party. For his part, Zakk was willing to give the G N' R dual lead idea a go, but told Slash in no uncertain terms that he and Axl would need to sort out their differences if they were ever going to take the band forward.

# YOU COULD BE MINE

'You Could Be Mine' was Guns N' Roses seventh single release, and the first to be culled from the band's *Use Your Illusion* albums.

'You Could Be Mine' was originally intended for inclusion on *Appetite For Destruction*, and the song's killer chorus line: 'With your bitch slap rappin' and your cocaine tongue/you get nothin' done,' features as a footnote on the debut album's liner notes. And contrary to popular belief, the song was never intended to be the official theme tune for James Cameron's 1991 Oscar-winning, blockbuster movie sequel, *Terminator 2: Judgement Day*, starring Arnold Schwarzenegger (who would subsequently befriend Axl and express his love for the Gunners' music in promotional interviews) and the director's then lover, Linda Hamilton. Indeed, Cameron's original script called for 'I Wanna Be Sedated' by the Ramones, but with Guns N' Roses being the biggest and baddest rock band on the planet, it made perfect business sense to incorporate the track and provide the movie with even more kudos. Aside from accompanying the closing credits, the song also appears in the movie itself in the scenes where Earth's future saviour – the teenage rapscallion, John Connor (played by Edward Furlong) – is seen tearing around town on his motorbike, and also during the high-speed chase scenes between Arnie and the T-1000 terminator, played by Robert Patrick. The band receives another plug – albeit subliminal – when Arnie pulls a secreted shotgun from a gift box containing red roses.

The accompanying promo video features Schwarzenegger moving through the audience at a Guns N' Roses show while the band is playing the song on stage (the video also includes brief clips from other G N' R live performances). With the gig over, the band – conspicuously minus Izzy – emerge through the backstage door onto the deserted parking lot to find Arnie waiting for them. The terminator assesses the threat potential of each member in turn – particularly Axl, who is then deemed to be a waste of ammunition. Such was the hype around both the movie and Guns N' Roses that 'You Could Be Mine' became one of the most requested videos of the summer. Sadly for G N' R fans, owing to the video containing several clips from the movie, legal machinations prevented it from being included on the *Welcome To The Videos* DVD.

# Z'

## ZILCH

Zilch was an alternative-industrial rock band which occasionally featured Duff McKagan as a guest musician.

Zilch was formed in Los Angeles, California in 1998 by ex-X Japan frontman Hideto "Hide" Matsumoto, former Professionals guitarist Ray McVeigh, ex-Killing Joke bassist Paul Raven, Danzig drummer Joey Castillo and a programmer known only as 'I.N.A'. The band, which will probably only be remembered for its select choice of guest musicians, such as Duff, Ian Astbury, Dave Kushner and Steve Jones (who had recruited McVeigh for The Professionals) was ready to release its debut long-player *3.2.1*, on the Avex Trax label when it suffered a fatal setback with the sudden demise of Hide Matsumoto.

Although the rest of the line-up staggered on with a little help from their friends and released two further albums: *Bastard Eyes* (1999), which was a remix based on the original debut album, and *Mimizuzero* (2001) as well as the single, 'Skyjin', the band never recovered from Hide's death and called it a day in 2002.

# ZUTAUT, TOM

Tom Zutaut was the man chiefly responsible for Guns N' Roses signing to Geffen Records on 25 March, 1986.

It had been Zutaut, whilst in his capacity as a junior A&R man at Elektra Records, who'd discovered, developed and subsequently transformed Mötley Crüe into the West Coast's – if not America's – premiere rock outfit. One might have thought his having unearthed the Crüe would have secured 'Zoot' – as the then 22-year-old, cherubic, blond-haired surf dude was affectionately known throughout the American music industry – a job for life. But sadly this was not the case, and as soon as David Geffen – who had once served as president of Elektra's sister company, Asylum Records – heard on the corporate grapevine that Zutaut was available, he stepped in. Geffen, fresh from his decade-long sabbatical and eager to re-establish his credentials within the music business, gave Zutaut but one objective: to find him a raw, rough-and-ready rock act to challenge Mötley Crüe's supremacy.

Geffen didn't have long to wait, for Zutaut, rather than sit around clutching a rosary and praying for lightning to strike twice, simply wandered into Vinyl Fetish, the trendy record store on Melrose Avenue which specialised in hard rock, and asked owner Joe Brookes for the low-down on the hottest groups currently strutting their stuff along Sunset Strip. There was, he discovered, but one name on everyone's lips: Guns N' Roses. And so the following Friday evening he followed the crowd to the Troubadour to see for himself.

The Gunners were barely into their third song when Zutaut surprised his fellow A&R execs by heading for the exit. He even stopped off to make some disparaging remark about the band's shortfalls. But this was merely smoke and mirrors, as he'd known from the moment he'd heard Axl in full rant that Guns N' Roses were going to be massive. He could barely contain his excitement over the weekend, and first thing Monday morning he put his case to David Geffen in person. Having won over the sceptical Geffen, who gave him the go-ahead to approach the band with a $750,000 offer, Zutaut purposely chose to make his pitch to Axl in person later that same day.

He'd come away from the meeting believing he had his band, but two days later Axl called him at his office to sheepishly explain how he'd offered Zutaut's female counterpart at Chrysalis a deal whereby the Gunners would sign with her label if she was willing to walk naked from Chrysalis' office to the nearby Tower Records. As it happened, Chrysalis' office stood on the same stretch of Sunset Boulevard as Geffen's HQ – with its front entrance directly facing Zutaut's office window. And although his partner, Teresa Ensenat, was dedicated to the Geffen cause and equally keen to procure the band's signatures, she wasn't prepared to bare her all on a city sidewalk. As Zutaut had arranged for the contractual signing to take place in David Geffen's office that coming Friday at 6pm, he spent an anxious couple of days watching out of his window to see if the Chrysalis chick would take Axl up on his offer. Needless to say, she didn't and Zutaut won the day.

Zutaut remained with Geffen/Interscope through to January, 1999, when he, along with a hundred or so other employees, were made redundant as part of the restructuring of the label by its corporate paymaster, Seagram. He was, however, subsequently rehired in 2001 as part of the label's attempt to coerce Axl into delivering *Chinese Democracy* before the year was out. Axl was initially thrilled to have an old and trusted friend back on the team, but his enthusiasm cooled somewhat upon discovering Zutaut had been offered a substantial bonus if the album was indeed completed. But by the time Guns N' Roses were taking to the stage at the Hard Rock Hotel in Las Vegas on 31 December, 2001, the finished album was still nowhere to be seen, and the only thing at an end was Zutaut's involvement on the project.

## Suggested reading

Danny Sugarman: *Appetite For Destruction: The Days Of Guns N' Roses* (Century) 1991

Mick Wall: *The Most Dangerous Band In The World* (Sidgwick & Jackson) 1991

Paul Stenning: *The Band That Time Forgot* (Chrome Dreams) 2004

Mick Wall: *W. Axl Rose: The Unofficial Biography* (Sidgwick & Jackson) 2007

Slash (with Anthony Bozza): *Slash* (Harper Collins) 2007

## Helpful Guns N' Roses related websites

www.mygnr.com
www.gnrontour.com
www.gnronline.com
www.heretodaygonetohell.com
www.rocksbackpages.com

And thanks to en.wikipedia.org for factual information: dates, faces, places etc.